BRIGHTON BELLES

A CELEBRATION OF VETERAN CARS

F 135
7

Brighton Belles

A Celebration of Veteran Cars

DAVID BURGESS-WISE

FOREWORD BY LORD MONTAGU OF BEAULIEU

THE CROWOOD PRESS

First published in 2006 by
The Crowood Press Ltd
Ramsbury, Marlborough
Wiltshire SN8 2HR

www.crowood.com

British Library Cataloguing-in-Publication Data
A catalogue record for this book is available from the British Library.

ISBN 1 86126 764 9
EAN 978 1 86126 764 1

Picture credits
All pictures by the author or from the author's collection except pages 9 (Julian Bennett); pages 153, 190B (Bonhams); pages 43A, 72A, 72B, 72C, 73B, 73C, 75, 76, 81, 94B, 98A, 98B, 98D, 99B, 99C, 137C, 167D, (Paul Burgess-Wise); pages 26, 28B, 29, 34B (Coachmakers Archive); pages 59A, 130A (Daimler Chrysler); page 105 (George Dorrington); page 131 (Dunhill); page 35 (Clive Friend); page 65B (Philip Hollis); pages 42B, 42C, 43D, 54, 147B, 147C, 148, 150, 177B, 179, 180A, 182, 183, 189B, (Louwman Collection); pages 32, 33, 34A (Ivan Mahy); page 70, 123 B, 147A (Michelin); page 123A (Renault UK); page 103 (Justin Sutcliffe); page 171B (Mike Timms); page 176 (Peter Venning).

FRONTISPIECE: Re-enacting a famous scene from *Genevieve* during a rally celebrating the film's 50th anniversary, De Dion-Bouton owner David Card has a Kay Kendall moment in the ford on Hawkswood Lane, a Brighton Road 'stand-in' a mere three miles from Pinewood Studios in Buckinghamshire.

Designed and typeset by Focus Publishing, 11a St Botolphs Road, Sevenoaks, Kent TN13 3AJ

Printed and bound in Malaysia by Alden Press Malaysia

Contents

Foreword

Veteran cars have played a large part in my life. When such cars were new, my father, 2nd Lord Montagu, was one of the very first people in Britain to own one. He bought his first Daimler – built by Britain's oldest manufacturer – in 1898. As a pioneer motorist, he was an ardent supporter in Parliament of the new means of locomotion, and founded and edited the prestigious weekly *Car Illustrated* magazine. He raced (and placed) his 1899 Daimler in the Paris-Ostend race that year, and when Britain won the Gordon Bennett Trophy in 1902, he piloted a bill through Parliament that allowed the race to be held in Ireland, despite a ban on racing on the roads of Britain.

It was as a tribute to my father's memory that I assembled a small collection of veteran cars and displayed them in the entrance hall when I opened my family home at Beaulieu to the public for the first time in 1952. That display was the root from which today's National Motor Museum sprang; the cars proved such a popular attraction that I opened Britain's first dedicated Motor Museum building at Beaulieu in 1955.

The first veteran to go on show at Beaulieu had been the little 1903 6hp De Dion-Bouton that my father had acquired before the Great War among the effects of a departing tenant. It first took part in the London to Brighton Veteran Car Run in 1930, and I made my Brighton Run debut with it in 1950. Since then, veteran cars from Beaulieu have been regular participants in the Run, underlining my philosophy that if a vehicle is in running order, it is better to use it occasionally than simply leave it to stand.

Several of those Beaulieu veterans feature in this book, which is a very personal account of a lifetime involvement with early motor cars. On that front, I share with the author a fascination with veteran cars. We also share the painful distinction of having suffered that now-rare but once-common form of broken wrist known as the 'chauffeur's fracture', acquired when crankstarting an early motor car; in both cases the doctor remarked that he hadn't seen such an injury for years!

Montagu of Beaulieu

OPPOSITE: *Motoring mythology:* L'effroi, *from a long-lost painting exhibited by Paul Gervais at the 1904 Paris Salon.*

RIGHT: *Lord Montagu's father bought this Daimler new in 1899. It was the first car to be brought into the Palace of Westminster and 105 years later Lord Montagu used it to deliver a petition against an 'annual registration charge' from Westminster to 10 Downing Street.*

Introduction

They say that it is better to be born lucky than rich, and in my case the luck meant that as a small boy, more than fifty years ago, we lived just a short bus ride from the A23. On a Sunday morning at the beginning of each November – generally a dank day – my father would take me on the 409 London Country bus, from Old Coulsdon down the curiously named Stoat's Nest Road, to watch the Brighton Run go by. I was lucky, too, that he considered the trip worth taking; at the time, the cars in action were already half a century old. Dad was in no way interested in cars, but for me it was the start of a lifelong fascination with very early automobiles.

In those early years I would carefully tick off the cars in the programme as they stuttered, burbled or chuntered by, so that, over half a century later, many of them seem like old familiar friends. I remember in 1952 watching the up-and-coming racing driver Stirling Moss go by on Fred Bennett's famous 1903 Cadillac, little thinking that many years later I would get to know him through my passion for motoring history – a passion that had been fired by watching those veterans go by every November. Nor did I imagine that one day I would be the editor of that programme. I still treasure my early copies of it, the start of a personal archive that now numbers hundreds of books and magazines covering the whole history of motoring.

My passion for the Brighton Run remains undiminished. One sunny Sunday in the 1960s, when the 1927 Clyno Royal Tourer that was then my only motor car was off the road, for some unspecified reason, I actually cycled the fifteen miles of give-and-take roads that lay between my home in East Sussex and the Brighton Road. My mount was a single-geared 1903 Rover Imperial Ladies' Safety Bicycle, which had an unyielding Brooks saddle and its original high-pressure beaded-edge tyres. I watched the veterans go by, followed them down the road to Crawley, and then cycled home.

After that trip, I could not sit down comfortably for some hours; those Imperial ladies must have worn iron-clad bloomers....

Although I have an interest in all periods of motoring, I have a particular fascination for the very earliest cars. They represent an astounding era when technological development was as rapid as it is in electronics today, when a car was obsolete almost as soon as its owner had bought it – often before he took delivery; in less than two decades, the motor car matured from a crude horseless carriage into a rapid and reliable means of transport, capable of crossing continents.

First things first: what *is* a veteran car? The basic answer is simple: to be classed as a 'veteran', a car has to have been built before the final stroke of midnight on 31 December 1904. (The day was a Saturday, so, even in that industrious age, the labour force would have to have been exceptionally hard-working!) To some extent, the choice of date was an arbitrary one, having been frozen in 1929 when the Brighton Run was open to cars of twenty-five years old or more. However, viewed

OPPOSITE: Veteran pin-up – these lovely ladies are promoting the 1904 15-19hp Beaufort car, a German make built in Baden but sold in England.

RIGHT: One of my earliest 'Brighton' memories is seeing Stirling Moss go by on Fred Bennett's 1903 Cadillac, the first of this marque to be imported into Britain.

Still with many horse-carriage features like unequal sized solid-tyred wheels, this stately 1899 Delahaye has its weather equipment in place for the very wet 2005 Brighton Run.

with hindsight, it was an exceptionally wise decision, for the transition from 1904 into 1905 was a technological tipping point at which car design matured from horseless carriage technology into a pattern that would remain recognizable for many years. It was, indeed, the point at which technical development began to put on the brakes....

Of course there were exceptions – there always are – and some cars of archetypal veteran design continued in production unchanged long after the end of 1904, while some cars built during the veteran era foreshadowed things to come. By and large, however, the differences between a veteran and cars of the following era are easy to spot.

Indeed, what makes the veteran period so fascinating is the vast variety of designs available from literally hundreds of hopeful companies, few of which achieved the hoped-for success or lasted more than a few financially fraught years. It was a period of enormous creativity, during which the engineering skills that had been perfected during the industrial revolution were applied to a totally new problem – the provision of reliable personal transportation independent of timetables and fixed routes. It was the start of a vast social revolution that is still in, for want of a better word, train....

There was personal transport on the roads before the coming of the car, but it moved at a speed that had been virtually unchanged for centuries. The advent of railways had certainly allowed people to move faster between fixed points, but at either end of the journey the passengers had to rely either on walking or on horse transport, both of which were limited in speed and range.

Conan Doyle's Sherlock Holmes stories give a good indication of how tightly travel in the Victorian world was ruled by the timetables of the various railway companies. Indeed, an intimate knowledge of Bradshaw's compendium of the complexities of those timetables was essential to planning a cross-country journey.

The growth of rail travel in the nineteenth century had seen a corresponding decline in road traffic and indeed regular travel by stagecoach had gone into a decline almost as soon as railways became established. As early as May 1838, less than a decade after Stephenson's *Rocket* went into service on the pioneering Liverpool & Manchester Railway, the Post Office announced that the mails to Holyhead, Manchester, Liverpool and Carlisle would in future be sent by rail from Euston.

Amazingly, even before the coming of the railways had driven the mail coach into history, the first age of the motor vehicle had dawned...and died....

CHAPTER ONE

Jurassic (Car) Park

The 1700s might have been called the Age of Enlightenment, but as far as transportation went, they were still very much the dark ages, for nothing moved faster than it had since Roman times. The horse was the sole form of power available for rapid transit, and millennia of breeding had failed to produce a beast that was noticeably faster than its distant ancestors. The highways were universally awful, for Thomas Telford had not yet embarked on his famous road-building programme, and long-distance travel by coach was both slow and inconvenient, relying on frequent relays of horses.

Typically, when Queen Anne's husband, Prince George of Denmark, set out to visit Petworth House in Sussex by coach, a distance of maybe 50 miles (80km), it took him fourteen hours over what a courtier described as 'the worst ways that ever I saw in my life'; the final 9 miles (14.5km) took six hours, and the coach was only prevented from overturning by the local peasants leaning against it.

But already the first stirrings of the industrial revolution had shown the tireless power of steam, and it would not be long before ingenious engineers sought to use steam to drive road vehicles.

The first authenticated steam-powered road vehicle was, perhaps inevitably, intended for use in war. In 1769 the French Minister of War commissioned a French engineer, Nicolas-Joseph Cugnot, to design a steam truck (or *fardier*) for carrying cannon. A scaled-down prototype tested early in 1770 was said to be capable of carrying four people at 2.5mph (4km/h), but it had to stop every 15 minutes for the boiler to be refilled. Cugnot's full-sized *fardier* was a clumsy three-wheeler that carried its boiler overhung on a massive iron frame ahead of its single front wheel, which was driven through a system of ratchets and levers from cylinders on either side.

It is difficult to envisage now, but when Cugnot built the *fardier*, the combination of crankshaft and connecting rod that is regarded as a basic component of any reciprocating engine had not been invented; in fact, it did not arrive until the 1780s. The *fardier*'s engine used the see-saw motion of a rocking beam linked to the ratchet arms to return the pistons to the tops of the cylinders after each power stroke. With no flywheel to damp out the motion, the *fardier* must have lurched along in a series of jerks.

The whole bulk of the engine, boiler and front wheel was pivoted on a single king pin. The hapless driver, seated on a kind of garden bench, was supposed to turn the massive power train through a flimsy-looking tiller that acted on a toothed quadrant and took thirty complete revolutions to go from lock to lock.

Designed to take a payload of 4–5 tons, Cugnot's *fardier* was finished by May 1771 at a cost of 20,000 *livres*, but by then the French Government had lost interest in the project.

There are tales (or legends?) that tell how the *fardier* (or maybe it was the scaled-down prototype) was involved in the first-ever motor accident when it hit a wall in the grounds of the Paris Arsenal; certainly the rudimentary steering linkage would have taken a very long time to have any effect on the single front wheel. Amazingly, the *fardier* survived the French Revolution and was, in fact, the first historic vehicle to be deliberately preserved, as L.-N. Rolland, Commissioner-General of the Army, recalled in 1800:

> During the Terror, a committee of revolutionaries wanted to take this carriage away and scrap it; I chased that committee out of the Arsenal, and the carriage was preserved there.
>
> When General Bonaparte returned from concluding his peace treaty, I spoke to him of this carriage; proposing to come and

Cugnot's clumsy fardier *of 1771 still survives despite its impractical design and overall lack of success.*

> see it, he sent Citizen Perrier of the Institute to examine it, after which he told me that by adding a little to its mechanism, you would get a very large horizontal force from it. So, as there were some repairs to be made, Citizen Brezin, son of the man who had built it, took it upon himself to make them free of charge, as he considered it the masterpiece of his father's forge.
>
> But, as General Napoleon had sailed for Egypt, the trials never took place.

In 1800 Rolland tried to persuade the authorities to conduct the tests anyway, and proposed building a track 'with gentle slopes' on private ground so that the driver could become accustomed to the steering before venturing on to the public highway. He had no success, and it was ordered that the 'fire machine' should be handed over to the newly created arts and crafts museum.

Although Rolland thought this order was condemning the *fardier* 'to purgatory', in fact, it was its salvation, and for the past two centuries, Cugnot's machine has been on display in the Conservatoire National des Arts et Métiers in Paris. Sadly, French museum curators seem to be an incurious lot, for no one since Cugnot's day has ever tried to make the *fardier* run – it only needs to be connected to a high-pressure air line – to see whether that primitive engine and its weird transmission really worked. Nor does its boiler seem practical; not only does it lack a safety valve but there is no way of feeding the boiler's fire once on the move.

Fortunately, we do know that the next serious contender for the title of the first successful road carriage worked, for full-size replicas of the pioneering road engines constructed by Cornish mining engineer Richard Trevithick have been built and operated in recent years. In engineering terms, this is the equivalent of the plot of the film *Jurassic Park*, except that these reborn monsters are solid wood and metal, not computer-generated animatronics!

Known as 'The Cornish Giant', Trevithick stood 6ft 2in tall and was immensely strong. Though he skipped school and had difficulty with his spelling, he was an intuitive genius who solved the most difficult mathematical problems. He came into his own when the Cornish mine owners fought the steam engine patent monopoly operated by James Watt and his partner Boulton. Trevithick realized that the Boulton & Watt engine, which operated at low pressure, was clumsy and inefficient, and developed a new steam engine that ran at a relatively high pressure.

Trevithick's engine was compact enough to fit into a simple carriage, and in 1800–1801 the ingenious Cornishman constructed his 'Puffing Devil', a rudimentary road locomotive – little more than a boiler and engine on wheels. On Christmas Eve 1801, it climbed part way up the 1:20 slope of Camborne Beacon, with seven or eight locals clinging on, before it ran out of steam. On 28 December Trevithick tried again, with the aim of travelling from Camborne to Tehidy House, a couple of miles away. Given the crudeness of the steering, it is hardly surprising that, when the front wheels hit a gully that ran across the road a few hundred yards from the start of the journey, 'the steering handle was jerked out of Captain Andrew's hand, and over she turned'.

Undaunted, Trevithick, his cousin Andrew Vivian (the unfortunate steersman) and the rest of the party pushed the steam carriage to a nearby hotel. They housed it under a lean-to before adjourning inside the building, where they 'comforted their Hearts with a Roast Goose and proper Drinks, when, forgetfull of the Engine, its Water boiled away, the Iron became red hot, and nothing that was combustible remained either of the Engine or the House'.

In the late 1990s the Council of the Trevithick Society backed the construction of a replica of Trevithick's 1801 road locomotive, which had its first public outing in Camborne on Trevithick Day (28 April) in the bicentennial year of 2001: It proved itself capable of travelling at a smart walking pace and, once 'nanny state' difficulties with the local police had been ironed out, successfully climbed Camborne Beacon just as its ancestor had done two centuries earlier (although it did get a bit breathless towards the very top).

Having proved that his ideas were valid with that one eventful run in 1801, Trevithick was anxious to promote his high-pressure engine. He was already planning a new carriage, which he described in the 1802 patent protecting his engine. The idea was to build and run the carriage in London to generate publicity. The great scientist Humphrey Davy was intrigued: 'I shall hope soon to hear that the roads of England are the haunts of Captain Trevithick's Dragons,' he wrote.

An engine and boiler were made in Cornwall and shipped to London at the end of April 1803, where coachbuilder William Felton, of Leather Lane, Holborn, had already built a chassis to take them. Felton added a body to seat eight (or ten at a pinch) above the engine, which had a 5½-in diameter cylinder with a 30-in stroke and ran at 50rpm: 'Much more power than we shall want,' remarked the optimistic Trevithick. A distinctive feature of Captain Trevithick's Dragon was the size of its driving wheels. These were eight feet in diameter, in an effort to even out the appalling road surfaces of the day.

A steersman and a stoker (or 'engineman') were needed to operate the carriage, whose historic first run – the first time that a motor vehicle designed to carry passengers took to the road – was made in the summer of 1803. With Andrew Vivian in control and carrying William Felton and his sons, the London Carriage travelled from Leather Lane through Liquorpond Street into Gray's Inn Road, passed Lord's Cricket Ground on its way to Paddington and Islington, and then returned to Leather Lane. It later made several journeys along Tottenham Court Road and Euston Square, and on another occasion Oxford Street was cleared of traffic to give the steamer a clear run.

On one trip, Andrew Vivian's 19-year-old son John was entrusted with the tiller. He later recalled the event:

> We started about four o'clock in the morning, and went along Tottenham Court Road and the City Road. There was a canal by the side of the road at one place, for I was thinking how deep it was if we should run into it.

> We kept going on for four or five miles, and sometimes at the rate of eight or nine miles an hour. I was steering and... Captain Dick came alongside of me and said, 'She is going all right.'
>
> 'Yes,' I said. 'I think we had better go on to Cornwall.'
>
> She was going along five or six miles an hour, and Captain Dick called out, 'Put the helm down, John!' and before I could tell what was up, Captain Dick's foot was upon the steering-wheel handle, and we were tearing down six or seven yards of railing from a garden wall. A person put his head from a window, and called out, 'What the devil are you doing there! What the devil is that thing?'

But even London's first motor accident failed to arouse any press interest, so the volatile Trevithick broke up his carriage and used the engine to drive a hoop rolling mill.

The brief adventure of Trevithick's London Carriage was quickly forgotten. As engineer Alexander Gordon explained in the first-ever motoring history, the *Historical and Practical Treatise upon Elemental Locomotion by means of Steam Carriages on Common Roads*, published in 1832, 'it will not be a matter of surprise that, at a period when turnpike roads were very ill-made...the inventor discontinued his attempts on common roads and confined his operations to a rail-way'.

A year after his trials with the London Carriage, Trevithick built the first steam railway locomotive, and again his efforts went unrecognized. Today, most people believe that George Stephenson – who lagged a quarter of a century behind the Cornish engineer – was the inventor of the railway locomotive. Trevithick bemoaned his fate in a letter to his friend Davies Gilbert:

> I have been branded with folly and madness for attempting what the world calls impossibilities, and even from the great engineer, the late Mr James Watt, who said to an eminent scientific character still living, that I deserved hanging for bringing into use the high-pressure engine. This so far has been my reward from the public; but should this be all, I shall be satisfied by the great secret pleasure and laudable pride that I feel in my own breast from having been the instrument of bringing forward and maturing new principles and new arrangements of boundless value to my country. However much I may be straitened in pecuniary circumstances, the great honour of being a useful subject can never be taken from me, which to me far exceeds riches.

In July 2003 George Grindey drove Tom Brogden's re-creation of Richard Trevithick's London Carriage down Leather Lane to commemorate the bicentenary of its first run.

Trevithick died in near-penury in Kent in 1833, but fortunately his achievement in building the first practicable self-propelled road carriage has at last been nobly recognized. Macclesfield engineer Tom Brogden has spent fifteen years creating a full-size replica of Trevithick's London Carriage, based on the 1802 patent and on a report by Simon Goodrich of the Navy Board, who sketched the carriage when he interviewed Trevithick. It all started, it seems, when Brogden's wife Ruth gave him a birthday card with a picture of Trevithick's carriage. Brogden's engineering brain began to wonder what such a machine must have looked like in action.

When building his replica, Brogden found that Trevithick had even put a

ABOVE: The 9ft diameter driving wheels of the Trevithick carriage were intended to give a smooth ride over the rough roads of 1803.

LEFT: Engineman Roger Lees fires up the Trevithick carriage to its working pressure.

deliberate mistake in the patent specification to prevent unscrupulous rivals from copying his invention; if the patent is followed to the letter, the engine will only run backwards! However, he persisted with the project, even building a replica body like the one shown in the patent drawing, copying it from a design in William Felton's *A Treatise on Carriages*, written in 1794 and one of the earliest books on coachbuilding. The body was slung – like the original – on short leather straps from long springs –guaranteed to make passengers feel seasick!

Tom Brogden had to cope with similar teething troubles to those that must have presented themselves to Trevithick back in 1803, according to his 'works driver' George Grindey: 'When I originally drove the carriage, it was virtually unsteerable, as there was so little load on the front wheel. That may be why young Vivian crashed into the railings in 1803. We needed extra water storage, so we added a 40-gallon barrel beneath the chassis to keep the front end down. In modern parlance, now it understeers.'

Roadholding problems solved, Brogden's 13-ft high steam carriage has been seen in action both in Britain and in Europe, and has even taken part in a veteran car rally round Lake Geneva. It develops 3 hp, working at a pressure of 30lb/sq in. That is enough to propel the carriage at 8mph (13km/h) on the higher of its two gears, so a more effective braking system has been thoughtfully added to supplement the minimal 1803 brake block on the flywheel.

On 6 July 2003 the replica was taken to Leather Lane to commemorate the bicentenary of the first run. With steersman George Grindey at the tiller and engineman Roger Lees feeding the boiler, Trevithick's reborn London Carriage ran majestically from the site of Felton's coachworks down Leather Lane and on into Hatton Garden. As Archivist of the Worshipful Company of Coachmakers and Coach Harness Makers – of which ancient City company William Felton, it seems, was a somewhat troublesome member – I was present at the re-enactment. I was delighted to meet Frank Trevithick-Okuno, a direct descendant of Richard Trevithick, who has been campaigning for years for greater recognition of his gifted ancestor's achievements. Ironically, when Trevithick was at last commemorated, on a British two-pound coin in 2004, it was for his invention of the railway locomotive rather than for his road carriages. British officialdom, apparently, has always preferred railway trains to road vehicles.

Having re-created Trevithick's long-forgotten London Carriage, the indefatigable Tom Brogden decided to bring back to life another extinct monster from the age of steam. Another of his heroes was Walter Hancock, one of the most accomplished engineers of the early 19th century, who between 1824 and 1836 built ten steam carriages, ran them successfully for thousands of miles at speeds of up to 25mph (40km/h) and even planned a chain of service stations to overcome the difficulty of finding fuel and water. (Endlessly inventive, Hancock also patented the process of vulcanizing rubber.)

Railway pioneer George Stephenson dismissed the idea of road-going steam engines out of hand, claiming that 'the idea of working steam carriages economically on common roads is entirely impractical'. He declared that steam engines would only work efficiently on level rails, with the consequent huge expenditure on tunnels and embankments.

In 1836 Hancock proved him wrong by running a regular bus service in London with four steam carriages. (One of them was named *Autopsy*, or 'See for Yourself', which was perhaps less worrying in an age when more people had at least some understanding of classical Greek.) *Autopsy* and Hancock's other carriages proved remarkably reliable, covering a total of 4,200 miles (6,760km) in twenty weeks and carrying around 13,000 passengers. Although he had proved that railways were hopelessly uneconomic compared with road traction, Hancock was forced to give up his work with steam carriages in 1840 when his backers failed to give him the necessary support.

Tom Brogden chose Hancock's 1832 carriage *Enterprise* as the model for his second re-creation. This second project took less time than the Trevithick replica to build as the team now had a better idea of how to solve the problems faced by Industrial Revolution engineers!

Many features that are now taken for granted, such as Ackermann steering, differential gears and roller chains, were not available in Hancock's day; his solutions are a measure of his genius. As he only had link chains to drive the rear wheels, Hancock devised a sort of negative sprocket with oval cavities to take the horizontal links. Because there was no differential, he normally only drove on one wheel, but could engage the second for extra traction by locking its hub to the driving shaft by threaded pins. Swinging arms located the back axle, just as they do on modern American Ford off-roaders, and kept the chains in the correct tension; the rear-mounted twin-cylinder engine was suspended, along with the rest of the carriage, on leaf springs, so that the passengers were insulated from vibration. And, because traditional cart wheels were too flimsy to take the side strains imposed by steam traction, Hancock invented a new kind of wheel, with iron nave plates pulled together by bolts to sandwich the wedge-shaped ends of strong wooden spokes. The design became known as the artillery wheel, and was still being used on motor cars a century later.

I rode aboard *Enterprise* at the 2001 Goodwood Festival of Speed, where Tom Brogden ran both of his amazing steam carriages, and was impressed by the practicality of Hancock's design – apart, that is, from the sheer physical effort involved in climbing aboard. The floor level is a yard or more above the road, and is reached by climbing two minuscule steps with only a brass grab-handle for assistance. It is hardly ideal for lady passengers in tight skirts, and the *Enterprise*'s intended use as transport from the car park to Goodwood House for the evening black-tie dinner attracted few takers. They missed a treat, however. Seated at the front of its roomy fourteen-seat body, I asked driver George Grindey, ensconced on the prow behind a horizontal steering wheel – Hancock was probably the first to employ this now universal device – what *Enterprise* was like to drive. '*Enterprise* uses an awful lot of coke and we only get 8 miles to 200 gallons of water…but it will climb a one in six hill easily,' he said. 'On smooth roads, she's a big pussycat, but you get a

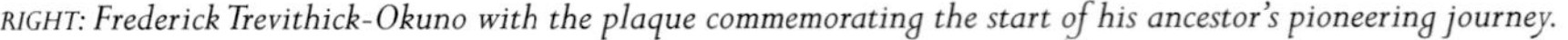
ABOVE: The location of the Trevithick carriage's first run has changed dramatically in two centuries.

RIGHT: Frederick Trevithick-Okuno with the plaque commemorating the start of his ancestor's pioneering journey.

A contemporary engraving of Hancock's carriages Autopsy, Era *and* Infant *in the rural Arcadia that is now the East End of London.*

lot of kickback with centre-point steering on rough roads.'

Because cart-type centre-pivot steering could easily be deflected by the potholes and pebbles of uneven roads, the ingenious Hancock fitted a pedal-operated brake that held the vertical steering column steady until the driver wanted to make a turn. Hancock also anticipated the supposedly very modern concept of 'drive by wire', with an overhead lever that signalled the driver's wishes to the engine room at the rear, where the engineer kept an eye on the boiler pressure and opened the throttle. However, as Roger Lees, the engineer of the replica *Enterprise*, explained, 'I can overrule George's commands if I think he's getting too carried away.' Too late for his steam carriages, Walter Hancock invented the flexible speaking tube in 1850.

Enterprise's firebox was at the very rear, and Tom Brogden plans to fit a hopper that will automatically feed coke into the furnace while the carriage is moving, as Hancock originally planned. 'At the moment, however, we progress a bag of coke at a time,' he says, 'though on long trips we have a third crew member who rides on the rear platform to tend the fire. He also commands an auxiliary hand-brake that pushes shoes against the iron tyres to supplement the braking efforts of the driver.'

Among the ingenious Hancock's many inventions was the steering wheel, but he still used cart-type centre-pivot steering, not the newly invented 'Ackermann' steering.

From the passenger's point of view, the cabin is both comfortable and weathertight, and the rear-engined configuration isolates its occupants from any sound or smell from the engines. The only sounds are subdued faraway rumblings from the iron-shod wheels, and the sensation is like riding in a land-locked paddle steamer.

On 31 October 1832, Hancock anticipated the Veteran Car Run by making the first ever-trip from London to Brighton in a self-propelled vehicle, using another of his steamers, the *Infant*. (At 3.5 tons, this was a lusty infant indeed!) One of his passengers was Alexander Gordon, whose short-lived *Journal of Elemental Locomotion* was the world's first motor magazine. Apart from complaints about the quality and availability of the coke that was needed to feed the boiler, the run was a great success, concluded Gordon. Typical was the steamer's ascent of Red Hill, still a testing climb for the veterans each November: 'As we approached Red Hill, the coke boxes getting low, the fireman came again to a small quantity of London coke, when the carriage immediately improved its speed, and carried us up the hill (a hill on which all the coaches in such weather require six horses) in fine style, at the average speed of six and seven miles an hour.'

Although that fuel problem caused the steamer to pause overnight after completing the first 38 miles (61km) of the journey, it arrived in Brighton the following morning 'apparently to the great surprise and satisfaction of a large concourse of persons who had by this time assembled'.

Even though the trial had been a success, Hancock's proposed London to Brighton steam carriage service never became a reality. Britain was in the grip of railway mania; fortunes could be made by speculating in railway shares, and many unprofitable branch lines were built on routes that would have been far better served by steam carriages. Moreover, many of the main roads were turnpikes run by trusts that, through either ignorance or malice, charged disproportionately high tolls on the few steam carriages that were built, making their operation uneconomical. A House of Commons Select Committee was set up to examine the whole question of 'Steam Carriages upon Common Roads' and produced a very favourable report, in which one of its members concluded the following:

> I think the roads will be considerably benefited by the change of impelling by steam instead of by horses. I think it will be a great public benefit when steam-coaches come into common use, and hence that it is expedient that a moderate bounty should be offered for the adoption of steam-carriages by giving them all possible advantage they can have without trenching on the interests of individuals. If they were allowed to run toll free, and duty free, until a certain number were in use, or during a certain time, it would much accelerate their introduction, because it would diminish the loss that must necessarily be incurred by running them before they are perfected in their construction.
>
> Small encouragements or discouragements have a considerable effect on new inventions in their infant and imperfect state. Steam-coaches will very well bear all tolls and taxes to which other coaches are subject, when they are able to carry passengers regularly and profitably; but they want encouragement now, instead of difficulties being thrown in their way.

I rode aboard Tom Brogden's re-creation of Hancock's Enterprise *at the 2001 Goodwood Festival of Speed. Passengers faced a steep climb to board the vehicle.*

In fact, concluded the Committee's report, the steam carriage was 'one of the most important improvements in the means of internal communication ever introduced'.

But the necessary encouragement was lacking, and by 1840 even dedicated experimenters like Hancock had given up the unequal struggle. All the effort, encouragement and investment went on railway travel, and, while Britain took an early lead in this field, the pioneering work of the steam-carriage builders was quickly forgotten. Britain's road system fell into disrepair, and when steam again appeared on the highways, it drove heavyweight traction engines and road locomotives. Their road-destroying activities were restricted by the infamous Red Flag Act, whose ultimate demise was to be celebrated by that first Emancipation Day Run of 1896.

Alexander Gordon was one of the steam carriage builders who believed that mechanical legs were needed to overcome wheel spin.

CHAPTER TWO

No Need for Mechanical Legs

Perhaps the most persistent of the steam-carriage pioneers after Hancock was Goldsworthy Gurney, another Cornish-man, who as early as 1822 had declared that 'elemental power is capable of being applied to propel carriages along the common roads with great political advantage, and... the floating knowledge of the day places the subject within our reach. I consider that ammoniac gas is usable. This gas can be used in the normal mechanism of a steam engine, without its requiring any great modification.'

However, having built a small carriage driven by ammonia, Gurney decided to construct a full-size carriage propelled by steam. Convinced that wheels would not have sufficient grip to drive the carriage, he fitted it with auxiliary steam-powered legs intended to push it along. Fortunately, tests showed that these were redundant – the carriage is said to have climbed Windmill Hill in Kilburn in 1825 – and he then built a second machine, which was reported to have made a 9-mile (14.5km) trip from London to Edgware.

However, the carriage for which Gurney is best remembered is the huge six-wheeled stagecoach intended for a regular London–Bath service, on which work started in 1826. At first, this was also fitted with 'propellers' to help it up hills, but after it climbed Highgate Hill in 1828 unaided, Gurney wrote that 'the wheels did not slip, nor was there need to use the mechanical legs for a single instant'.

Stopping was another matter. Coming down Highgate Hill, the carriage ran away and ended in a ditch.

Designed for a London to Bath service, Goldsworthy Gurney's six-wheeled carriage only made the journey once, in 1826.

At this 1829 demonstration of Gurney's steam drag, the Duke of Wellington was one of the passengers.

In 1828 Gurney drove this carriage to Bath – it made just the one journey there, even though it carried the words 'London and Bath – Royal Patent' on its sides – and had to pause every 4 miles (6km) to refill its thirsty boiler. Fortunately, this was one road where water was not a problem. In Regency times, Beau Nash had established a chain of huge pumps (some of which still survive alongside what is now the A4) to allow the roads to be kept well watered. This stopped the route being too dusty for the carriages of the smart set, who regularly drove down to Bath, where it was fashionable to take the cure at the city's ancient springs.

It is said that Gurney's carriage broke down on the outward journey, and was ignominiously dragged to its destination by a team of horses, but on the return leg it is reported to have covered the 84 miles (135km) from Melksham to Cranford Bridge – not far from the present-day Heathrow Airport – in ten hours, 'including stoppages'.

Gurney then turned his attention to a far more practical design: a light four-wheeled tractor unit intended to pull a passenger-carrying trailer. He called it a 'steam drag' and in size and concept it was far more like a modern car. He gave several public demonstrations of this machine, including one at Hounslow on 12 August 1829 when a Gurney Drag hauled a 'Barouche…containing the Duke of Wellington and other Persons of Distinction'. Railway pioneer Robert Stephenson was another 'person of distinction' who rode behind a Gurney Drag at one of these demonstrations, while Sir George Cayley, 'the father of British aviation' and the constructor of Britain's first successful glider, was a keen collaborator on Gurney's steam carriages.

Astoundingly, the chassis and engine of a Gurney Drag survive today in the Glasgow Museum of Transport in the Kelvin Halls, presented to that institution as long ago as 1889. Without doubt the oldest British self-propelled road vehicle in existence, the Drag – apparently one of two sent to Scotland in 1830 – was found in a barn near the Paisley Road. If any historic British vehicle deserves a sympathetic restoration, this unique relic is surely it!

This 1838 cutaway shows the mechanism of Gurney's steam drag.

CHAPTER THREE

Captain Bordino's Coach

There is only one place to go to see what a British steam coach in all its glory looked like; paradoxically, that place is central Turin, where the Biscaretti Museum's impressive collection of early cars includes a massive steam coach built by an Italian military engineer named Virginio Bordino. After spending several years studying engineering in England on behalf of the Sardinian Army, Bordino returned home to Italy where he planned five experimental steamers to test the viability of steam power for military use, three of which were built in the Turin Arsenal. There remains no trace of the first two, but the third, built in 1854, is the massive steam coach that is today the pride of the Biscaretti Collection; bizarrely, Captain Bordino must have been a slow learner, for his coach was around twenty-five years out of date even when it was new!

Powered by a twin-cylinder underfloor engine like Gurney's stage coach, Bordino's carriage had a range of about two hours, consuming around 130lb of coal and travelling at a fast walking pace.

Virgilio Bordino's steam coach was decades out of date when it was built in 1854.

CHAPTER FOUR

Red Flag Days

Amazingly, the first press report of a vehicle that would be recognized as a motor car today appeared over 140 years ago, in the French weekly paper *Le Monde Illustré*. Reporter Emile Bourdelin described in 1860 a new type of engine powered by lighting gas, 'available everywhere nowadays, whose infinitely reduced price gives rise to the hope of a truly fabulous saving'.

Already in use by small workshops to power machines such as lathes, the engine had been invented by a Belgian named J.-J. Etienne Lenoir (who had previously designed a 'vehiculo-motor' powered by a horse walking on an endless belt) and used an electric spark 'pistol' to ignite town gas in a cylinder. Having described the engine, Bourdelin went on to say, 'Let's forget stationary engines and visualize the new invention from the point of view of the services it could render as a power unit on board ships or as the engine of all kinds of vehicles...in which would be fitted a tank storing a small volume of gas.'

He went on to describe an illustrative engraving:

> [it is of] a carriage recently built by M. Lenoir. The casing that houses the engine does not inconvenience the travellers. The gas is contained in the tank A. The motion is communicated to the rear wheels by an endless chain which runs over two sprockets. The carriage is steered by a wheel on a vertical shaft placed ahead of the driver. This shaft carries a pinion at its lower end that acts on a semi-circular rack gear. This rack is fixed to the front wheel, which it forces to turn left or right, altering the direction of the vehicle. A crank handle applies a brake to reduce the speed, and as soon as the gas tap is closed, the machine stops moving.

Bourdelin went on to envisage a network of 'filling stations' producing gas for vehicles in areas where there were no public gasometers, however, there were few customers for Lenoir's gas engines, which proved hopelessly inefficient.

The carriage that Bourdelin described in 1860 as 'recently built' was, in fact, only a paper project, and work did not begin on it until 1862. It made a few out-and-back journeys from Lenoir's workshops in the Rue de la Roquette in Paris, one of which Lenoir recalled many years later: 'I made, in '63, an automobile carriage with which, in the month of September, we went to Joinville-le-Pont. An hour and a half to go, the same to come back. The 1.5 horsepower engine turned at 100 revolutions a minute, with a pretty heavy flywheel.'

It would be fascinating to know how Lenoir managed to make his wildly inefficient engine drive a car, apparently without any form of transmission. As the Lenoir engine gobbled 3166 litres of gas per horsepower per hour (equal to some 45 cu ft of uncompressed gas for every mile so laboriously covered), used four times as much water as a steam engine, and needed oiling every ten minutes, it can hardly have been the ideal power unit for a car!

I discovered a curious postscript to the Lenoir story in the mid-1960s when I was working on *Motor Trader* magazine. Leafing through the early numbers of the paper to prepare the Diamond Jubilee issue, I found a 1906 news story that papers had come to light in Paris detailing the sale of Lenoir's carriage to Tsar Alexander II of Russia in 1864. Apparently, the car was taken from Paris to the railway station at Vincennes to begin its long journey to St Petersburg, but after that nothing more was heard of it; when enquiries were made in 1906, no trace of the Lenoir carriage was found. Maybe it is still mouldering in some cellar in one of the Tsar's palaces; who knows?

We do know, however, that Lenoir's carriage was perfectly practical, for in 1907 Henry Ford built a car powered by a non-compressing Lenoir engine to

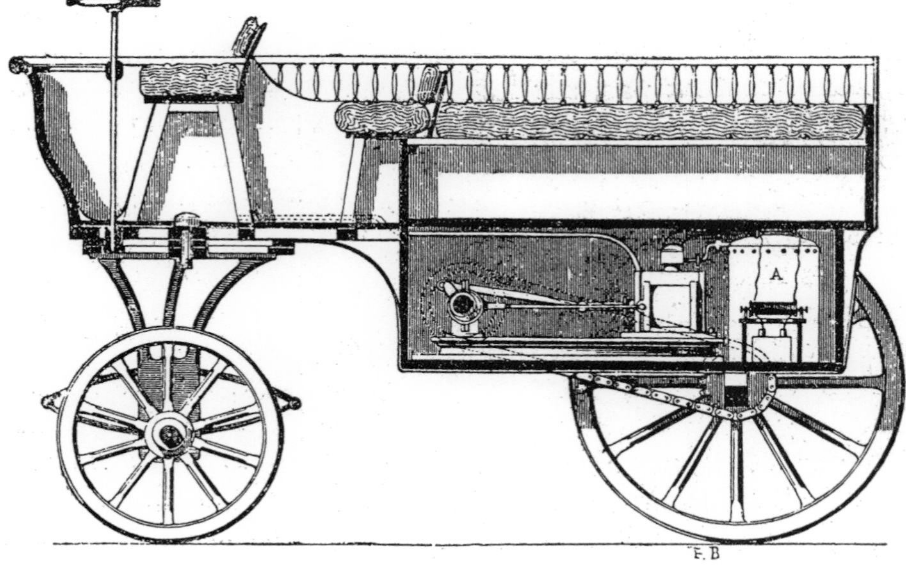

This 1860 engraving of Lenoir's carriage was based largely on imagination; the carriage did not run until 1863.

prove that internal-combustion-powered cars existed prior to an 1877 'master patent' in the name of George Baldwin Selden. The Association of Licensed Automobile Manufacturers had taken Ford to court on the grounds that he had infringed the Selden patent, by which they hoped to control the American motor industry.

In July 1907 pioneer car builder Charles Duryea described a ride on the Ford-Lenoir in New York:

> When I first saw it, it was on the second floor at the Ford garage and the operator very kindly started it for me by giving the starting crank about one turn, much as a modern auto would be started. He then stopped it by shutting off the spark, and soon after, by connecting the current, started it by use of the spark and not using the crank, as modern four-cycle autos frequently are started.
>
> We drove up Broadway into the Park, around a number of curves and up and down some grades at a speed that I should think fully averaged ten miles an hour, sometimes going faster, sometimes, of course, slower.

The car's longest non-stop run was over 8 miles (13km); two Selden carriages had also been built as evidence in the trial, but neither could run a mile without breaking down.

This spectacular performance by a fifty-year-old design was one of the factors that led to Ford's eventual victory in the court case, and freed the American motor industry from the ALAM's crippling attempts to establish a monopoly.

There were other constructors of private road carriages active at around the same time as Lenoir, but to a man they relied on steam. In 1860 Thomas Rickett of the Castle Foundry in Buckingham built a 'common road steam carriage', designed for the Marquis of Stafford by J.E. M'Connell of the London and North Western Railway. Like Lenoir's carriage it was a three-wheeler, with two driving wheels behind and a single steering wheel in front, but it was capable of carrying three passengers at 10mph (16km/h). This was the second carriage that Rickett had built: in 1859 he had constructed a similar machine for the Earl of Caithness, which had successfully made the difficult journey from Inverness to John O'Groats.

These were handy vehicles much the same size as a modern family car – about 11ft long and 7ft wide, in which the passengers sat ahead of the boiler ('as the passengers are in front of the chimney, neither steam nor smoke can create any discomfort for them'). Ingeniously, the main chassis frame consisted of two sheet-iron tanks that held the water supply.

The chief practical difficulty with such machines, declared the *New York Coachmaker's Magazine*, which kept a close watch on the development of steam carriages on both sides of the Atlantic, was 'passing horses, and this will always be a difficulty, for it is hardly to be expected that the horse will ever learn to pass automatic machinery without fear and trembling. At present, at any rate, frequent stoppages are necessary to allow the animals to pass.'

It was inevitable that in a country as 'horsey' as Britain, the legislators would view these newfangled steam carriages with suspicion. Since the existing Turnpike Acts did not cover self-propelled vehicles, in 1865 the Liberal government imposed a 4mph (6.4km/h) speed limit on all 'road locomotives'. Perversely, it lumped together neat private carriages such as the Ricketts steamers with the massive traction engines whose great bulk wrought havoc with Britain's poorly maintained highways, which had been neglected by the authorities since the coming of the railways. Every 'road locomotive' had to be attended by three people, with one walking ahead of the engine to warn of its approach, carrying a red flag in the daytime and a red lamp at night. It was an ignorant political decision that was to retard the progress of motoring in Britain by many years.

The law was amended in 1878 to remove the requirement for the red flag, but local authorities were given the option to insist that it should still be carried – and many of them still exercised that option after the first motor cars made their hesitant way on to the road.

In the mid-1960s I met a man who must surely have been the last surviving 'red flag boy', a remarkable octogenarian named Frank Hunt who lived in a terraced house in Putney, in south-west London. Gordon Crosby illustrations clipped from *The Autocar* in the late 1920s had been glued straight on to the walls of his home, barely recognizable under a quarter-inch accumulation of grime. Miss

In October 1860 the Earl of Caithness drove this steam carriage from Inverness to his seat at Borrogill Castle, near John O'Groats, boasting, 'On the level I got 19mph!'

Havisham would definitely have approved! Mr Hunt retained a broad and virtually impenetrable Oxfordshire accent after more than sixty years living in London. In the 1890s, he had ridden against William Morris in a cycle race (and won) and helped to repair one of the very first cars on the roads of Britain – it was such a novelty, it was an exhibit with a travelling circus. In 1915 he had helped to build the very first Aston Martin car.

Frank Hunt had begun his working life in 1890, at the age of ten, carrying a red flag in front of the traction engines of the Oxfordshire Steam Ploughing Company (his job also included scaring crows from the crops with a rattle!). Despite such eyewitness evidence, however, 'barrack-room lawyers' in the Veteran Car Club tried to prove that, as there was no legal compunction to carry a red flag, there can have been no such thing as a red flag man after 1878. Their tunnel vision blinded them to cases such as that of pioneer motorist Leon L'Hollier of Birmingham, who in December 1895 was prosecuted for 'driving an autocar, or horseless carriage… at between five and six miles an hour… [with] no one in front of it to warn of its approach'. In court, L'Hollier's barrister declared that 'it could not be the intention of the legislature to see that every vehicle used in the ordinary way with the most perfect guiding gear, as in this instance, must be preceded by a man with a red flag… it was 'manifestly absurd… [to] get a man to go on in front with a Red Flag…'.

Deterred by the introduction of the Red Flag Act 4mph speed limit, engineer Richard Tangye exported his steam carriage Cornubia *to India.*

Alfred Yarrow, aged 19, designed this steam car in collaboration with his 20-year-old friend J.B. Hilditch. It was built by William Cowan of Greenwich and shown at the 1862 South Kensington Exhibition, but won no prizes because the judge for carriages thought it was an engine, and the judge for engines thought it was a carriage…

Manifestly absurd though it was, the law restricting all self-propelled vehicles on British roads to walking pace deterred all but the boldest pioneers. Robert Neville Grenville was one of these. In 1875 he built a three-wheeled steam carriage in the well-equipped workshop at his home, Butleigh Court, Glastonbury, Somerset, helped by his lifelong friend George Jackson Churchward, who in 1902 became chief mechanical engineer of the Great Western Railway. Both men had been engineering pupils with the South Devon Railway and, inevitably, the Grenville carriage had many features in common with railway locomotives. Indeed, some components, including the solid teak 'Mansell' wheels, may have been made in the GWR workshops at Swindon under Churchward's supervision. Grenville developed his carriage over a fifteen-year period, replacing the original single-cylinder engine with a more powerful twin-cylinder unit.

To comply with the law, the carriage had a driver, a brakesman and a fireman. Despite its consumption of five gallons of

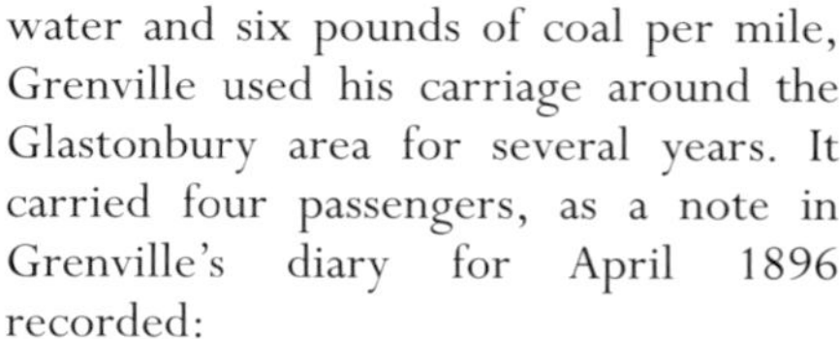

ABOVE: Robert Grenville's 1875 steam carriage is still in full working order, as demonstrated at the 1996 Victorian Extravaganza at the National Motor Museum at Beaulieu. A few years later, it took part in the Brighton Run.

RIGHT: Tricycle or locomotive? Victorian law classed the lightweight Bateman steamer to be as much a locomotive as a ten-ton traction engine.

water and six pounds of coal per mile, Grenville used his carriage around the Glastonbury area for several years. It carried four passengers, as a note in Grenville's diary for April 1896 recorded:

> Mr Pinney came at 9.30 am and we started with steam carriage at 9.45, George Mildred with me in front, and Noble firing, Mrs. N.G. and Mrs. Audry with us as far as the Horse and Lion; went on through Glastonbury and to Polsham; stopped there for five buckets of water, and on to Wells, arriving at the Palace at 10.50 – ten miles in sixty-five minutes including stops for horses, water, and at railway level crossing. Called on the Bishop (of Bath and Wells) as I promised, and took him and some friends for a run round the Palace.

Two years later, Grenville converted his carriage into a stationary engine to drive a cider mill. It was not used after 1902, but after Grenville's death, in 1936, the carriage was completely overhauled and put back into running order. Today it is displayed in the Bristol Industrial Museum, the oldest running vehicle in the world.

Even though they were designed as private carriages, such machines were hardly motor cars like today's. They were far lighter and manoeuvrable than the massive traction engines that weighed many tons, but the legislators classified them all as 'road locomotives'. The lunacy of the law was clearly demonstrated in the case of Parkyns v. Priest, referenced in the handy pocket compendium *Police Duty – Catechism and Reports*, which included many case-law Q & As that were intended to guide the Victorian bobby in his unhappy lot:

> Ques. When may a tricycle be said to be a locomotive ?
>
> Ans: When propelled by steam. (Parkyns v Priest, 72 BD, 313.)

The sad tale behind those lines was told in the catalogue of the first-ever motor museum, which opened in London's Oxford Street in 1912 (and, after relocating to the Crystal Palace, was closed down in August 1914 when its display space was requisitioned to store munitions for the Great War):

> This curious old vehicle, the original English steam tricycle, was patented by Sir Thomas Parkyns, Bart, in 1881. It was made by Arthur H. Bateman, engineer, East Greenwich, London SE.
>
> These were the dark days when the law demanded that motor vehicles or steam carriages, as they styled them – having traction engines in mind – should only be driven when the wheels were 4 inches wide, when there were three men in attendance, two on the machine, and one ahead carrying a red flag, the pace not to exceed 2mph (3km/h). It need not be pointed out that with this machine it was impossible to fulfil the two first conditions, so the inventor was fined one shilling for breaking the law. He appealed to the Queen's Bench, but the appeal was dismissed, the Act stating that any vehicle 'propelled other than by animal power' came under the heading of 'steam carriage'. Sir David Salomons had a similar machine on order at the time. Owing, however, to this decision, the order was never completed.
>
> This decision had the effect of holding back all further development of motor traffic until the passing of the Emancipation Act of 1896, which was largely obtained through the exertions of [Sir David Salomons] the donor of this exhibit.

However, Sir Thomas's tricycle did make a more positive mark on history, for when the Stanley Bicycle Club held its fourth annual 'exhibition of bicycles, tricycles and accessories', at London's Holborn Town Hall in February 1881, the little steamer was displayed on the farthest corner of the platform in the 'Tricycle Room'. It was the very first motor vehicle to go on show at a public exhibition anywhere in the world.

CHAPTER FIVE

The Cautionary Tale of Edward Butler

But for the stultifying effect of the law, Britain might have led Europe in the development of a practical light motor car. In 1884 an inventor from Erith, Kent, named Edward Butler, exhibited drawings of a 'Petro-Cycle' at the Stanley Cycle Show, although the machine itself probably was not completed for two or three years after that. It was a three-wheeler with a twin-cylinder engine, the two horizontal cylinders being placed one on either side of the single rear wheel with the piston rods facing forward. Each rod was linked directly to a crank on the rear axle by a long curved connecting rod projecting over the cylinder; this arrangement, however, proved unsatisfactory, and an epicyclic reduction gear was later incorporated in the rear hub.

Butler was assisted by an engineer named Charles Crowden, who recalled that 'between the steering wheels was fixed a seat for the rider and on each side were fitted two handles for the rider to steady himself at high speed and at the same time manipulate the steering wheels. Each steering wheel was fitted with a powerful band brake actuated by a foot lever. Another foot lever was also provided for raising the driving wheel from the ground to start the motor running.'

This, in effect, was the Petro-Cycle's clutch; once the engine had been started – presumably by pulling the rear wheel round – the driver gently took his foot off the lever to lower the driving wheel to the ground. This must have given a rather jerky start as the spinning tyre gripped the road!

The rear mudguard incorporated a water tank that held water for the cooling jackets round the cylinders, while 'petroleum' was carried in a small tank under the seat, supplying 'a novel form of vaporizer' (apparently a crude form of carburettor) 'and thence to the cylinders as required'. Initially, a small Wimshurst machine was fitted to supply the ignition sparks, but this was soon abandoned in favour of coil and battery ignition.

It appears that Butler's machine was tested and ran 'fairly satisfactorily', but could not legally be used on the road because of the restrictive requirements of the Locomotive Act. It all ended in tears, recalled Crowden, who in 1896 became works manager of the Great Horseless Carriage Company: 'The syndicate that had found the money to build the machine refused to have anything more to do with it and all further developments of this little motor carriage were abandoned.'

A lost opportunity: Edward Butler's practical 'Petro-Cycle' could not be used on the road because of the Locomotive Act.

CHAPTER SIX

Bells and Smells – The Bollées of Le Mans

There are some visits that I am reluctant to repeat for fear that the magic that existed the previous time might have been broken by some change in the interim. So it was with my visit to the Compiègne Museum in the winter of 1978. It was a bitter winter in France that year; we were delivering new Ford Capris to Bordeaux for the model's press launch, and snow had fallen there for the first time, it seems, within the living memory of most of the inhabitants. On the way to our overnight halt at Blois, I diverted off the *autoroute* to revisit the carriage museum at Compiègne, which houses some of France's oldest and rarest motor vehicles.

The collection is kept in the ancient chateau of Compiègne and my wife and I were, apparently, the first and only visitors that day. Instead of being allowed to stroll through the collection on our own, we had to be shepherded from room to room by a warder with an enormous bunch of ancient keys, solemnly locking and unlocking each of the massive doors as we passed from section to section.

We saw the little Renault that claimed to be France's first saloon car, the 1895 Delahaye owned by France's first lady driver, the Duchesse d'Uzès; the little Sigma roadster that once belonged to France's First World War ace of aces Georges Guynemer; and, like something from Victorian science fiction, *La Jamais Contente* ('Never Satisfied'), the torpedo-shaped electric land-speed record car on which in 1899 the red-bearded Belgian racer Camille Jenatzy had been the first man to top 60mph (97km/h) in a motor vehicle. (Alas, poor Jenatzy came to a bizarre end when he crept up outside a hunting lodge and imitated a wild boar in order to frighten a friend inside. Apparently, he did it too well, because the friend fired out of the window at the supposed boar and killed Jenatzy instead.)

The 1895 Delahaye kept at Compiègne once belonged to France's first lady driver.

But the greatest thrill of all came when we arrived in Compiègne's central courtyard, which had been covered over with a glass roof, to see two of the most significant steam vehicles of the nineteenth century: Amédée Bollée's *La Mancelle* and the great steam coach he had built for the Marquis de Broc. Like all the cars and carriages displayed in the central courtyard, they were badly in need of cleaning and dusting, yet even in their scrofulous state they were magnificent.

Their builder was aged only 28 when he started work on his first steam carriage, *L'Obéissante* ('The Obedient One'), in 1872. The descendant of a long line of bell-founders who had established a factory in Le Mans in 1842, Amédée Bollée had seen Michaux velocipedes and a steam bus at the 1867 Universal Exhibition in Paris, then spent some time working in the Lotz factory in Nantes, studying armament production (and also looking at the traction engines built by that company).

The twelve-seater *L'Obéissante* was unlike any steam carriage previously built; although it looked rather like a mobile bandstand, it possessed geometrically perfect steering. Each rear wheel was driven by a separate vee-twin steam engine and the carriage could travel at almost 20mph (32km/h), consuming 136 gallons of water and 110lb of coke per hour.

ABOVE: The torpedo-shaped body of La Jamais Contente *was clad in an aluminium alloy called Partinium; in 1899 it reached 65.79mph (105.86km/h), the first car to travel over a mile a minute.*

RIGHT: Two early Renaults at Compiègne. The 1900 model on the right is claimed (incorrectly) to be the world's first saloon car.

With ten local dignitaries on board, young Bollée gave a demonstration run through Le Mans, but, going down a muddy hill, he had to apply the brake suddenly. *L'Obéissante* failed to live up to its name and skidded violently through 180 degrees, ending up facing back up the hill. Worried about the effect on his passengers, but saying nothing, the driver set off again in the direction in which the carriage was facing, drove back to the central square and stopped, whereupon his passengers applauded him on the ease with which *L'Obéissante* could be manoeuvred.

After some opposition from the authorities, Amédée Bollée got permission to drive to Paris on condition that he give three days' advance notice to the chief highway engineers of the *départements* through which he intended to travel. On 9 October 1875 he set off,

ABOVE: Although it looked like a mobile bandstand, Bollée's 1871 L'Obéissante *was a technological triumph, with geometrically perfect steering and independent front suspension. Amazingly, it was still in perfect working order half a century after it was built.*

BELOW: Setting the pattern for motor cars to come, Bollée's La Mancelle steamer had the engine under a bonnet in front driving the rear wheels.

making the 145-mile (233km) journey in 18 hours including halts to refill the boiler, meal breaks and half-hour pauses as he entered each *département* to obtain the necessary passes. During the trip in Paris, Bollée picked up seventy-five tickets from police officers. He arranged an interview with the Prefect of Police the following day, gave the Prefect and several of his officers a ride in *L'Obéissante*, and the tickets were all cancelled.

Young Bollée became the toast of Paris, and crowds of onlookers applauded him when he drove through the city. *L'Obéissante* was a perfectly practical vehicle, but, although Bollée received several enquiries from prospective customers, he did not consider the machine suitable for untrained owners, nor was he ready to go into production. At the grand age of fifty, the steamer was demonstrated during the 1921 French Grand Prix on the Sarthe circuit south of Le Mans; a film of its demonstration plays continuously in the motor museum alongside the 24-hour circuit to this day. Today, the steamer stands near Cugnot's *fardier* in the Conservatoire Nationale des Arts et Métiers in Paris.

After a trial with a steam tram, financed by another bell-founder named Dalifol, Bollée developed another steam carriage named *La Mancelle* ('The Girl from Le Mans'). This carriage set the pattern for generations of motor vehicles to come, with the engine at the front under a bonnet driving the rear wheels. Like *L'Obéissante*, it had a steering wheel – many early petrol cars had the far less satisfactory tiller steering – and independent front suspension.

Both steamers were shown at the 1878 Universal Exhibition in Paris, after which a rich industrialist from Alsace, Gustave Koechlin, ordered a *Mancelle*. His vehicle was delivered in May 1879 and remained in service for over twenty years. Other *Mancelles* were built under licence by a firm named Wöhlert in Berlin, while Amédée Bollée continued to build 'one-off' steam carriages: the massive 20-ton *Marie-Anne* of 1879, which had an auxiliary shaft drive to the wheels of its trailer, making it capable of pulling a 100-ton load; *La Nouvelle* of 1880, with its enclosed passenger accommodation; the low-built *La Rapide* of 1881; and, in 1885, an amazing eighteen-seat 'Mail Coach' for the Marquis de Broc, who used it to travel between his home at Parigny-le-Poulin (Sarthe) and his other chateau at Turbilly (Maine-et-Loire). The body alone – made by leading Parisian coachbuilder Mühlbacher – cost the Marquis the equivalent of £1500, a huge sum in 1895. He retired the coach in 1896, when he bought a three-wheeled voiturette built by Amédée Bollée's younger son.

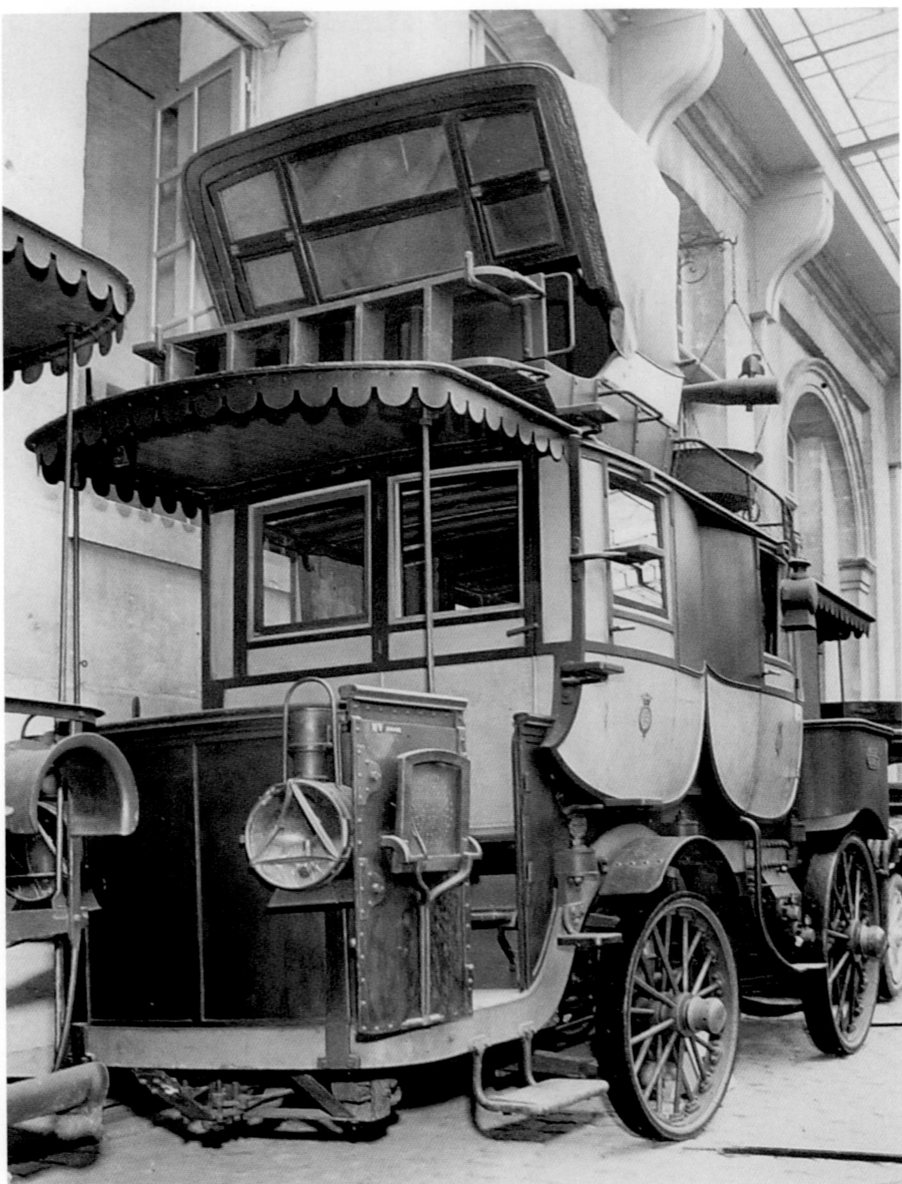

Dominating the glass-roofed courtyard at Compiègne is the massive steam coach that Amédée Bollée had built for the Marquis de Broc in 1885. Its elaborate body alone, by the Parisian coachbuilder Mühlbacher, cost the equivalent of £1500.

After ceasing production of road-going carriages, Amédée Bollée – known with some justification as 'the father of the automobile' – built steam trams as well as, in a sort of reversal of the normal evolutionary progress, manufacturing some three hundred 'anti-vibrator' pedal bicycles in 1895. Both his sons – Amédée Jr and Léon – were to make their mark on the petrol car world; their father's only fault, it seems, was being born too soon.

Made by a famous sewing machine company in Cleveland, Ohio, this 1903 10hp White steam car has a twin cylinder compound engine famed for its hillclimbing abilities.

Built at Neuilly-sur-Seine in France, the Boyer light car became famous when one was driven from Paris to Barcelona without breaking down.

This 1903 De Dion-Bouton is typical of the racing voiturettes of the veteran era.

Now owned by the Royal Automobile Club, this 1901 Mors was originally delivered to Fernand Ruillard of Chaumont, France, in September 1901.

This 1904 6hp Siddeley was found in a dump in Devon in the 1930s. It has a single horizontal cylinder.

Once owned by a famous Parisian piano maker named Gaveau, this 1902 5.4-litre four-cylinder Panhard-Levassor started life as a racing car and was fitted with its present Double Phaeton bodywork in 1904–5.

The elegant body on this 1902 Renault competing in the 2003 pre-Run concours is known as a Double Phaeton.

A twin-cylinder Panhard & Levassor arrives safely in Brighton at the end of the 2002 Veteran Car Run.

CHAPTER SEVEN

A Ride on 'La Marquise'

Forget the popular idea that the Germans Daimler and Benz were the fathers of the motor industry: the first company in the world to issue a catalogue offering motor vehicles for sale was French, and those vehicles were powered by steam.

While browsing in the Paris Flea Market in the 1960s, Lord Montagu of Beaulieu discovered some correspondence dating from 1886 regarding the steam carriages built by Trépardoux et Cie of Puteaux. Clipped to the letter were loose sheets from the company's catalogue showing drawings, specifications and prices of a steam phaeton, a dog-cart, a tramcar, a lorry, an eighteen-seat omnibus and an elegant 'Berline de Voyage', as well as a photograph of a little four-wheeled steam carriage.

The Trépardoux name was being used as a front for the automotive activities of a rumbustious young aristocrat named Count Albert de Dion, whose family disapproved of his involvement with self-propelled vehicles. His father, the Marquis de Dion de Malfiance, had even tried to restrain the son whom he thought crazy with a court order. But Count Albert – a formidable duellist and celebrated man about town with an equally formidable reputation as a ladies' man – was no fool. Described as 'the despair of mothers, the terror of husbands and the best of friends', he had been obsessed with *'l'idée du dada Automobile'* since the mid-1870s, when he had been studying German in Munich and had apparently built himself a model steam engine.

The idea bubbled to the surface in December 1881, when the 25-year-old De Dion was strolling through Paris looking for presents for a ball that he and the Duc de Mornay were organizing. Visiting a novelty shop in the fashionable Boulevard des Italiens, the Count noticed a little model steam engine in the window and asked who had built it. 'Georges Bouton,' replied the shopkeeper, 'who works with his brother-in-law Trépardoux in the Passage Leon.' The young aristocrat hurried to the tiny back-street workshop where Bouton and Trépardoux were struggling to make a living making model engines using outdated machinery.

'How much do you make a day?' he asked.

'Seven francs,' came the mournful reply.

De Dion immediately offered the pair ten francs a day if they would help him develop a light steam car, and set them up in a run-down house in the Rue Pergolese in Paris. Their first task was to develop a sufficiently compact boiler, which also proved suitable for use in light steam launches; orders from maritime customers such as the French Navy provided a handy source of income while work proceeded on a prototype carriage.

After experimenting with a little steam engine attached to a pedal tricycle, in 1883 De Dion, Bouton & Trépardoux built the Veloce, 'a little Victoria with rubber-shod 47¼ inch metallic front wheels driven by twin belts; between them the vertical water-tube boiler with removable vaporizer; 3 horsepower

The first steam vehicle built by De Dion, Bouton & Trépardoux was a powered quadricycle with belt drive to the front wheels.

When the liquid fuel spilled on to the drive belts and set them on fire, the resulting blaze was greeted with enthusiasm by the bystanders.

The Comte de Chasseloup-Laubat at the controls of an 1885 dog-cart; his passenger is Georges Bouton, the engineering genius of the partnership. The front wheels were driven by chains and the rear wheels steered.

The Comte de Dion at the wheel of a steam carriage built in 1885 for Albert Menier. This was, said De Dion, 'a genuine touring carriage that allowed its owner to spread amazement among the population'.

twin-cylinder engine, 300 revolutions a minute; ... Above the two steerable 31½ inch rear wheels is a bench seat, with a water tank beneath it. Speed: 12–18mph...'

De Dion recalled the Veloce as 'quivering and spitting fire...one day when running at full speed, the liquid fuel in the burner spilled on to the belt and the result was a magnificent flaming punch which the spectators greeted with a great deal more enthusiasm than I did'.

In August 1884, journalist Louis Bonneville of the Paris cycling paper *Le Sport Vélocipédique* visited the little factory to prepare a story on the Veloce and was impressed:

> Not only does this machine run, but it runs effectively, contrary to the opinion of my velocipede-riding friends. Perhaps they haven't given the machine the full attention it deserves? Would they also perhaps have greeted this novelty with cries of enthusiasm if it had come from abroad? It's eternally true that a prophet is without honour in his own country.

Soon afterwards, De Dion, Bouton & Trépardoux unveiled a four-passenger light steam car that steered with the front wheels and had a separate tandem-compound engine driving each rear wheel through connecting rods and cranks.

'This vehicle,' proudly declared De

In 1892 De Dion had this steam tricycle, originally built in 1888, fitted with the recently invented Michelin detachable pneumatic tyres. According to the Count, the increased comfort made this 'the little vehicle of individual transport for which we had been working for several years'.

Dion towards the end of his long life, 'can be considered as the embryo of the first touring automobile. It had four seats; it was already a family car.' He named it 'La Marquise' in honour of his mother.

Importantly, the little company began to sell steam carriages, and soon had to move across the river to a more spacious site at Puteaux: 'There was no lack of room; we could employ as many men as we liked – 12, 15 and sometimes even 20 workers!' crowed De Dion.

One of De Dion's first customers, the Count de la Tour du Pin Vercluse, recorded his impressions of buying a car in the very dawn of motoring:

> I had always considered it would be highly interesting to become the owner of a horse-less carriage and on reaching the workshop at Puteaux, I met Monsieur Bouton and immediately asked him if he could make me one.
>
> 'But you must see what we are making; if you will come with me I will show you our cars,' said M Bouton with a smile. After walking through a badly kept garden full of weeds, we arrived in a large yard round which were sheds covered with tarpaulins which served as workshops. We entered the largest of them, where a poor, tired-out stationary steam engine was puffing with all its might to painfully work a few lathes and other machinery.
>
> In a corner was a forge which threw a red glare upon the scene and filled the shop with smoke, from which a few rare workmen occasionally came and went. Across the yard was an open-fronted shed where three or four men were busy assembling a sort of dog-cart with rear steering wheels. In other sheds I inspected a phaeton and a quadricycle. I afterwards helped with the testing of a small lorry which was being driven around a

A De Dion, Bouton & Trépardoux steam quadricycle displayed at Compiègne.

Patience was rewarded when, after almost an hour's preparation, Tim Moore took me for a ride on La Marquise.

With a full head of steam, the 1884 De Dion, Bouton & Trépardoux quadricycle is capable of speeds up to 35mph (56km/h).

large tree planted in the centre of the grounds.

After having had the working of each vehicle explained to me, Bouton gradually guided me towards the office in which we discussed the possibility of making me a dog-cart similar to the one I had just seen. Before leaving the works, I gave my firm order, accompanied by a cheque as a deposit. I was absolutely charmed with my visit to Puteaux and delighted with the idea of soon becoming the owner of a steam car.

It was an early summer's day in 1993 when I rode on what was then the oldest roadworthy car in the world, Tim Moore's 1884 De Dion, Bouton & Trépardoux steam quadricycle *La Marquise*. Nowadays, a car should start at the first turn of the key; in the past, the car owner had to be much more patient.

On that summer's day, the starting procedure began in bright sunshine at 2.40pm. Tim Moore removed the lid on top of the circular boiler and stuffed the firebox with screwed-up newspapers, topped with firewood and coke. He then set light to the paper and, as smoke started billowing from the firebox, lifted the damper – a sort of hollow plug in the long flue pipe, which passed through the floor and exhausted at the rear of the vehicle – and opened little side doors at the top of the combustion space to force the draught through the boiler. An air scoop beneath the firebox would take over this task once the steamer was in motion.

Twenty-five minutes later, he added more fuel and sat back to wait for the boiler gauge to reach the operating pressure of 150psi. By 3.30pm, when the gauge reached the magic figure, grey clouds were covering the sky. Using a tall brass hand pump, he pumped more water into the boiler to maintain the level in the sight-glass. Then he and his mechanic energetically rocked the quadricycle backwards and forwards to clear water from the cylinders and finally – almost exactly an hour after lifting the firebox lid – *La Marquise* was ready to go chuffing down the farm track in front of Tim's house (which was, incidentally, once owned by electrical engineer William Crampton, who started a motoring legend by persuading his friend Henry Royce to buy a 10hp Decauville, which inspired Royce to try to build a better car). By now, rain had started to fall.

The car's performance proved surprisingly good, touching 35mph (56km/h)on the open road. The quadricycle is steered by a spade-grip handle on the right of the driver, which operates twin intermeshing geared sectors that work the steering. On the driver's left is a second spade-handled lever controlling the amount of steam fed to the engines. A third 'simpling' lever admits live steam into the low-pressure cylinder, to boost the speed.

Putting the De Dion away at the end of the run is also an alien experience. It is not a case of simply switching off the engine. The steam pressure needs to be released and the mechanic has to pull out the grate to empty the glowing embers on to the ground. And that is not the end of it. 'After 20 hours' running,' instructs a brass plate on the boiler, 'have the flue swept… every 100 hours empty the boiler under pressure to clear out the mud.'

Eventually, the little Puteaux-based company built about thirty of its light steam cars, of which several survive, as well as heavier machines, including a 'Boggie à Vapeur' heavy tractor unit intended to free horses from the cruel burden of pulling heavy carts. This project earned sponsorship of a thousand francs from the Animal Protection Society when it ran in the 1895 Paris-Bordeaux race.

But, by then, engineer Bouton was already working on a high-speed petrol engine….

Bouton's masterstroke was the design of a high-speed petrol engine, fitted from 1885 to petrol tricycles. A trailer was sometimes added; the unfortunate passenger got all the dust and fumes, and the combination was highly unstable. (The tricycle upended itself a few seconds after this photograph was taken…)

CHAPTER EIGHT

Denmark's Oldest Car

As a 12-year-old grammar-school boy back in November 1954, I waited eagerly beside the Brighton Road at Purley in the early hours of a bright Sunday morning, solemnly ticking off the veterans in my programme as they chuntered past. A keen aircraft spotter, I also noted in the margin the leisurely passage overhead of the rare 1930s Hirtenburgh HS-9A parasol monoplane 'G-AGAK' on its way to nearby Croydon Airport. Eventually, the car I had been waiting for trundled uncertainly down Russell Hill on its iron-shod wheels to the incessant ringing of a big brass bell mounted atop a shaft rising from its steering wheel. Claimed to be the world's oldest roadworthy automobile, the sombre black machine adorned with a mass of metal curlicues was the 1886 Hammel motor carriage, 'the first motor car ever made in Denmark'.

Its slightly erratic progress was due to the fact that – in contrast to just about every other road vehicle ever built – turning the steering wheel to the right made the Hammel turn left, and vice versa.

It had been built for Albert Hammel, owner of a gas engine factory in Copenhagen, by his foreman Hans Urban Johansen and, according to a local newspaper report, was 'intended for Mr Johansen to drive Mr Hammel all the way to Skovshoved [a seaside suburb ten miles away] where he lives, if they can get that far'.

Albert Hammel had been making gas engines for several years, so he would have known what was going on in neighbouring Germany in a field that was at the time extremely high-tech. The engine of his carriage reflected contemporary stationary engine practice: it was a stolid constant-speed unit governed to run at a steady 500rpm. If it exceeded this pre-set rate, the supply from the primitive carburettor was interrupted until the engine speed was back to normal.

Probably completed in 1887, the Hammel seems to have performed adequately over that limited distance for some time, although by the time Albert Hammel died, in 1903, it had been abandoned as 'unserviceable' in the factory yard and was valued at a mere £1.50. Miraculously, it survived, was exhibited in 1926 to celebrate the Silver Jubilee of the Danish motor industry, and then presented to the nation's technical museum. Brought out again 'in a deplorable state' in 1951 for the Danish industry's 50th anniversary, it was found to be missing certain vital components, so the decision was taken to have it returned to running order by the chief mechanic of Bülow-Service, Copenhagen's General Motors agency. He fabricated a new piston and connecting rod for its 2.7-litre twin-cylinder engine and reassembled the ancient machine, whose 1954 trip to Brighton was probably, at some 57 miles (92km), the longest journey it had ever undertaken.

Starting 30 minutes before the other entrants 'so that as many people as possible along the route have the chance to see it before nightfall', the Hammel (which only has one forward speed plus reverse) took twelve and a half hours to complete the Run at an average speed of just under 5mph (8km/h), eventually arriving on Madeira Drive at 8pm by the light of its one-candlepower carriage lamps.

Concentration was needed to drive the Hammel car, for its steering worked the wrong way round.

CHAPTER NINE

Daimler and Benz – Petrol Pioneers

Although the non-compression Lenoir engine of the 1860s had arrived at a technological dead end, it was the catalyst for the separate careers of two young Germans, who together were crucial to the invention of the automobile as we know it. When 26-year-old Gottlieb Daimler read of the Lenoir engine in 1860, he gave up his job as an engineer at the Grafenstaden locomotive works in Alsace and travelled to Paris in the hope of collaborating with Lenoir. Meanwhile, in Cologne, a 28-year-old commercial traveller named August Otto was inspired to try and invent a 'miraculous motor'.

When Daimler arrived in Paris, he realized that there was no future in Lenoir's design, so he found another job at the Perin woodworking machinery company before travelling to England to study engineering progress there.

Otto, on the other hand, joined forces with an engineer named Eugen Langen, and the pair devised a stationary engine in which a gas mixture was exploded, raising a piston attached to a long toothed rack in the cylinder to rotate a flywheel. Back in the 1980s, one of those early Otto engines was displayed on the steps of the grandiose railway station at Deutz, the Cologne suburb where Otto and Langen had their factory. This inefficient and weighty device needed a tremendous headroom to operate, and although it found some limited industrial applications, it would have been no use at all to propel a vehicle. Certainly, the Otto & Langen engine had little commercial success until Gottlieb Daimler joined the company as works manager, in 1872.

Otto and Daimler proved to be quite incompatible as personalities, and their frequent clashes threatened to split the company. To act as a buffer, Daimler recruited a new chief engineer named Franz Rings, who designed a successful four-stroke engine. Perhaps unfairly, the principle on which this engine operated became known as the Otto cycle; perhaps it was just as well, since a 'Rings Cycle' would have sounded too much like a Wagner opera.

After ten years with Otto & Langen, Daimler resigned in 1882 to pursue his quest for a universal power source, developing a neat internal combustion engine that he applied to a motor-cycle test-bed in 1885, following with a motorized carriage in 1886. He was aided by his protégé Wilhelm Maybach, the former chief designer at the Deutz factory, who was the engineering genius who translated Daimler's ideas into functioning machinery.

Daimler, however, was not so much interested in producing motor cars as in providing a self-contained 'universal power source' that could be applied to everything from industrial machinery to motor boats. In a way, this would prove more valuable to the development of the motor car than if he had concentrated on the manufacture of complete vehicles, for the Daimler engine was to be the power source of two of the most significant French marques of the veteran era.

Gottlieb Daimler at the start of his quest for a universal power source.

Daimler showed his prototype 'Stahlradwagen' ('steel-wheeled car') at the 1889 Paris World's Fair that marked the centenary of the French Republic; the exhibition was almost over by the time the Stahlradwagen was delivered, but its cycle-like construction soon attracted the attention of cycle manufacturer Armand Peugeot, who was showing a steam tricycle his company had built to the designs of Léon Serpollet. At once Peugeot terminated his arrangements with Serpollet, negotiated with Daimler for the manufacturing rights to the steel-wheeler and negotiated with Panhard & Levassor, the French agents for the Daimler engine (and, incidentally, successors to the Perin company where Daimler had once worked), for a supply of power units. It was the general layout of the steel-wheeler, with a rear-mounted Daimler engine, that would dictate the design of the first few years of Peugeot manufacture.

The guiding genius of Panhard & Levassor was Emile Levassor, who had married Louise Sarazin, widow of the original French importer of Daimler engines. Having seen the plans for the proposed Peugeot quadricycle for which his company was to supply engines, he decided to go ahead with the construction of a motor car. He had already sketched out some of the details; his

Prominent in this reconstruction of Gottlieb Daimler's workshop are a model of his first motorized carriage of 1886, and a re-creation of the motor-cycle test-bed that he built in 1885.

Daimler's 1889 'Stahlradwagen' was the inspiration for the first Peugeot cars.

prototype was to have its engine mounted in the centre of the body between back-to-back seats, a layout known to carriage builders as *dos-à-dos*.

Worldwide communication is instantly available at the touch of a button today, so it is impossible to appreciate how insular things could be 120 years ago. In Mannheim, just a few miles from Daimler's workshop in Cannstatt, yet totally unknown to him, another young engineer was building internal combustion engines and working towards the construction of a three-wheeled horseless carriage. That engineer was named Carl Benz.

Benz's vehicle made its first appearance in the brief interval between the Daimler motor cycle and carriage. It was the first petrol-powered car designed as an entity, and among its advanced features was electric ignition on a system devised by Benz himself. Its single-cylinder engine was mounted at the rear with its single cylinder facing forwards and it had no crankcase: the crankshaft simply turned in the open air. Moreover, the crankshaft was vertical so that the flywheel turned horizontally. Benz was fearful that the gyroscopic effect of a vertical flywheel would affect the steering so that the car would be unable to turn. He designed and fitted a differential gear to the back axle but, apparently ignorant of the invention of his fellow countryman Lenkensperger, who had devised a system of pivoting stub axles, he used a single front wheel held in bicycle-like forks. (Lenkensperger's system subsequently became known, rather unfairly, as 'Ackermann steering', after the London printmaker who took out the English patent on his design.)

From the summer of 1886, Carl Benz began making cautious short test runs around Mannheim in an attempt to iron out any problems. He improved the design, and by 1888 had developed the more powerful 'Model III', with a rudimentary front seat over the steering fork and a simple two-speed belt drive. It had a curious double chassis, with an unsprung lower frame linking the steering head to the rear axle, and a sprung upper frame carrying the body and engine. Fearful of ridicule, Benz kept to the same short test route in the late evening, then gave up even these brief outings to work on a car to be shown at the September 1888 Munich Industrial

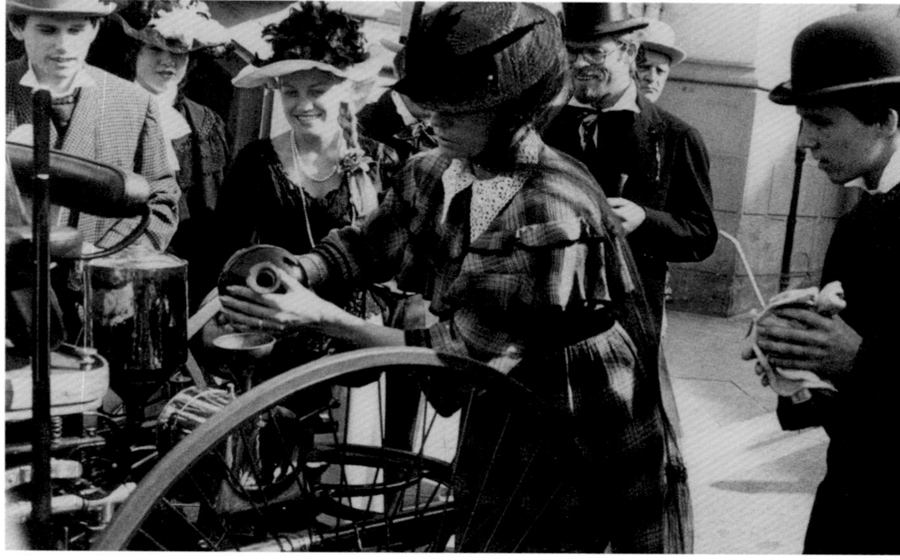

In 1978 this replica of the first Benz car of 1886 took part in a rally to commemorate the 90th anniversary of Berta Benz's pioneering journey from Mannheim to Pforzheim. Here, the 1978 'Berta Benz' re-enacts the purchase of fuel from a chemist's shop.

Machinery Exhibition. However, his wife Berta had greater ambitions for her husband's new invention, which she realized would have to prove itself as a viable touring machine before anyone was likely to place an order. She hatched a plot with her two sons, 13-year-old Richard and 15-year-old Eugen, telling Benz that she was going to take the boys to visit her mother at Pforzheim, more than 100 miles (160km) away. As they would be leaving the house early to catch the first train, there was no need for him to get up to see them off.

'Eugen and Richard were right up to date with all the modifications and new fittings on the car,' she remarked. 'During their outings with their father, they had learned to drive and maintain the car, and they knew its mechanism almost as well as he did.'

Bright and early one fine August morning, Berta and her sons set out on the world's first long-distance tour by motor car aboard the borrowed Model III prototype, with young Eugen at the wheel. They had no map; they simply followed the course of the railway line.

All went well as far as Heidelberg, about 20 miles (32km) out, and for as long as the road remained relatively flat. Then they came to Wiesloch, where they managed to buy a couple of litres of 'ligroine oil' (that was what they called the volatile spirit they used as fuel) from the local chemist. After Wiesloch, the road climbed, and Eugen and his mother had to get out and push the car while Richard steered. Downhill gradients were a worry, too, for the brakes were simply leather-faced wooden shoes pressing against the iron tyres of the back wheels. When the leather wore down, the intrepid tourists called on village shoemakers to replace it. Then a driving chain jumped the sprockets and had to be replaced by a village blacksmith, as wondering villagers gathered round and marvelled at this strange vehicle that moved without horses to pull it.

When the car stopped because its fuel feed was blocked, Berta's hatpin was used to clear the obstruction. When the electric ignition short-circuited, Berta sacrificed one of her elasticated garters to insulate the wire.

The three travellers pushed for hours in the dark until at last they saw the lights of Pforzheim in the valley below. Covered in dust and grease, they pulled up outside Grandma's house, where a casserole was produced to greet them. Berta happily sent a three-word telegram to Carl: *'Pforzheim glucklick ankommen'* ('Safely arrived at Pforzheim').

Carl's reply was typical: 'Send back the chains by express!' He needed them, he claimed, for the car that he was preparing for the Munich exhibition, although he did send another set a few days later so that the travellers could return home.

Amazingly, the exploits of Berta and her sons aroused little interest, although nearly three-quarters of a century later there were still elderly peasants in the villages along her route who recalled that August day back in 1888 when the first horseless carriage had passed through.

Benz produced a few examples of the Model III for sale, but there was no response from Germany; only an adventurous French entrepreneur named Emile Roger showed any interest. Fortunately, a carefully restored 1888 Benz Model III three-wheeler bearing the plate of Roger's Paris agency survives in running order as part of the collection of the Science Museum in London. As a schoolboy, I used to visit the museum every time I was in London to admire the historic cars and aircraft on display. Sadly, while the museum has a considerable number of early motor cars in its ownership, in recent years the bulk of the collection has been rehoused in its long-term storage facility in Wiltshire, greatly diminishing the status of the Kensington Land Transport Gallery.

Although the Science Museum bought the Benz from a private owner in 1913, its early history and the story of how it found its way to England remain a mystery. However, some years ago, I found a possible clue in *The Old Flying Days* by Major C.C.Turner, a rare book from the 1920s on the early history of aviation in Britain, discovered in a second-hand bookshop in Lewes. It relates the story of G.H. Handasyde, one of the founders of Martinsyde Aircraft:

> He spent two and a half years on the Atlantic, and, eventually settling down, became manager of the Edinburgh Car Company. From Edinburgh he came to London and took charge of the garage of the London General Omnibus Company, which had just been formed. After spending seven months there he joined Friswells, and then went to Mass Cars, where he remained two years. It may be mentioned incidentally that he was the owner of the third petrol car in Great Britain, a three-wheeled Benz. This varied experience with motor cars was, of course, of great value to him when he tackled the problem of aviation and the aero engine.

Oddly, I have never found any contemporary reference to Handasyde's Benz in the motoring press of the 1890s, which was usually voracious in gathering every scrap of information about the tiny motoring community.

Fortunately, it is known how the 1888 Benz performs, as in 1957 and 1958 the Science Museum entered it for the Brighton Run. The 1957 outing was not deemed a success. The Benz, its wooden brake blocks failing to work in torrential rain, ran away on Russell Hill in Purley – a deceptively sharp drop down to the Brighton Road that has even caught out drivers of modern cars – and demolished its front wheel against a modern bumper.

The following year, with an auxiliary band brake fitted to its countershaft, the Benz tried again. Once more, it poured with rain, but, after starting ahead of the pack, at 7.00am, the Benz reached the top of Russell Hill, 13.5 miles from Hyde Park, by 8.20am. Not anxious to tempt fate, its crew then dismounted and manhandled the car down to the bottom of the slope, where its fuel, oilers and water tanks were topped up and the Benz continued on its leisurely way.

Its driver, C.F. Caunter, recalled the events in 1958 as follows:

> The steering and brakes are its worst features. There is little or no 'feel' in the simple rack-and-pinion, single-wheel

The Model III Benz of 1888, the first petrol car offered for sale.

The Science Museum's 1888 Benz is one of four built by Carl Benz in 1887–88 and was sold by Emile Roger of Paris. It was purchased by the Science Museum for just £5 in 1913!

steering, and the inherent flimsiness of the three-wheel design with its 'penny-farthing' bicycle form of pivoted front fork steering adds considerably to instability. Up to 15mph (24km/h) on the level the steering is comfortable, but at speeds downhill in excess of this there is a marked indication of uncontrollability, of the kind which Dr. F.W. Lanchester in his early aerodynamic experiments called 'catastrophic'. The crude horse-carriage block brakes fitted are quite inadequate, and have to be used with the greatest circumspection.

On the other hand, the fast-and-loose pulley belt-shift clutch and the two-speed layshaft gear were both found to be effective and reliable. These, with the quite reliable if very low-powered engine which, nevertheless, had an unexpected ability to 'hang on' until the summits of the hills were reached, gave the vehicle a modicum of flexibility which materially assisted its successful completion of the run.

The first real hill for which it was anticipated assistance might be needed was Redhill, a maximum gradient of 1 in 12, but, after the passenger had dismounted, this was climbed successfully. So the run proceeded without trouble or incident; three more stops were made, principally to replenish the radiator-less cooling system, and the hills at Pease Pottage, Handcross, Bolney and Pyecombe were successfully surmounted.

At the third replenishing stop, a stretched primary belt was replaced; the fourth stop at the foot of Pyecombe was undertaken more to ensure a final non-stop run to Brighton than because it was really necessary. The finish at Madeira Drive was reached at 2.40pm.

Of the total of 7 hours 40 minutes taken for the journey, about 1.5 hours were absorbed by the four replenishing stops; running time was therefore 6 hours 25 minutes – an average speed of 8.8mph (14.2km/h) for the 56.5 miles.

Three gallons of 0.680 specific gravity petrol – kindly supplied by the Shell Company, Ltd – and five gallons of water were consumed. The petrol consumption was thus about 19 mpg; this high consumption was due to the great deal of low-gear running necessary with this car, as well as the poor thermal efficiency on a compression ratio of 3 to 1. No trouble of any kind occurred, either from mechanical failure or the continuously wet weather.

Carl Benz

Despite his early start in manufacture, Carl Benz remained firmly rooted in the horseless carriage mode. He did not introduce a four-wheeled model until 1892–3, calling it the Viktoria, to commemorate his victory over the knotty design problem of the steering layout. It was the first car to carry a model name. A smaller model, the Velo (short for 'velocipede'), followed in 1894, and proved more popular than the Viktoria. Benz sold 181 Velos in 1896, making the company the industry leader, but the firm's dominance rapidly evaporated as other makers came forward with more advanced, nimbler, designs. Although the Benz design, with slow-turning rear engines and belt drive, was widely copied, other makers regarded this as just a starting point and rapidly moved on. The obstinate Benz clung on to his outdated layout until 1902.

Three generations of the Goodman family aboard their 1900 Benz vis-à-vis, one of the final variations on the Velo theme.

This Benz Viktoria was built in 1898, revealing how little progress Benz had made compared with the rest of the industry.

ABOVE: The late Bernard Garrett, a great advocate of primitive motor cars, urges his 1893 Benz Viktoria on to Brighton in 1977.

OPPOSITE, TOP: The International Benz was a Benz with an English body. This 1899 car was originally owned by J. Miles of Brighton. He kept it until 1934, when it was acquired by C. S. Burney, who entered it for that year's Brighton Run.

OPPOSITE, BOTTOM: This 1899 Benz Mylord Victoria is powered by the flat-twin 'Contra-Motor' introduced in 1897, which was smoother and more powerful than the original single-cylinder engine.

ABOVE: This lofty 1899 Benz 5hp Phaeton, with optional green-and-white striped 'summer awning with curtain', is a true horseless carriage, powered by a 2916cc single-cylinder engine at the rear of the chassis. It is believed to be the actual car shipped from the island of Java in 1924, where it had been the property of local dignitary the Soesoehoenan of Soerakarta, for exhibition at Holland's RAI show.

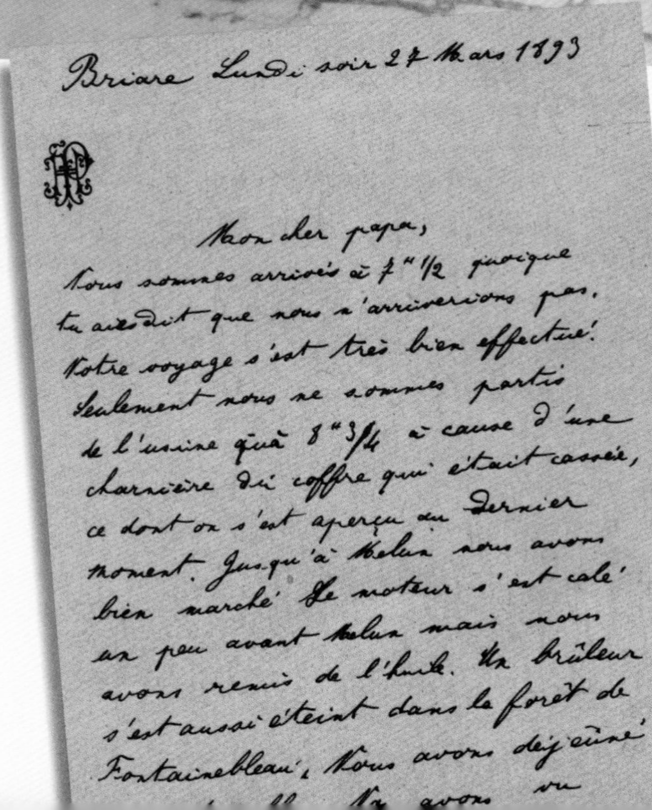

Briare Lundi soir 27 Mars 1893

Mon cher papa,

Nous sommes arrivés à 7h 1/2 quoique tu ais dit que nous n'arriverions pas. Notre voyage s'est très bien effectué! Seulement nous ne sommes partis de l'usine qu'à 8h 3/4 à cause d'une charnière du coffre qui était cassée, ce dont on s'est aperçu au dernier moment. Jusqu'à Melun nous avons bien marché. Le moteur s'est calé un peu avant Melun mais nous avons remis de l'huile. Un brûleur s'est aussi éteint dans la forêt de Fontainebleau. Nous avons déjeuné

... Nous avons vu

ABOVE: The 1892 Panhard & Levassor used by young Hippolyte Panhard for his pioneering journey from Paris to the Mediterranean. On the return trip, hours of mountain climbing wore out the steel bristles of the primitive clutch, and the car, 'in semi-disgrace', had to be put on the train at Digne. However, it continued in regular service for the next five or six years, covering some 12,000 miles.

LEFT: A diligent correspondent, Hippolyte wrote detailed accounts of his journey to his father in Paris.

CHAPTER TEN

An Epic Journey

What was it like to go touring by car in the days when there were fewer than a couple of dozen motor vehicles on the road? Amazingly, a record survives of what must have been the very first car journey from Paris to the Mediterranean, a route now followed by millions of tourists every year. It began at 8.45am on Monday, 27 March 1893, when 23-year-old Hippolyte Panhard and his uncle, Georges Meric, set off from the Panhard & Levassor works, in the Parisian suburb of Ivry. They were bound for Nice aboard the tiller-steered 2hp Panhard & Levassor *'Dos-à-dos'* (its two rear seats were normally folded down into the boot), which Hippolyte's father René had bought on 28 August 1892 as a present for his son. It followed the pattern adopted by Emile Levassor after tests with two experimental mid-engined *vis-à-vis* cars had shown him the disadvantages of that layout; its engine was mounted in front under a bonnet, driving the rear wheels through a multi-ratio gearbox.

As a director of Panhard & Levassor, René Panhard had been entitled to a discount on the car's list price of 4800 francs; he actually paid a total of 4318 francs (including 104 francs for the parasol) for the car. Its solid rubber tyres would also have been classed as an extra (500 francs for a four-seated car), since the standard wheels in those pre-pneumatic days were iron-shod; as the Panhard jolted along beside the Seine on the cobbled quays at Alfort, which had not been resurfaced since the reign of Louis XIII some 250 years earlier, Hippolyte and his uncle must have been glad of even the limited amount of extra comfort afforded by the optional rubber-wear!

Final drive was by chains. While the car had Levassor's sliding gear transmission, similar in basic principles to the modern gearbox – although obviously devoid of such aids to easy changing as synchromesh – its three speeds ('a short, a middle, and a long one', according to the sales leaflet) were totally exposed; a separate 'reversing lever' giving the car three speeds backwards, too. Because the 1.1-litre V-twin power unit ran at a fairly constant 600rpm, variations in speed were obtained by using the gears rather than by moderating the speed of the engine.

Once the car reached the Melun road, Hippolyte engaged the third (top) speed, allowing the Panhard to rattle along at a little over 10mph (16km/h). 'It is possible to attain a speed of 12.5mph, but such high speeds require considerable attention on the part of the driver and are not always advisable,' cautioned the Panhard catalogue.

The travellers joined the southbound Route Nationale 7 before making an involuntary stop in the forest of Fontainebleau to relight one of the ignition burners which had blown out. They lunched at Fontainebleau, where the local inhabitants stood open-mouthed at the sight of the strange machine that moved without the pulling power of horses, then carried on through Nemours, Fontenay and Montargis. They halted for the night at Briaire, where they arrived at 7.30pm, having covered 87 miles since leaving the factory. At every stop, Hippolyte and his uncle handed out leaflets advertising the Panhard & Levassor range.

That night, the diligent Hippolyte sat down to write the first of a regular series of reports of the day's adventures to his father:

> We arrived at 7.30, even though you said we wouldn't arrive at all. Our journey went very well, although we didn't leave the factory until 8.45 because of a broken bonnet hinge, which we didn't notice until the very last moment. We went very well until Melun. The motor overheated a

The Daimler engine of Panhard & Levassor's first prototypes built in 1890 was mounted amidships, a position quickly abandoned in favour of the front engine layout.

An early attempt at weather protection on an 1893 Panhard & Levassor.

> little before Melun, so we put some more oil in.
>
> Everything is working satisfactorily, though I often had to use second gear because of the ups and downs of the terrain.

The next morning, as on the following days, the motorists set off at daybreak. At Bonny-sur-Loire, a few miles down the road, they paused to take down that optional parasol 'because it caught the wind'. Finding adequate supplies of fuel along the road was a major problem in an era long before service stations, so the travellers were glad to buy five gallons of motor spirit that morning from the owner of an oil-engined plough at Pouilly, between Cosne-sur-Loire and Nevers.

'Driving through villages,' wrote Hippolyte, 'the children, dogs, cats and chickens ran noisily after us. It was a frightful commotion.'

They followed the road along the north bank of the Loire which was 'better swept than the Avenue de l'Opéra', halting for the night at Decize: 'For dinner there were five exquisite courses, much appreciated by my uncle Georges. Dinner, two rooms, stabling for the vehicle and breakfast cost us 10 francs in all. It really isn't expensive!'.

The next leg of their journey took them through Bourbon-Lancy, Digoin and Marcigny to Roanne, 'a fine big town where the Grand Hotel has a glass-covered yard for oil-engined carriages'. At Roanne, an element of farce intruded: 'Unfortunately, when I went to buy some motor spirit at a grocer's shop, I stopped behind his hand-cart. Whilst alighting, I pushed the clutch lever and the car jerked forward, tipping over the grocer's cart. Cost: 10 francs'.

From Roanne, the little Panhard & Levassor plugged steadily south through Neulise, Balbigny, Feurs and la Fouillousse to the industrial town of St Etienne, noted for the manufacture of firearms and ribbons ('the workshops of Mars beside those of Venus'), where, in 1830, Barthelemy Thimonnier had invented the sewing machine.

South of St Etienne the formidable Col de la République rose to a height of around 3700ft, but the adventurers climbed the hill at a steady 4mph (6.4km/h) 'without alighting from the car'. On the way down, they freewheeled 'silently, like running on velvet', but the brakes overheated and almost caught fire, so Uncle Georges 'held a bucket of water between his legs and kept the brakes cool with a wet rag'.

They ran down the Rhone Valley, through Saint-Vallier, Valence, Montelimar and Orange, where Hippolyte noted, 'We saw a triumphal arch, and regretted that we couldn't drive under it – then there was the Roman theatre by moonlight. Magnificent!' Passing through Avignon and Salon, Hippolyte and his uncle reached the Mediterranean at Marseille, then headed east along the coast to Toulon and Hyères, where Belhomme, a mechanic from Ivry, replaced Georges Meric.

Finally, after eight days on the road, Hippolyte drove his Panhard & Levassor into Cannes beneath 'a blue sky worth a king's ransom'. Aided by Belhomme, he carried out necessary greasing and maintenance on the Panhard, using spare parts forwarded from Paris, following instructions cabled to him by Emile Levassor. The mechanical problems worried him a little, as he wrote to his father: 'M Levassor will say that I drove the car badly, but I can assure you that I was most careful and did not try to climb hills faster by slipping the clutch.'

Hippolyte was instantly the centre of attraction on the Côte d'Azur, showing off his travel-stained car to prominent personalities at the best hotels, theatres, casinos along the *promenades* of Cannes, Nice and Monaco. The confused Belhomme, his personal Passe-Partout, addressed everyone of the society folk they met as 'My Lord' or 'Your

OPPOSITE: This 1892 Panhard & Levassor belonging to Brian and Ruth Moore was rescued from a museum in Arkansas and restored to running order. Ruth has driven the iron-tyred veteran several times to Brighton.

AX55

This amazingly original Panhard & Levassor private omnibus discovered in Avallon in 1950 was built for a leading maker of car components named Lemoine in 1896, and is believed to be the only surviving example of this model.

Abbé Gavois

The sixth Panhard-Levassor made was the choice of the first motoring priest, Abbot Gavois of Allery, in the Somme department of France. 'When the world was scoffing at the possibility of a horseless carriage ever being practicable,' he is reported to have said, 'I prayed my patron saint to provide me with the means for purchasing an automobile. My prayers were heard, for fate put me in touch with the Mayor of Troyes, who had purchased a Panhard-Levassor in 1891 and who after four years' service had grown tired of his acquisition.' The Abbot bought the car for 1800 francs (about £70) and for the next thirty-three years he solemnly chuntered about his parochial business at the tiller of the iron-tyred veteran, before presenting it to the Automobile Club of Picardy in exchange for a donation towards a seminary for young priests.

Highness'. Hippolyte reported certain concerns to his father:

> I met a number of English people and the Grand Duke of Mecklenburg, cousin of the Grand Duke Michael, [whose] wife wanted a car to drive herself. They want me to drive them to the Golf Club of which the Grand Duke is president. There will be three or four of them and I understand that they are all big and fat. However, I shall try to put a wedge behind the clutch spring, which may get it to engage better. It would be so embarrassing to fail in front of these personalities.

But he needn't have worried, for everything went very well.

After all the success and the celebration, Panhard and Belhomme left Cannes on the morning of 20 April to return to Paris by an ambitious itinerary along the Route Napoléon to Grenoble, Bourg-en-Bresse and Chalon-sur-Saône.

After lunch at Grasse, they set off into really mountainous country and at 4000ft the hard-working engine began to gasp for breath. Then, on the serpentine Pas de la Faye, just after St Vallier, the clutch failed. The automobilists, who had been told there was an inn some ten miles further on at the Logis du Pin, found a man with two horses to tow them the four and a half miles to the top of the hill, where they thought it was only a matter of freewheeling down to the inn.

But the freewheeling descent only took them another mile and a half; it was 7pm, night was falling and they still had more than four miles to go. Belhomme went stumbling off over the rocks to look for help. He came back three-quarters of an hour later having found another man with a horse that would tow them to the isolated Logis du Pin.

'At the inn, they baked bread every eight days and we had to arrive on the seventh!' concluded Hippolyte. 'But, after all, it was a very picturesque journey!

CHAPTER ELEVEN

No Unnecessary Pedalling – The 1894 Bremer

Just before Christmas 1963 I set off to see what was said to be the oldest surviving British-built car, which was being restored by a couple of Veteran Car Club members in North London. It seemed that at the end of the 1880s, a teenaged cycling enthusiast named Frederick Bremer had decided that he could save himself a lot of unnecessary pedalling by fitting a gas engine to his bicycle. One thing led to another, and in 1892, still aged only 19, he began work on a motor car based on what he knew of the work of Carl Benz. He could well have seen a Benz car on a trip to Germany with his father, who had been born in Berlin. A gasfitter and plumber by trade, Bremer worked on his project in the little workshop at the rear of his mother's house in Connaught Road, Walthamstow.

Late one December afternoon I arrived in Walthamstow, where the Bremer car that belonged to the local museum was kept in one of the outbuildings of the town hall. John Trott, who was mainly responsible for its restoration, wheeled it out for me to inspect; what immediately struck me was how small – almost toy-like – it was. Young Bremer seems to have used whatever materials he could lay hands on to build it, and would not have been surprised to learn that its little wire wheels had come from a perambulator.

The little car was certainly laid out on similar lines to a Benz, although it was more like the little Velo that Benz introduced in 1894 than anything that was available from the German company in 1892. I would guess that Bremer began by making the engine before developing the rest of the car. Bremer's engine was a brilliant piece of work, using a single iron tube as the cylinder and a larger-diameter tube encircling it as a water jacket. There was a cast cylinder head at one end and a cast plate to carry the crankshaft at the other, the whole being pulled together by four long studs. There was no crankcase, just a wick oiler to lubricate the exposed big end, and the automatic inlet valve was unusual in being held shut against a tension spring rather than using a conventional compression spring. The only way of controlling the speed was by a little lever that advanced and retarded the ignition; although there was a throttle, it had very little effect.

Bremer mounted his engine beneath the seat and, since there was no such thing as a spark plug in the early 1890s, he made his own, using pipeclay as insulation. The range of the car would have been limited by the cooling system, which had no radiator, just a small water tank on either side of the body.

The two-speed transmission was along similar lines to the Benz, with primary transmission by fast-and-loose belts controlled by two small handles on top of the dashboard. There was one handle for each forward speed, and no reverse. Final drive was by chain.

Bremer used a tiller, unlike the tiny

On a December night in darkest Walthamstow in 1963, I photographed the diminutive Bremer car, which had first run on the road almost exactly 99 years earlier.

John Henry Knight

Another British pioneer who fell foul of the asinine Locomotives Act was John Henry Knight of Farnham, Surrey, who in July 1895 completed a three-wheeled motor car powered by a single-cylinder engine of his own design and manufacture. He converted it to four wheels (with independent front suspension) in April the following year and ran it at the Crystal Palace Exhibition in May 1896. However, in 1895 he was fined for using his car 'at a speed greater than 4mph'. He was almost certainly the first person to appear in court on a motoring charge. Nevertheless, he continued using his car locally for two and a half years and it was still running in 1910. It survives and is on display at Beaulieu.

The 1895 Knight was later fitted with four wheels.

steering wheel of the Benz, while the braking was basic, with a long lever pulling spoon brakes against the solid rubber rear tyres.

The car apparently first ran on the road in December 1894, although the body was not completed until the following month. Bremer used the car very little, and always after dark, to avoid the legal requirement for a red-flag man walking in front. He put the car away in about 1903 and forgot about it until 1912, when he presented it to the new Motor Museum that was housed in the galleries of Waring and Gillow's furniture store in Oxford Street. It was displayed in the window along with the 1896 Pennington Torpedo Autocar. When the museum (which had by then moved to the Crystal Palace) was closed on the outbreak of war, in 1914, Bremer got his car back. He put it in the garden shed and forgot about it once again until 1929, when he heard that the Walthamstow Corporation was forming a museum; he presented the car to them the following year.

The Bremer car stayed with the Walthamstow Corporation until 1962, when permission for its restoration to running order was given. It was in remarkably original, if decrepit, condition and needed very few new parts, apart from upholstery, tyres and petrol tank; Hepolite made new piston rings to the original pattern. When the thick layers of brown paint were removed from the body, the original green livery was discovered underneath, and new paint was matched to it.

Because the car had never been registered for road use, the Construction and Use regulations would have treated it as a modern car, so an amendment to the law was needed before it could be taken on to the roads. Nevertheless, when I went to see it, it had already covered several miles on private ground, running on volatile Pratt's Perfection Spirit, which was still available from Esso. It had displayed no worse mechanical vice than a tendency for the exhaust tappet clearance to open up suddenly after about four miles' running, although the harsh springing and tremendous vibration generated by the single-cylinder engine had opened up the rear body joints. John Trott told me that all the nuts and bolts on the chassis had been either brazed or pinned in position by Bremer to prevent them from shaking loose!

The Bremer had been entered for the 1963 Brighton Run but had not been allowed to start because the Ministry of Transport had not got around to changing the law. With revised regulations in place, it did take part in the run in 1964–65 and showed everyone the viability of Frederick Bremer's pioneering design.

CHAPTER TWELVE

The Man Who Invented the Garage

The first private 'automobilist' to defy the law and make a long cross-country journey without a man walking in front was the Hon Evelyn Ellis, a son of the late Lord Howard de Walden. He brought the Daimler-engined 4hp Panhard & Levassor – 'a neat and compact four-wheeled dog-cart with accommodation for four persons and two portmanteaux' – that he had been using in France into Britain at the beginning of July 1895. In order to do this, he had taken out a licence to operate the Panhard on British roads from the Daimler Motor Syndicate, established in London in 1893 by an English entrepreneur named Frederick Simms. Simms was a fluent German speaker, born in Hamburg, where his Brummie grandfather had founded a trading company to equip the Newfoundland fishing fleet. His aim in setting up the syndicate was to market German Daimler petrol engines as a self-contained power source for industrial machinery and motor launches.

The engine was the only German-made component of Ellis's tiller-steered Panhard & Levassor, which was made in Paris, where the company had built around 100 cars by the time Ellis took delivery of his vehicle in 1894. It had 'hot tube' ignition, in which petrol Bunsen-burners heated platinum tubes projecting into the combustion chambers to fire in petrol/air mixture. The cogs of the simple three-speed gearbox were exposed to the open air and side chains transmitted the drive to the rear wheels. In standard form, Panhards ran on iron tyres, but Ellis opted for the more costly option of solid rubber tyres. Despite the caveat by the car's cautious makers that 'great speeds demand great attention', the daredevil Ellis threw caution to the winds and drove at breakneck speeds – sometimes up to as much as 20mph (32km/h).

His cross-country trip had been planned as a deliberate act of defiance against the regulators. He wanted to demonstrate the stupidity of applying a speed limit designed for steam-powered monsters to light, manoeuvrable petrol cars and was prepared to go to court to prove his point. Bringing the car to England from France, he had started his long journey home in Marseille, driving all the way across France to the cross-Channel ferry.

Ellis's willing accomplice Frederick Simms joined him on Friday 5 July at Micheldever Station in Hampshire, and the two set off for Ellis's home in Datchet at 'exactly 9.26am'. They took the old coaching road to London – today's A33/A30. It was in ideal condition for their run, as steady overnight rain had laid the dust usually thrown up by the solid tyres of passing carriages; 'Thus,' according to Simms, 'we had every prospect of an enjoyable journey.'

Simms was anxious to see motor cars become a common sight on British roads and was particularly diligent in observing

The Hon. Evelyn Ellis on his 1895 Panhard & Levassor, which made the first long journey by a petrol car in Britain without a man walking in front.

Ellis bought a new Coventry Daimler in 1897 and fitted the body of his Panhard to it before making the first climb of Malvern Beacon, with his daughter Mary and two Daimler officials as passengers.

the effect the Panhard had on the horses that used the road. 'Out of 133 horses we passed on the road,' he noted happily, 'only two little ponies did not seem to appreciate the innovation.'

The little car chuffed steadily onwards under cloudy skies, passing through Basingstoke – then a little town of well under 10,000 inhabitants – at 11.00am. Twenty minutes later the travellers stopped in the village of Mapledurwell-hatch to top up the car's cooling system with water (and themselves with something more stimulating). After thirty minutes, they took to the road again.

'In every place we passed through, we were not unnaturally the object of a great deal of curiosity,' remarked Simms. 'Whole villages turned out to behold, open-mouthed, the new marvel of locomotion. The departure of coaches was delayed to enable their passengers to have a look at our horseless vehicle, while cyclists would stop to gaze enviously at us as we surmounted with ease some long and (to them) tiring hill.'

The Panhard, already obsolete at the age of two, was converted into a fire engine for use on Ellis's estate at Datchet.

Their progress was steady, through villages such as Nately Scures, Phoenix Green and Hartley Wintney, and then the Panhard plugged inexorably down the long straight across Hartford Bridge Flats to Blackwater, 'passing a great many vehicles of all kinds, as well as cyclists'.

The motorists paused briefly and left Blackwater at 1.55. Simms noted the 'very steep hills' the Panhard encountered on its way to the 'pretty country place' of Bagshot. The car laboured on upgrades that a modern vehicle would scarcely notice, taking 52 minutes to cover just over four miles. Putting Bagshot behind them 'at exactly 2.47', noted the meticulous Simms, 'We met on our way to charming little Sunningdale several officers on horseback, apparently engaged in surveying duty.' Putting duty before curiosity, the soldiers ignored the first motor car they would ever have seen. It was a very different story a year or two later, when another pioneering motorist, the Hon John Scott-Montagu – the future Lord Montagu of Beaulieu – encountered a party of mounted troops near Aldershot at the tiller of his first Daimler. The horses took fright and bolted through an orchard in which family washing was hanging out to dry, and all sorts of unmentionable garments ended up wrapped around the fleeing horses and their riders.

The weather was improving all the time, and the sun had come out. Simms recorded that 'it was a very pleasing sensation to go along the delightful roads towards Virginia Water at speeds varying from three to twenty miles per hour. Our iron horse behaved splendidly!'

Virginia Water was reached at 3.28, and Ellis and Simms took a late lunch 'and also fed our engine with a little oil'. At 4.30 they departed again, turning off the London Road towards Windsor at Englefield Green at 4.47. It sounds as though the previously reliable Panhard played up a little at this point, for Simms made a rather terse note in his report: 'We remained there until 5.25.'

Then it was downhill all the way into Windsor and Datchet:

> We arrived in front of the entrance hall of Mr. Ellis' house at Datchet at 6 o'clock, thus

> completing our most enjoyable journey of fifty-six miles – the first ever made by a petroleum motor-carriage in this country – in 5 hours 32 minutes exclusive of stoppages. The average speed we attained was 9.84 miles per hour, the usual travelling speed being from eight to twelve miles per hour.

In 1996, the carefully conserved Panhard made its first appearance outside the Science Museum since 1912, at a centennial commemoration of the first London-Brighton Run.

Their usual speed was two to three times the legal speed limit, but Ellis had failed in his original intention of making the law look an ass, for the police completely ignored the Panhard's daredevil drive.

In order to house the Panhard at Datchet, Ellis had erected a specially built motor house, which he christened a 'garage' from the French verb *garer* ('to store'); his impromptu coinage beat all the other early names that were considered for this now universal building – 'carhome', 'carrepose', 'carrest', 'cardomain', 'cardom', 'dock', 'motor mews', 'motories' or 'motostore' – and remains in everyday use more than 110 years later.

The little Panhard's running costs were said to be 'a little over a halfpenny a mile', and Simms is said to have added another word to the infant motoring lexicon when he referred to the specially refined oil fuel that Carless, Capel & Leonard of London supplied for his new-fangled internal combustion engines as 'petrol'.

Ellis's brother Lord Howard de Walden did not approve of his kinsman's Panhard & Levassor. 'If you must bring that infernal thing here,' he complained, 'kindly bring a little pan to put under it to catch the filthy oil it drips.'

'Certainly,' replied Ellis, 'if you'll bring a big pan for your carriage horses when you visit me!'

Already the first motor car to be imported into Britain, Ellis's Panhard continued to make history: it was exhibited at the first motor show in Britain (in Tunbridge Wells on 15 October 1895); it was the first car ridden on by a member of the Royal Family (the Prince of Wales, in February 1896); and it took part in the 1896 Brighton Run.

In 1967 Ellis's daughter Mary Critchley Salmonson, who often rode in the Panhard with her father, told me, 'Its average speed was eight miles per hour. He took King Edward VII for his first drive in that first car, and old King Edward said to my father, "Evelyn, don't drive so fast, I am frightened!".'

Shortly after that, Ellis bought a new Coventry Daimler and fitted the Panhard's body to it. The Panhard was converted into a fire engine for use on the Datchet estate. In 1908, Evelyn Ellis sold the old Panhard, now reunited with its original bodywork, to a consulting engineer. A. Vaughan-Williams paid just £3 for the ancient machine; by then, an 1895 car was as out of date as a 1930s car would be today, so rapid had been the development of the motor car. Vaughan-Williams was obviously more interested in the car as an historic relic than as a cheap means of transport, for he loaned it to an exhibition of early cars in London's Imperial Institute, where it attracted the attention of the Royal Automobile Club and the Science Museum. (Incidentally, Evelyn Ellis had proposed the formation of the club at a meeting in 1897, with the caveat that 'my own opinion is that it's not wanted'.) The Science Museum had been looking for an early motor car for several years, and the historic associations of the Panhard persuaded them that it was the right car for their collection. The astute Vaughan-Williams sold the Ellis Panhard to the Royal Automobile Club for £50 and in 1910 the RAC presented it to the Science Museum.

For many years, the car looked dull and faded but, as it attained its centenary, the Royal Automobile Club sponsored its restoration. The Science Museum's specialists used techniques more usually associated with conserving Old Master paintings to reveal the startlingly original state of the paintwork, which had been miraculously preserved under ancient coats of linseed oil.

In November 1996, there was a re-enactment of the start of the 1896 Brighton Run outside the former Metropole Hotel in Whitehall Place. The Panhard made its first appearance outside the walls of the Science Museum for more than eighty years, much to the delight of the Ellis family, who attended the re-enactment in force!

The model no one could copy

Now in the magnificent automobilia collection of my friend Evert Louwman of the Dutch National Motor Museum at Raamsdonksveer, near Rotterdam, is this silver model of the Ellis Panhard, commissioned by its owner from a London silversmith, Albert Barker of New Bond Street, as a table centrepiece. In 1967 I corresponded with Ellis's daughter Mary Critchley-Salmonson, who told me: 'A couple of years ago the county (Somerset) wanted to make a presentation model of my model of the first car to give to Her Majesty the Queen in remembrance of my father who had taken King Edward VII for his first drive but no craftsman could be found to copy it in silver and they had to give her an inferior model in bronze and brass.'

CHAPTER THIRTEEN

The First Motor Show

According to his entry in the 1903 *Motoring Annual*, an invaluable register of the great and the good in Edwardian motoring, Sir David Salomons was 'a very early advocate and leading pioneer of the horseless carriage in Great Britain... many times held up on the road by the arm of the law, for neglecting to provide a snail's-pace signalman waving a scarlet flag'.

A wealthy baronet who lived just outside Tunbridge Wells in Kent, Sir David Salomons was a barrister by profession, a director of the South Eastern Railway, a past Vice-President and Treasurer of the Institution of Electrical Engineers and a respected amateur scientist – 'a Fellow of the Astronomical, and half-a-dozen other learned societies... [and] the author of many learned books and widely read pamphlets on electrical installations and allied subjects'. He possessed 'a rare talent and skill in all mechanical matters, and to take a motor to pieces or to design a novel type of car he regards as a labour of love'. He was also an enthusiastic carriage driver ('a splendid whip [who] can manage a four-in-hand skilfully').

In 1895 Salomons, then Mayor of Tunbridge Wells, became the owner of one of the first cars to come into Britain, a rear-engined Peugeot *vis-à-vis*. He decided to hold the first-ever public demonstration of motor cars in Britain on his home town's agricultural showground.

At the time, there were very few British car owners available to take part in such an event, and only Evelyn Ellis was able to bring his Panhard & Levassor along on the day, 15 October. It was doubtless the energetic Frederick Simms who provided a manual fire engine, with a pump powered by a Daimler engine, which was to be demonstrated by the Tunbridge Wells fire brigade. Salomons had strong connections in France, however, and secured two vehicles from De Dion & Bouton (the third partner, Trépardoux, had left in a huff when Bouton began experimenting with petrol engines): the new De Dion petrol tricycle, and a steam-powered tractor unit known as a Steam Horse. According to a rather sniffy report in the recently founded *The Autocar* magazine, the latter was 'really only an improved, albeit greatly improved, form of traction engine, [and] hardly comes into the category of motor vehicles'. Also promised was another French vehicle, a motor tricycle made by the Gladiator company, which failed to turn up.

A teenaged eyewitness, one of the crowd of 5000 who flocked to see the horseless carriages, later recalled the events of 15 October:

> Sir David Salomons had gone to a great deal of trouble to get these cars and tricycles over from the Continent, also getting special police permission to take or drive these 'things' – they had no name – over the two to three hundred yards of public road from the London, Brighton and South Coast railway station to the Show Field, a soft grassy meadow on a considerable incline – hopeless conditions for these newly born infants to show what they could (or couldn't) do. They just sulked!

In the opinion of *The Autocar*, the condition of the ground in the show ring hardly constituted fair play, but the cars did their best, circling the grounds and 'exhibiting very remarkable speed capacity considering the soft and lumpy nature of the turf'.

Sir David Salomons was undoubtedly the star of the show. The onlookers

Sir David Salomons and a party of local dignitaries demonstrate the capabilities of his 1895 Peugeot on the Tunbridge Wells showground.

Peugeot

Peugeot today is the world's oldest car maker still in family control. It all began when Jean-Georges Peugeot built a watermill at Sous-Cratet in the Montbéliard region of France, close to the Swiss frontier, in 1793. His son Jean-Pierre expanded into textiles, paper-making and oil processing, and in 1810 Jean-Pierre's elder sons Jean-Pierre and Jean-Frédéric transformed the mill at Sous-Cratet into a metal works. In 1810 they founded the 'Peugeot Frères Ainés' company to specialize in metal forming, eventually diversifying into the production of tools, household goods, crinoline hoops and corset stays from a network of factories in the region. Armand Peugeot, who had learnt to ride a penny-farthing while serving an apprenticeship in a metal works in Leeds, inspired a venture into bicycle manufacture, and in 1889 the company built four steam three-wheelers for Léon Serpollet.

In the same year Gottlieb Daimler and his French licensee Emile Levassor demonstrated the V-twin Daimler Stahlrad quadricycle to Armand Peugeot at his Valentigny factory. The result was the construction by Peugeot of five Daimler-engined prototypes (two front-engined, three rear-engined), followed by the start of real production in 1891. In 1894 output reached forty, and 156 cars left the factory in 1898, by which time Peugeot was making its own power units.

The 1894 Peugeot Type 5 is typical of the company's earliest production models, with a rear-mounted V-twin Daimler engine with hot-tube ignition. Ingeniously, Peugeot used the tubular chassis as a reservoir for water to cool the engine. In 1894, this car competed in the Paris-Rouen trial, the first true competitive event for motor vehicles.

cheered as he drove round, and he responded by stopping to give them a description of his Peugeot. This was a complete novelty to everyone present, and although motoring had yet to develop a lexicon of its own, *The Autocar* did its best to inform its readers about the Peugeot's technicalities:

> The carriage takes the form of a Victoria body with a seat for two in front; the back seat, also accommodating two passengers, is raised considerably above that facing it, in order that the *directeur* may have a good view ahead. His starting and stopping lever, and his speed variation lever, is placed close to him on the right, and a foot lever is conveniently fitted for the purpose of throwing the engine out of gear, and for actuating the brake on the shaft that carries the gearing.
>
> A lever brake is also fitted which has several actions; it throws the engine out of gear, brakes the gear shaft, and both driving wheels. The engine is 3¾ horse-power, but will develop more if required.
>
> The average speed on a good level road is about eight miles per hour, but fifteen miles per hour is attainable when desired. The engine, etc., is all neatly packed away under the back seat, and, except for the driving chain running naked at one side, there is no indication of machinery in

connection with the vehicle, except the slight noise and smell of warm spirit as it passes, and the somewhat serious vibration when the carriage is stopped.

The steering is done by a bicycle handle-bar in front of the *directeur* which actuates the front pair of wheels, which run free of each other on a fixed axle. The axle of the rear driving wheels is fitted with differential gear to allow of independent rotation when turning. The vehicle weighs 13 cwt., and will run from 180 to 200 miles without a fresh charge of petroleum.

The petroleum reservoir is well removed from the motor, being formed under the front seat. Five gallons of benzine, costing about 11d per gallon, is stored in this tank, from which it is pumped by a small pump into a smaller vessel which supplies the fuel for the two burners which keep the small platinum ignition tubes at a red heat.

This having been done, a pump like a syringe is attached to the small tank, and, all tubes having been closed, is worked until the pressure reaches a certain point indicated by the gauge, then a little spirits of wine is poured on the cups, one of which surrounds each burner. This when lighted heats the burner, and in two minutes the valves may be opened and the burners lighted.

Very quickly the ignition tubes are red-hot, and the engine is ready to start. The engine is started, and the driving gear thrown into gear after the *directeur* has taken his seat. To stop the vehicle the gear is thrown out, and, though the vehicle stops, the engine rattles on as though it had not another moment to live, and causes so much noise and vibration that one is heard with difficulty, while the vehicle appears seized with a species of Brobdingnagian ague.

This, we were informed, is to be averted in future by the fitting of a band-brake, which will cause the motor to moderate its transports when let loose for a while. In order to make the explanation clearer, we might say that, except for special fitting, these motors are practically the same as gas engines, except that the petroleum is vaporized at the moment of employment, and that it is the explosion of the gas so produced which gives the necessary impulse.

After the motor cars had been circling the show ring for some time, Sir David Salomons flexed his mayoral muscles and 'steeled himself to dare the majesty of the law, for the carriages left the ring and came out upon the excellently laid highway which stretches between the Agricultural Show Ground and the town. Directly the wheels of the automobiles revolved upon the surface of the high road, the serious handicap imposed upon

This horse-drawn firepump powered by a Daimler engine was operated by the Tunbridge Wells fire brigade.

their movement of propulsion by the rough turf of the ring was plainly apparent.'

A whispering campaign against cars said that they were a danger to pedestrians and horses but 'the motor vehicles were shown to be under perfect control, and not one of the horses so much as lifted an eye as the horseless carriages sped somewhat noisily by'.

Britain's first motor show had been a triumph for Sir David, and *The Autocar*'s somewhat long-winded claim that 'a new era in vehicular propulsion on the high roads of this country' was dawning seemed more than justified.

'When the day arrives – and by all surrounding signs the time is not far distant – for many purposes a horsed vehicle will look as quaint as did the horseless chariots seen by us at the Wells,' decreed the magazine. But the horse-drawn vehicle was not quite ready to give up the ghost.

London's first motor show took place at the Imperial Institute in Kensington early in 1896, followed soon after by an exhibition at the Crystal Palace.

Hot-tube ignition

The idea of an engine being fitted with spark plugs is so familiar today that the notion of using a naked flame to provide the ignition seems quite bizarre. Many of the earliest cars employed this method, but Gottlieb Daimler evidently did not trust it. In 1883 he patented 'hot-tube' ignition – initially used on his stationary engines – to replace an earlier method of ignition in which a slide valve (a simple device that acted something like the lid of an old-fashioned pencil box) opened briefly to expose the fuel/air mixture in the cylinder to a naked flame.

Daimler's invention was simple and effective: it consisted of a hollow platinum tube with a closed outer end screwed into the combustion chamber and heated by a Bunsen burner supplied with petrol from a closed fuel tank pressurized by an air pump. When the piston rose in the cylinder, it forced the fuel/air mixture into the closed tube, where the heat exploded it. The drawback with this system was that the engine would only run at a more or less constant speed, and a governor had to be fitted that prevented the engine from exceeding a predetermined limit. The only way of varying the speed of the engine or enabling the car to climb hills was to fit a gearbox with suitable ratios.

This was the invention of Emile Levassor, who based his variable-speed transmission on the mechanism of a lathe. Its revolving gears operated in the open with a minimum of lubrication.

Levassor countered criticism of his design with a famous saying: *'C'est brusque et brutal, mais ça marche.'* ('It's crude and brutal, but it works.') And so it did, and the majority of manual transmission cars today still use gearboxes employing the basic principles laid down by Levassor almost 120 years ago.

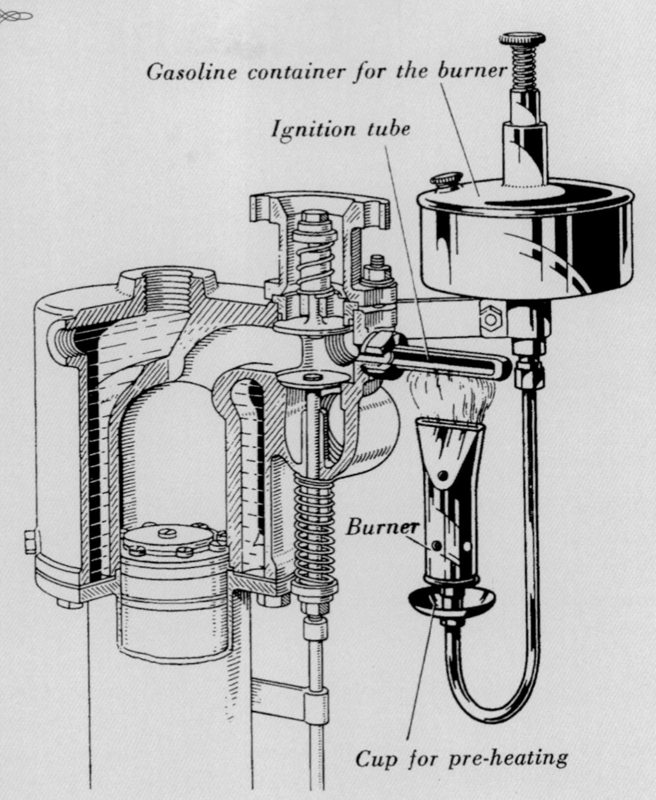

ABOVE RIGHT: Hot tube ignition used a platinum tube heated by a burner instead of a spark plug.

RIGHT: The burners of this 1892 Panhard & Levassor are contained in a fire-proof metal safe.

CHAPTER FOURTEEN

Emancipation Day

In the mid-1890s there were maybe a dozen cars on the roads of Britain, yet one man – who has as good a claim as any to being the founder of Britain's motor industry – envisaged a future in which special roads, hotels and restaurants would be built to cater for car users, out-of-town land prices would rise because the motor car enabled people to commute 20 miles to work from the suburbs, the police and Post Office would rely on motor vehicles and a motorized army 'would no longer need to waste money on horsepower'.

Just 5ft tall and slightly pop-eyed, this unlikely prophet was Harry John Lawson, the son of a preacher. Lawson founded Britain's first motor manufacturer, the Daimler Motor Company, on 14 January 1896, made a huge personal fortune out of the many companies he founded, but ended his glittering career in poverty and disgrace.

Lawson started modestly enough, making bicycles in Brighton during the 1870s. He claimed to have made the first safety cycle, and as early as 1880 he had patented a gas-propelled tricycle, which he later claimed to have been 'the first British motor car'. He moved to Coventry, which had become the centre of the cycle industry, and in 1887 he helped convert Rudge Cycles into a joint stock company. The venture was so successful that he made a career out of floating companies. The pattern was always the same: a beguiling prospectus attracted investors with the promise of spectacular dividends, and, certainly for the first couple of years, Lawson's over-capitalized companies paid out generously, but then they would crash into insolvency and Lawson would move on to another company promotion.

By the end of 1895 Lawson had made huge profits out of fifteen such over-capitalized flotations, often working with the notorious company promotor Terah Hooley, who stuffed the boards of his companies with impoverished noblemen whom he recruited on a sliding scale, paying £10,000 for the use of a duke's name, £5000 for an earl, and so on. In one famous promotion of the early 1890s, when Hooley bought the Dunlop Pneumatic Tyre Company for £3 million and floated it as a new business for £5 million, Lawson was said to have made half a million out of the deal.

Harry John Lawson may have been a conman, but he was also a visionary, and he realized that, as soon as it became legal to drive motor cars at faster than walking pace, a huge demand would be created. The man who controlled the motor industry that was bound to develop would make an immense fortune. Scenting that a change in the law was inevitable, in mid-1895 Lawson formed the British Motor Syndicate, with the aim of buying all the key patents covering motor vehicles so that he could extract royalties from the owners of every motor car in Britain.

Since 1893, businessman and inventor Frederick Simms had been importing Daimler power units from Germany for industrial use, several of which were installed in motor boats; Lawson snapped up Simms's Daimler Motor Syndicate for £35,000 and relaunched it as a manufacturer of motor cars.

The City financiers, many of whom who had burned their fingers in Lawson's previous company launches, were wary of this new venture, but nevertheless the launch was over-subscribed; typically, of the £100,000 invested, £40,000 ended up in the pockets of Lawson and the other directors of the British Motor Syndicate. Energetically lobbying Parliament to repeal the law that restricted motor vehicles to 4mph (6.4km/h), Lawson set about constructing a house-of-cards empire of car companies. Early in 1896 he organized an exhibition of motor vehicles in the Imperial Institute in Kensington, where the future King Edward VII first rode on a petrol car. He spent lavishly in accumulating 'master patents', investing an estimated £400,000 on more than seventy inventions, of which many eventually proved to be quite worthless. He founded the Motor Car Club 'for the protection, encouragement and development of the motor-car industry', and, when the speed limit was raised from 4 to 12mph (19km/h), on 14 November 1896, he held an 'Emancipation Day' run from London to Brighton in celebration.

Like so much of what Lawson did, the details of the Emancipation Day run are cloaked in mystery and legend. Consequently, reports of that first Brighton Run vary widely, although they do all agree that the weather was appalling: 'A drenching rain had fallen steadily for hours, the roads were soft and muddy, while a mist – heavy enough to be almost described as a London fog – hung about the streets in the vicinity of the river.' (That 'soft and muddy' road surface was one of the most unspeakable features of an era when urban transport relied heavily on horse traction. Every year each one of the hundreds of thousands of horses that used the streets of London produced 6.5 tons of all-too-evident exhaust pollution and deposited a large part of it on the highway. Crossing sweepers and watering carts fought a losing battle trying to keep this filthy tide at bay. The equine miasma fouled everything in winter, while the summer sun

OPPOSITE: Lawson's promotional leaflet for his British Motor Syndicate illustrated – not always accurately – the many claimed advantages of the 'coming change in the world's traffic'.

The Coming Revenue of the British Motor Syndicate.

Sole Owners of the Master Motor Car Patent in this Country.

EXCITING FINISH—PARIS-MARSEILLES GREAT MOTOR RACE.
Started Friday, September 24th—continued ten days through the wildest weather, all kinds of roads. 1000 miles. Average speed about sixteen miles per hour. Fifty-two Motors competed; winners first, second, third, fourth and fifth were British Motor Syndicate Patents, thus finally proving the enormous value and superiority of our patents.

THE FAMOUS MOTOR—THE "NEW TIMES" OF THE LORD MAYOR'S PROCESSION.
Latest Motor Landau to carry six people (5½ h.p.), belonging to the President of the Motor Car Club. (British Motor Syndicate Patents).
Described by the *Daily Telegraph* as representing "the great incident of Her Majesty's long reign."
* The detachable Motor may be added to the rear of the Carriage shown.

MARGATE POLICE MOUNTED on MOTORS.—An incident.
Motors are already wanted in every direction—for why? Machinery is always more certain and sure than any animal—works any length of time without fatiguing. (**De Dion Tricycle:** British Motor Syndicate Patents).

BOLLEE MOTOR TANDEM
(British Motor Syndicate Patents), now being erected in hundreds at **Coventry**, under Licence to the Syndicate.

All the New Motor Works besieged with Orders now pouring in.

IT MEANS THIS—
The saving of 75% over Horses.
IS IT WORTH **YOUR** CONSIDERATION ?

Business houses decide for Motors!

IT MEANS THIS—
The saving of 75% over Horses.
IS IT WORTH **YOUR** CONSIDERATION ?

MOTOR PARCELS VAN
Now building for **Peter Robinson**, 204 to 212, 214 to 228, Oxford Street, London, W.
Indicating the Enormous Revenue of the British Motor Syndicate.

The coming change in the world's traffic begins in earnest.

MOTOR PARCELS VAN,
As supplied to **Vel Vel**, St. Paul's Churchyard, London, E.C.
Motor Vans are wanted in all directions.

MOTOR PARCELS VAN,
Now on order for **Messrs. Liberty**, 142 to 144, Regent Street, London, W.
Hundreds of Parcels Vans are on order with motors instead of horses (British Motor Syndicate Patents).

THE GREAT FUTURE.—Wanted in all Large Towns Self-Acting Motor Broughams and Carriages.
(British Motor Syndicate Patents)

MOTOR SOCIABLE, TO CARRY WHOLE FAMILIES.
Now building at Coventry. (British Motor Syndicate Patents).

Royal Patronage.—H.R.H. THE PRINCE OF WALES rode British Motor Syndicate Patents.

* The Motor may be attached at the rear of the above Carriage.

Fifteen Reasons

. . WHY . .

A Motor Car is better than a Horse-drawn Vehicle.

Because . . .

1.—It wants no stable—the coach-house is enough.

2.—It needs no daily grooming, consequently

3.—No man need be kept specially to look after it.

4.—There is no manure heap to poison the air.

5.—It cannot shy, kick, or run away.

6.—It has no will of its own to thwart the wishes of its driver and cause disaster.

7.—It is more absolutely under control than any horse.

8.—It costs nothing to keep, and cannot "eat its head off in the stable."

9.—It consumes only when working, and then in exact proportion to the work done.

10.—It cannot fall sick and die.

11.—**It will do more work than any two horses,** and will travel **twice as fast as any one.**

12.—**It is only a fraction of the cost in working.**

13.—It can be stopped with certainty and safety in half the distance.

14.—No cruelty is inflicted by climbing a steep hill with a full load;

15.—Nor can distress be caused by high speed travelling.

Several of Lawson's publications contained this list of fifteen reasons why the car was better than the horse.

transformed it into disease-bearing dust that polluted everything it touched.)

The rain could not keep the crowds away from the start of the heavily promoted run to Brighton, which began from the Hotel Metropole in London's Northumberland Avenue, just off Trafalgar Square. The intrepid automobilists partook of a hearty breakfast, at which Lord Winchilsea – a director of Lawson's Great Horseless Carriage Company – 'tore into tatters one of the red flags which have hitherto been carried in front of traction engine and motor bicycle alike', before climbing into the racing Panhard 'No 8'.

Among those present was young Montague Grahame-White, whose run to Brighton on a borrowed De Dion tricycle would be cut short when the front wheel got stuck in the tramlines outside the Brixton tram depot, twisting forks and wheel beyond repair. He recalled that 'not the least prominent among the passengers were several street urchins who had surreptitiously clambered on to the tailboards and steps of the cars in order to claim to posterity they had taken part in the first motor race in England'.

The prevailing gloom lasted until shortly before the official start was to be signalled to the drivers. There was an atmosphere of reeking exhaust gases and a constant melange of explosions due to back-firing in silencers, followed by clouds of thick smoke. This emanated for close on two hours from the exhausts of a score or more engines receiving final adjustments at the hands of drivers and mechanics. Pandemonium reigned in the street while distinguished guests of the Motor Car Club at the Metropole breakfast were labouring to make their speeches heard. Grahame-White recalled his securing of a precious souvenir of the events:

> Whilst awaiting the arrival of a supply of Carless, Capel and Leonard's petrol, which I knew was reliable, I slipped into the Metropole for a cup of hot coffee. As I entered the now-deserted breakfast room, I encountered a waiter collecting discarded menu cards and other decorations, such as miniature enamel lapel badges of the Motor Car Club, and the symbolic Red Flag previously carried by a pedestrian in front of a mechanically propelled vehicle when travelling on the highway. It had been ceremoniously torn in half by the Earl of Winchilsea an hour or so earlier. Placing half a sovereign in the palm of his hand in exchange for this bundle of bunting I drank my coffee, and have ever since retained in my motoring collection this historical flag.

The exact number of cars that took part remains a mystery over a century later. The official programme listed an impressive fifty-four entries, some of which had been displayed in Wembley Park to publicize the event, but it was evident that some of those entries were there just to swell the numbers, and some of those listed were almost certainly fictitious. Some accounts claim that out of fifty-eight cars entered, thirty-three set off to Brighton, while others declare that only twenty-two took part officially.

ABOVE: On 14 November 1896 the participants in the Emancipation Day Run set off from the Hotel Metropole in Northumberland Avenue.

RIGHT: Each driver in the Emancipation Day Run was given route instructions, which warned against 'any rashness or carelessness which might injure the industry in this country'.

BELOW: At the 1996 centennial celebrations of Emancipation Day, the current Lord Winchilsea re-enacted his ancestor's act of ceremonially ripping up a red flag.

Motor Car Tour to Brighton.

FIRST MEET OF THE MOTOR CAR CLUB.

Saturday, November 14th, 1896.

Instructions as to Route & Itinerary.

GENERAL RECOMMENDATIONS. Owners and drivers of Motor Vehicles taking part in the Tour

Should remember that Motor Cars are on their trial in England, and that any rashness or carelessness might injure the industry in this Country.

Should see that their Motor Cars appear in thoroughly good clean order, and are never left unattended on the route.

Should be fully provided with sufficient lubricating and motor oil.

Should see that passengers are provided with proper protection against bad weather, such as mackintoshes, etc., and with light provisions.

Should use the greatest care as to speed and driving, so as not to endanger ordinary traffic.

Should treat the Police and other Authorities on the route with polite consideration.

UNIFORM. Special Caps and Armlets can be provided to Members of the Club driving Motor Vehicles who wish for them on application to the Secretary.

PILOT CAR. Mr. Harry J. Lawson, the President of the Club, will drive the Pilot Car, from which directions will be given. Drivers are requested not to pass this Car unless by necessity, so that directions may be communicated to those taking part in the run.

OIL. A supply of motor oil (spec. 6·80) and also of lubricating oil will be found at the "White Hart Hotel," Reigate

WATER. Water can be obtained at the "Horse & Groom," Streatham, "Wheatsheaf," Thornton Heath, "Greyhound," Croydon, "Windsor Castle," Purley, "The Star," Horley, "White Hart," Reigate, "The George," Crawley, "Black Swan," Peas Pottage, "Red Lion," Hand Cross, "Queen's Head," Bolney, "King's Head," Albourne, "The Plough," Pyecombe, and the "Black Lion," Patcham.

MEET OF CARS. The Motor Cars should assemble in front of the Whitehall Entrance of the Metropole Hotel, not later than 9 a.m. Breakfast takes place at 9.30 sharp in the Whitehall Rooms of the Hotel Metropole. Tickets 10/- each, including Wine.

Back in the 1960s, when I lived in East Grinstead in Sussex, I used occasionally to meet an elderly gentleman named Herman Volk – son of the man who built the electric railway along the Brighton seafront in Victorian times – who lived in a private hotel at the far end of town. He told me that as a youth he had accompanied his father, Magnus Volk, on the Emancipation Day Run aboard an experimental electric carriage, and that they had followed the official entries for part of the route.

However, the Volks were not part of Lawson's entourage, and so they were not mentioned in any of the official reports, which (although vague on details of the journey) wax lyrical about the start of the run. The cars were led away by the Panhard & Levassor 'Old No 5', which had won the 1895 Paris-Bordeaux-Paris race. Flying the violet and gold banner of the Motor Car Club, the Panhard was driven by Otto Mayer, with Harry Lawson as passenger. Lawson was wearing the flamboyant costume of the Motor Car Club, a sort of fancy yachting uniform that made him look, as one insider put it, 'like an admiral in the Swiss Navy'.

Next in line came the huge Daimler barouche 'Present Times', which had run in the Lord Mayor's Show a week earlier. Its passengers included Frederick Simms, who had founded the Daimler Motor Syndicate in 1893 to import German-built Daimler engines, and Gottlieb Daimler himself. Then there was another racing Panhard, 'No 6', followed by Evelyn Ellis's 1895 Panhard, three Léon Bollée voiturettes, a New Beeston tricycle and racing Panhards 'New No 5' and 'No 8'.

The great self-publicist Herbert O. Duncan, who drove a Léon Bollée three-wheeled voiturette, declared that the entry was completed by a couple more Bollées, several 'Daimlers' (actually Daimler-engined Panhards), several electric vehicles (most of which actually rode to Brighton aboard a train), two American Duryeas, four Roger-Benz cars, the prototype Arnold 'motor dog-cart', and a Pennington four-seated tricycle driven by Edward Joel Pennington himself. This, however, somewhat suspiciously, 'got lost in the crowd at the start and had to join the procession at a later point'.

The Pennington was unsuitable for any sort of journey, as is obvious from a view of the fine example of the Torpedo Autocar – possibly even the very one driven by Edward Pennington in 1896 – that survives today. One of the early cars that was preserved by the late R.G.J. Nash, it was displayed for many years at the National Motor Museum at Beaulieu. (But for the folly of local planners in refusing permission for development, because they found historic cars and aircraft of no interest, it would have found a home in a motor museum that Nash tried to build in Surrey soon after the Second World War.)

Before the Great War, it was acquired by C.A. 'Bath Road' Smith, the former racing cyclist who ran the White Lion hotel at Cobham, and in 1912 it went on show in the very first motor museum in Oxford Street. The catalogue was suitably cynical about Pennington's design skills:

> This is a tandem tricycle. It was very fast – for those days. It would do about 40mph (64km/h), and was undoubtedly the fastest thing on wheels at the time – while it ran.
>
> The machine, like all Pennington machines, was most original, bicycle steering and the bicycle forks carrying both steering wheels being about the only

This Panhard & Levassor, which had won the 1896 Paris-Marseilles-Paris race, took part in the 1896 Motor Car Tour to Brighton 'carrying a party of Parisian automobilists'. It was bought by Harry Lawson, who sold it to the Hon. C.S. Rolls late in 1896. Rolls kept the car until his death in a flying accident at Bournemouth in 1910. At the 1996 celebrations, it was driven by former world champion racing driver and antique-car enthusiast Phil Hill.

features of conventional cycle design of that period. There are two very large, sloping, tubular 'backbones', running from steering heads to back axle, a rider at each end, and the engine in the middle.

The engine is very simple, each cylinder being made of steel tubing, with a very shallow water jacket, worked by natural circulation from a tank above it. There was never any need for a radiator – the engine would not run long enough to boil the water. Petrol was fed direct into the combustion casting, and mixed with the air there. Paraffin was supposed to be the fuel, but Pennington bluffed on the public ignorance of the difference between paraffin and petrol.

The great feature of the engine was stated to be the 'long mingling spark', about which raged a great controversy. Pennington claimed his ignition to be so hot and so long drawn out that it would vaporize even crude oil or paraffin wax; but he took care never to experiment publicly!

Actually, the ignition consisted of a flat spring projecting into and half across the cylinder, with a spade-handle striker on the end of the piston. This made contact on both strokes, rubbed all along the surface of the spring, and sparked as contact broke. Pennington tried to persuade the public it was sparking, with one long-continued flame, all the time of contact. The rapidly repeated deflections of the spring within the combustion chamber let down the temper, and after 10 to 30 minutes' operation it broke, and the engine went out of action. With a reliable ignition, Pennington might have made a success of the machine. As it was, over £100,000 was lost to no purpose.

Over a hundred years after Emancipation Day, I had the chance – the first ever, I believe – to 'test drive' the 1896 Pennington Torpedo Autocar, even though it has not actually run under its own power for at least eighty years. I had to gauge its curious dynamics by virtue of gravity assistance (and energetic pushing from Phil Sexton, one of the National Motor Museum's hard-working volunteers), but I think that I have ridden the Torpedo Autocar further than any man living. On the gentle down slopes of the museum's rally field I was able

Harry Lawson's stately Cannstatt-Daimler landau 'Present Times' was a prominent entrant in the London-Brighton Run, with Gottlieb Daimler as passenger. A week earlier, it had been the first motor car to take part in the Lord Mayor's Procession through the City of London.

The author 'test drives' the 1896 Pennington under gravity at the National Motor Museum; its steering was, to say the least, extremely odd.

ABOVE: Grand Prix driver Graham Hill drove the Pennington-inspired 1896 Ford Quadricycle replica on the Crystal Palace race track, where its total lack of braking was no problem, in 1963.

LEFT: It was steam power –courtesy of the London, Brighton & South Coast Railway – that enabled Walter Bersey's Electrical Landau to reach Brighton in 1896. The problem was, it arrived too clean…

to explore the ride and handling of this unwieldy tricycle at more than adequate speeds.

Fortunately, I had not long before driven Ford-Britain's replica of the 1896 Ford Quadricycle, whose power unit is a close copy of the Pennington power unit, and this enabled me to imagine how perfectly uncontrollable the Pennington would seem with the engine running. Despite the manifest shortcomings of Pennington's engine, Henry Ford had read about it in the *American Machinist* magazine and took it as the pattern for the engine of his first motor vehicle, which he built in a shed at the bottom of his yard in Detroit.

In one rather basic respect, the Ford Quadricycle was even more terrifying than the Pennington, for it numbered among its many deficiencies a total lack of brakes (Ford was so anxious to get it running that he forgot about making it stop, and I made the painful discovery that the only way to arrest its progress on a gentle down slope was to hit a concrete wall head on). Despite this fundamental design flaw, once his experimenting was done, Henry Ford managed to sell the Quadricycle to an eager buyer named Charles Ainsley for $200, proving indisputably that there is at least one born every minute. This time, it seems, there were two, for Ainsley, boasting of 'extraordinarily good service', sold the little car on to cycle dealer A.W. Hall, who in 1899 wrote a glowing account of the service it had given him.

Like the Pennington, the Ford had a curious 'make-and-break' ignition system, in which adjustable studs on the pistons made contact with insulated 'igniter' plugs in the cylinder walls that carried the low-tension ignition current, with the 'long-mingling' spark occurring as the plugs and studs separated. Neither machine had a throttle or even a carburettor, just simple needle valves that allowed gasoline to dribble into the intake manifold; the speed of the Pennington engine was controlled by a desperately inadequate advance-and-retard knob for the ignition. Nor was there an ignition switch on the Pennington, whose engine 'kill' knob pulled on a metal strip that prevented the inlet valves from opening; the Ford, on the other hand, had a brass household-type switch to turn off the ignition.

Either way, control was limited, and you have to wonder about the wisdom of – in Pennington's case – trying to drive the machine from London to Brighton, or – in Henry Ford's case – of running around the streets of downtown Detroit after dark.

Every model – and there were several – designed by Edward Joel Pennington is worthy of inclusion in a list of the worst cars of all time, but the three-wheeled Autocar preserved at Beaulieu is particularly awful. It boasts cylinders with only nominal cooling and has neither suspension nor bodywork, just cycle saddles. The driver sits at the absolute rear of the Pennington on a tiny cycle saddle, uncomfortably like a ladies' model, and, despite the fat 'unpuncturable' tyres that provide the machine's only suspension, feels every pebble in the road through the seat of the trousers. Moreover, back in 1896, the view ahead would have been obscured by the backs of the three passengers sitting on angled saddles encompassed by semicircular armrests.

Pennington may have been a craft company promotor, but he obviously had little idea of steering geometry. The front wheels, controlled by a sloppy rod-and-chain linkage from the driver's handlebars, assume the most amazing angles on full lock. Moreover, the toe-in varies visibly as the car runs along.

There are two gears, controlled by in-and-out levers that lock sprockets of different diameters to the rear hub. It is quite easy to engage both speeds at once, and the handbrake, which noisily wraps wooden brake blocks on to a steel drum, is not to be relied upon as a means of stopping the Torpedo Autocar if top speed is engaged, for the handbrake and gear lever foul one another.

If the means by which the Pennington reached Brighton in 1896 remains obscure, it is a certainty that the elaborate Bersey 'Electrical Landau' made the journey by courtesy of the London, Brighton & South Coast Railway; conveniently, the train line ran parallel to the route.

In 1896 Bersey had boasted of the 'prominent part' that the Landau had played in 'the memorable run from London to Brighton'; at the dinner after the 1935 Brighton Run, however, he confessed the truth:

> As I knew the batteries of my electric brougham would not have got me to Brighton, the machine was hurried off the course to a station, then entrained to a spot near Brighton, where it was hidden round a corner to await the other competitors. The difficulty was the discovery that the other competing machines had become covered with mud, which entailed frantic efforts to discover mud with which to clothe the electric car!

Some thought had, in fact, been given to providing breakdown cover, in the shape of a Panhard & Levassor van packed with tools for emergency use. However, according to its young passenger Charles Jarrott (who later became a famous racing driver and a founder of the Automobile Association), 'The one thing we did not carry for use in emergency was the one thing we required ourselves when the van broke down!'

Competitors in the modern-day Brighton Run are well used to rain, but few could visualize the hellish conditions endured by the participants in the 1896 Run, when torrential rain turned the surface of the untreated Brighton Road to liquid mud. A.O. Bradley, who was driving a twin-cylinder 5hp Panhard & Levassor, recalled the conditions:

> As the run progressed, the weather became worse and worse; we were all soaked to the skin and every time I stood up the water ran down my legs into my boots.
>
> On arrival at Reigate I found five or six cars in front of me, but I did not stop long because I was anxious to get to Brighton as early as possible. My poor old Panhard kept steadily mud-plugging through the rain for hour after hour until darkness set in, when I was obliged to stop to buy some candles for the lamps.
>
> Shortly after this my troubles began. Within ten miles of Brighton I was unfortunate enough to break a link in one side chain. A stone had been thrown up by one of the wheels, and this became jammed

Swerving to avoid a frightened horse, H.O. Duncan's Bollée voiturette hit the bank and hurled its unfortunate passenger into a muddy ditch!

Whatever happened to Harry Lawson?

Although the British Motor Syndicate had declared a 30 per cent dividend on its first year's trading before it had actually built a single car, Lawson's next venture, the Great Horseless Carriage Company – which had raised £750,000 in mid-1896, of which £500,000 went to the British Motor Syndicate – was liquidated at the end of 1897. Its illustrated prospectus, according to *The Autocar*, 'would have done credit to an H.G. Wells or a Jules Verne'.

Daimler, fortunately, had already broken free of Lawson's control. That enabled the company to avoid the knock-on effects of the depression which hit Coventry in 1898, when the reckless overproduction by the cycle industry as a result of all those extravagant company promotions brought down Lawson's mentor Terah Hooley. However, while Hooley filed for bankruptcy, he managed to hold on to around £200,000, most of which he had secretly put in his wife's name.

Preacher's son Harry Lawson was a visionary confidence trickster who had patented a curious gas-driven tricycle in 1880 and had been a prime mover in the bicycle boom of the early 1890s.

Lawson, on the other hand, seemed unstoppable, making a profit of more than £50,000 in 1898 from the flotation of an ambitious scheme to provide London with a steam bus service that never materialized. But, behind the scenes, all was far from well; those expensively acquired patents were proving increasingly difficult to enforce (and some, including the most expensive of all, which had cost him £100,000, were proving absolutely worthless).

It was the American bunco artist Edward Joel Pennington who had sold Lawson those worthless patents, and so Lawson decided that America promised rich pickings and the chance to escape the irate investors who had lost money in his ventures. Calling himself 'Sir Harry', he arrived in the United States in 1900, where he persuaded the country's leading bicycle maker Colonel August Pope to produce a gawky front-wheel-driven three-wheeler called the Lawson Sociable in Chicago under the name 'Trimoto' (America's first licence-holding lady driver owned one). He did try and sell his Coventry-built Sociables in England, but without success – the market had moved on.

The 'master patents' monopoly bubble finally burst in 1904, and Lawson and Hooley were tried for fraud over their Electric Tramways Construction Company, which the Crown condemned as a 'paper' concern through which large sums of money subscribed by the public had found their way into Lawson's hands. Hooley, who was brilliantly defended by the great Rufus Isaacs, a future Lord Chief Justice, was acquitted, but Lawson was found guilty of making false statements and sentenced to twelve months' hard labour.

You cannot keep a good conman down, and a decade later Lawson resurfaced in the aviation industry with a blanket company known as

between the sprocket and the chain itself. Unfortunately I had no spare links, and was benighted by the roadside, unable to move another yard. Meanwhile, the rain was pouring down in torrents.

I tried to fix things up with the aid of one of the candle lamps, but the situation was quite hopeless, and as I was then feeling exhausted after this long and tiring drive I suggested to my companion that we should try to find a cottage where we could get a shake-down for the night.

Eventually I found a farmer, who lent me a horse to tow the car to the nearest village, which was some distance away, and we stayed at the local inn for the night. Next morning, feeling somewhat stiff, I took a link out of the unbroken chain, adjusted the radius rods and was soon on my way again to complete the journey.

The weather and slippery road conditions also defeated H.O. Duncan's Bollée, which had to swerve to avoid a frightened horse and hit the bank, hurling Duncan's passenger, W. McRobie Turrell, into a muddy ditch: 'We held our sides with laughter at Mr Turrell's grotesque appearance. That worthy gentleman was wearing white ducks – one half covered with mud while the other preserved its pristine whiteness.'

It is difficult, too, to imagine the amount of interest caused by the sight of a handful of motor vehicles ploughing down to Brighton through rain and mud. *The Daily Telegraph* remarked that 'from Charing Cross to the West Pier at Brighton spectators assembled – by hundreds of thousands in the Metropolis – by thousands in the towns, by hundreds in the villages, and by scores at almost every yard of the country roads traversed. The Motor Car, by its triumphal progress, was received with astonishing enthusiasm, unanimous from the beginning to the end of the journey.'

Those lucky enough to ride on the cars were entranced by the experience. One journalist, who sped down Handcross Hill aboard a racing Panhard, was full of enthusiasm: 'To rush through the air at the speed of a torpedo-boat destroyer, down a narrow, curving road enclosed with hedges, and without being able to see what was to the front of us, was a novel and thrilling experience!'

Some on the day had foreseen the huge change in society that the motor car would bring about, like the enterprising

Lawson, wearing his curious Motor-Car Club uniform, poses with a group of his associates after the Emancipation Day Run of 1896.

the Army & Navy Contract Corporation. In May 1915 it floated a £200,000 company trading under the respected name of aviator Louis Blériot, first man to cross the English Channel in an aeroplane; Blériot, of course, knew nothing of Lawson's company. The Blériot Company lasted just eight months, and at an extraordinary meeting prior to its winding-up, angry shareholders threw missiles at Lawson, who escaped through a side door.

'There was nothing to show for the money of the shareholders and no hope of any dividend,' declared the Official Receiver when winding up yet another of Lawson's contemporary ventures.

In March 1916 Lawson survived the torpedoing of the cross-Channel ferry *Sussex* in the English Channel by a German U-Boat, but ironically was unable to attend the London Bankruptcy Court that August as he was still in hospital.

By November that year, when *The Autocar* celebrated its twenty-first birthday, Lawson was well enough to write a prickly letter claiming that the 'huge motor works which I established with so much hard work became the birthplace of the motor industry of the country'. He added: 'Perhaps these very works will help to win the war. They are running night and day on munitions. The Government are depending on the outputs of nine of the factories I raised the money for by prospectuses to establish the industry. Mark the latest Government appeal in this crisis for more works. Lawson could get them, he believes, even now.' The Government wisely ignored.

Lawson, acknowledged by many to be 'a man of great ideas and great energy', died, forgotten by the motor industry he had founded, at the age of 73, on 12 July 1925 in Harrow-on-the-Hill. He had just £99 left out of the hundreds of thousands of pounds he had extracted from a gullible public.

wheelwright who displayed a hastily painted notice claiming 'Motor-Cars Repaired While You Wait' outside his workshop near Reigate. In his neighbourhood, the streets were packed six or seven deep with spectators on either side, leaving only a narrow path clear for the motor vehicles to pass through. Crawley – then only a small village – hung out a banner proclaiming 'Success to the Motor-Car'.

Some things change little. The *Star* newspaper seemed more interested in the lady cyclists following the run than in the cars:

> Two charming girls, one with flaxen hair, another black as jet, attracted every eye as they 'pedalled' just behind the procession in bloomers. Nice blue serge blouses and baggy knickerbockers of good cut made a very pleasant picture of the human or leg motor, now to be swept away by the intelligent foreigner and his steam bicycle. One of the bloomer girls was with a young fellow on a bicycle made for two, and she didn't mind at all when the crowd called her 'Dysy'.

Inevitably, the crush of spectators caused at least one accident. At Three Bridges, one of the two Duryeas that had come over from America for the run clipped the small daughter of a local publican named Dyer when she leant too far into the road, and knocked her down, where a cyclist following the cars 'fell on her with his machine'. Happily, the child was not seriously hurt.

One of the Duryeas, driven by J. Frank Duryea, one of the two brothers behind America's first production car (thirteen were built in 1896), became the first four-wheeled car to reach Brighton after a brace of Bollée three-wheelers, for it had not stopped for lunch at Reigate with the other cars. Harry Lawson had rashly promised a gold medal to the first man home, but the Duryea was not one of the makes covered by his patents monopoly. A quick rejigging of the rules followed; Frank Duryea got his gold medal, and the next seven cars home, all Lawson-backed makes, were awarded gold medals too!

Duryea's medal is now in the possession of the Smithsonian Institute in Washington DC, while another gold medal, awarded to Otto Mayer, was acquired by the Veteran Car Club in 2004.

But how many cars actually arrived in Brighton that Saturday night? Harry Lawson issued an official report after the run:

> Owing to the crowd, no real start could be made until Brixton was reached, when twenty-two cars only were started, as they arrived at long intervals... The following cars duly arrived at Brighton: First at 2.35 a Bollée voiturette; 2.47 Bollée Car (British Motor Syndicate Patents). Neither of these followed their instructions to wait at Reigate; their time record, however, was extraordinary, as they each carried two persons and were not racing.
>
> The Pilot Car and three British Motor Syndicate cars were all four in their proper places at Preston Park, Brighton, punctually at 4.30, where they were received by the Mayor. A Duryea American car, following the two Bollées, had also gone through, and a New Beeston Motor Cycle, making eight cars in all, which were in good time. The next hour brought four more, making

The Léon Bollée Voiturette was the sports car of its day. This 1897 Bollée bravely tackled the testing 85-mile circuit followed by the 2005 Gordon Bennett Centenary Rally.

twelve; the whole of the rest of the twenty-two cars arrived in Brighton at intervals during the evening with two exceptions – one broke down at Patcham, the valves being choked with mud; the other stopped at Reigate and came in during the night.

All these motors behaved splendidly, with the exception of the one referred to. No accident of any kind happened to our cars. The Crawley accident was caused by the Duryea American car, through no fault of the driver.

After the banquet, the Committee had the satisfaction of examining twenty motor cars in Messrs. Du Pont's stables, and beyond the lower half of each vehicle being smothered with mud, they were in perfect condition, and ready to take to the road again immediately.

An American Duryea was the first four-wheeled car to reach Brighton. Driver and designer Charles Duryea was – grudgingly, perhaps?– presented by Lawson with a gold medal, which is preserved in the Smithsonian Institution in Washington, DC.

In contrast, *Punch*, the cynical chronicler of the Victorian scene, had already revealed that 'many of the guests of the Motor Club went to Brighton on Saturday last by a horseless carriage – supplied by the LB & SC Railway'. In addition, a 'diary item' on 'Automobilistic Brighton' by a fictitious Frenchman named Auguste described a less magnificent arrival in Brighton:

And see there, after to have attended during three quarters of an hour, without anything to see excepted the crowd, all to blow, *tout à coup*, I smell an odour of oil – ah but, an odour of the most disheartenings, *écoeurantes*, and I perceive a little carriage, conducted by a man, in costume of 'yachtman', with a droll of bonnet, *galonné* of gold. The little carriage is followed of two other carriages and of two other odours of oil, still more disheartening, and, after some time, of an electric carriage, absolutely without odour. *Voilà tout!* All the world has passed one hour or more by a frightful time, for to see to arrive four carriages, absolutely covered of mud, and one distinguishes them at pain in the obscurity, excepted by the odour of the oil and by the *vacarme* of the mechanism. Truly it is an historic occasion, the inauguration of the carriage of the future, but extremely disagreeable by a so villain time!

'Auguste' also hinted in the article, not very subtly, that most of the cars actually arrived on the 16th (not too unlikely, given the Victorian's strong views on Sunday observance). Certainly, the photographs of the cars at Brighton must have been taken after the 14th, as they were all shot in full daylight, and the cars and their occupants were clean and dry.

In 1935, the then Mayor of Brighton, who as a young journalist had covered the 1896 run for a London daily newspaper, recalled that Harry Lawson had sent the papers a report of the event a day or two before it actually happened: 'Not the least of the joke [was] Lawson's description of how well his own car performed in this preamble, as against its actual performance in the run.'

Despite the comments of various detractors, the public had shown how much it liked the motor car, a view reflected by the report in the popular illustrated paper *The Graphic*:

Saturday's great London–Brighton test has proved that we may travel much faster, much easier and at less cost. A four-in-hand makes five changes and employs twenty horses to do what one little Motor can easily accomplish.... The Railway excitement and wild mania of our forefathers will soon be entirely eclipsed by a greater public Motor boom than has ever been witnessed.

London to Brighton Album

Headed by a 1902 7hp Panhard & Levassor, veterans await the start of the 2004 Brighton Run alongside the Serpentine.

The German Adler company was already famous as makers of typewriters and bicycles when it built its first cars in 1900. This vis-à-vis seated Adler dates from 1901.

Feeding time? Engine accessibility is no problem on this 1902 8hp De Dion-Bouton.

This wonderfully-original 1899 Henriod won the Judges' Special Award in the 2005 pre-Run Concours in Regent Street. It was built at Neuilly-sur-Seine, near Paris.

This 1902 10-hp MMC was built in the famous Motor Mills at Coventry.

ABOVE: The fire screen-like condenser in front of this 1902 White once owned by Sir Charles Ross of Balmagowan Castle, Scotland, enables the steamer to travel further on a tank of water.

RIGHT: The identity of this de Dion-engined veteran found in a garage in Kirriemuir, Scotland, in the 1960s was a mystery for many years. It is now known to be a 1901 Colliot, built in Soissons, France.

The two De Dion-Boutons of Ecurie Gonfalon, the father and son team of the Banner family, arrive together at the finishing line on Brighton's Madeira Drive.

CHAPTER FIFTEEN

By Steam Cart to Brighton

One of the most remarkable people I have come across since I became involved with early cars was a Norfolk farmer named George Milligen. I first met him in the 1960s when I was freelance editor of *Old Motor* magazine; he would call in at the offices on his weekly forays to London to chat about early cars. A diffident chap, he kept his private life very private, but I learned that his weekly routine involved a visit to his elderly mother and a night at a jazz club, for music played an important part in his bachelor life.

George Milligen had a quite remarkable collection of cars at his farm in Norfolk, many of them perhaps the sole surviving examples of very rare makes, but few people ever got to see it in its entirety. I was lucky enough to be shown round on several occasions; even though I was a writer, George trusted me not to write about anything he did not want mentioned in print. Despite his obvious wealth, he was not an ostentatious man; he used to receive visitors wearing carpet slippers and an ancient camel overcoat tied up with string. He was also notorious for the shorts he wore most of the time, with the legs rolled up so far that the pockets hung below their hems.

My first view of the Salvesen Steam Cart, piled with rubbish, including old oil lamps and the number plate from one of George Milligen's Facel Vega cars.

On one occasion, George entrusted me with bidding on his behalf at a Veteran Car Club auction sale for a fine pair of Polkey Paraffin Headlamps to go on his gorgeous Labourdette-bodied 1904 Gardner-Serpollet steamer. 'If I start bidding in person, they'll just rack the price up,' he told me. I got them for £160, which seemed quite a high price then, but was an absolute bargain in hindsight; certainly George was very pleased.

George's collection was kept in the several brick and stone barns surrounding his handsome farmhouse, and I remember a curious and very primitive steamer stored amid a considerable amount of detritus in one of the smaller barns. George had bought it at the second sale of vehicles from the famed Sword collection in Scotland in the mid-1960s. It had been built in the mid-1890s by Henry Adolph Salvesen for use on his Lathallan estate at Polmont, near Grangemouth, the second port on the River Forth adopted by the Christian Salvesen company. (His father Christian Salvesen had come to Scotland from Norway in the mid-19th century to found a shipping and trading company in the port of Leith, on the Forth near Edinburgh.)

Henry Salvesen, it seems, was a skilled amateur mechanic, as recorded by the *Falkirk Herald* in his obituary in May 1924: 'as a craftsman with his hands, working in iron, or steel, or wood, he was equal to any trained mechanic'. He built two steam cars to run about the estate, the second of which was later converted into a steamroller for use on his tennis courts.

The only clue to the age of the steamer in George Milligen's barn was its axles, which were obviously the same as those used on the first Coventry Daimlers. Given that the first company to start assembling Daimlers from chassis components sent up by rail from Coventry was the Scottish coachbuilder

On its maiden voyage in 2003, the Salvesen Steam Cart arrives at Crawley, the mid-point of the Brighton Run.

John Stirling, of the Hamilton Carriage, Motor Car & Cycle Works, just 20 miles from the Salvesen estate, it seems likely that Salvesen would have obtained the axles from them rather than from the Motor Mills in Coventry. It is known that the first 'Stirling Daimler' ran in January 1897 (although this was a hybrid vehicle powered by a French Panhard engine, as the Motor Mills was still working on the development of its own power units.) In 1896 Henry Salvesen had ordered his own Daimler from Stirling; its first run was still clearly remembered more than half a century later, in the RSAC Jubilee history of 1949:

> It was a 4½hp job, with tube ignition, tiller steering, the car fitted with solid tyres. The Salvesens, father and son, had a glorious first journey from Hamilton to Polmont, a distance of about 20 miles. An employee of the Company drove, and he was accompanied in the front seat by another representative of the makers.
>
> Mr Salvesen, senior, commented on the fact that this second official in the front seat, with a splendid detachment and an attitude of indifference to this new experience for the owner, read a newspaper as the car moved along! The people in the villages through which they passed stared with astonishment at what seemed to them a portent. Going up hills, the speed was four miles an hour. Children encountered by the wayside at these points were able to run alongside, holding on to the car.

Aside from the axles, which were probably ordered from Stirling at the same time as the new motor car, Henry Salvesen used a Merryweather vertical boiler and an underfloor twin-cylinder engine, fitting them in a sturdy channel steel chassis that was far stronger than the average frame used in motor cars at the time.

George Milligen took a long-term view over the restoration of the cars in his collection, prioritizing them on a 'need to use' basis. He did drive many thousands of miles in some of them and kept many models all his collecting life, which was certainly a long one. He received a 30-98 Vauxhall as a gift of on his 17th birthday in the 1920s, and carried on collecting right up until his death early in 2004, at the age of 94. The Salvesen was one of a handful of cars that he planned to 'get around to one day'. He had apparently driven it around his estate, and at some stage the original tiller had been removed and a big red iron steering wheel from a traction engine had been substituted, but it was otherwise still just as he had bought it back in the 1960s. It stood on blocks next to an early Albion fire engine, still covered with old starters, coach lamps and even the number plate from one of his Facel Vegas!

As a consultant to the Bonham's auction house, I was given the agreeable task of cataloguing George's cars for the sale of the bulk of his collection (a handful of his favourite cars, including the birthday Vauxhall, were kept by his family). I was delighted to discover the original steering tiller under the seat; it was quickly refitted, in place of the incongruous steering wheel. The sale, at the 2004 Goodwood Revival Meeting, was the auction event of the year. His 1929 Mercedes-Benz SSK 38/250 set new records with a selling price of almost £4.2 million. Compared with this, the unique Salvesen Steam Cart seemed a relative bargain at a shade under £70,000, but would it retreat again into the obscurity in which it had dwelt for most of its long life?

Not a bit of it. The sale was in September and a few weeks later I was astounded hear that the Salvesen had been entered for the Brighton Run, at the beginning of November. Surely its new owner John Brydon was showing an excess of optimism, given that the Steam Cart had probably only covered a few hundred yards since the start of the 20th century? However, on the appointed day, there was the Salvesen at the start of the run in Hyde Park with steam up and its first-ever licence plate (it had never previously been registered for the road), ready to set off for Brighton.

John Brydon, already the owner of a big 1905 CGV racing special, told me how he had put his 'sleeping beauty' back into running order:

> It was in a remarkably complete condition, and it soon became very apparent that the vehicle had done very little work since it was built, for the drive gears were like new.
>
> I went through the vehicle and stripped most of it down, particularly the boiler which is of considerable age, if not original to the cart. After having had some internal repairs carried out by Taylors of Leeds and being tested, we successfully steamed the boiler on Friday 29 October.
>
> Thankfully, George Milligen had maintained the cart very well and stored it in dry and well-oiled condition, and it was really due to him that we were able to get it running so quickly. The two cylinders had no form of lubrication at all; all the bearings relied on a hand-held oil can. Clearly this would not allow many minutes of running time, so I fitted a Manzel twin-feed lubricator of the correct vintage, with wick oilers to the bearings and screw greasers to the eccentrics. Hopefully, this should give us a mile or two before the oils need checking!
>
> It was a very tight schedule; we were only able to give the cart its first road test last Friday!

Some four hours after leaving London, with its owner gamely stoking the boiler,

Proud owner John Brydon acted as stoker for the Brighton Run and found the Salvesen to be encouragingly economical in its consumption of anthracite and water.

the Salvesen Steam Cart puffed gently into Crawley, to be photographed at the midway staging point. Later that afternoon, as dusk started to fall, a few minutes before the 4.30 deadline, it crossed the finishing line on Madeira Drive in Brighton. John Brydon was a worthy recipient of the medal 'for punctual arrival' that is the sole but much-coveted reward for every successful entrant in the run.

At least the Salvesen had a happier fate than the Daimler that shared the Polmont garage with it back in the mid-1890s. After giving satisfactory service for thousands of miles, it was eventually sold for just £25; rapid depreciation is certainly nothing new when it comes to motor cars.

Many years later, Henry Salvesen's son was in Edinburgh, where he passed one of the superannuated Stirling Daimlers that operated a bus service in the town waiting for passengers at the top of the Waverley Steps with its engine running. Something familiar in the note of the engine caught his ear; surely it was the old Daimler that he used to drive?

Journey's end – with fifteen minutes to go before the deadline, the Salvesen Steam Cart arrives in Brighton.

Even though the external appearance of the car had been altered – the original tiller had been replaced by a wheel and there were wooden mudguards in place of the patent-leather originals – Major Salvesen recognized the household light switch that his father had fitted to the car when the ignition had been converted from hot-tube to electric-spark. Some of his father's other gadgets were still fitted, too. It was like meeting an old but much-changed friend.

On the spur of the moment, Salvesen told the driver that he had driven thousands of miles in the old Daimler and would like to drive it once again. The driver agreed, and, when the bus was full a few minutes later, Major Salvesen took the wheel and drove the car as fast as he dared down Princes Street. History does not recall what the passengers made of it all.

CHAPTER SIXTEEN

The Old Adam

In the mid-1960s, I interviewed a rather crotchety chap named J.M. Turner, who lived in a pebbledashed bungalow in Peacehaven, a community of single-storey homes fit for heroes built high on the Sussex cliffs after the First World War. He had had a long career in the motor trade, which he had recorded in laborious handwriting in a series of exercise books. A motoring pioneer – he had ridden a Darracq motor tricycle as early as 1900 – and one-time owner of an 1899 Panhard & Levassor that is still a Brighton Run regular ('You can still see the repair to a front mudguard where I took the guts out of a cab horse before the Great War,' he assured me), Turner had run a garage in the Ealing area of London in the late 1920s. There he had known an elderly electrical engineer named H.J. Dowsing, who had in his shed a veteran car he called 'Adam'.

Dowsing had owned the car since the late 1890s, and had fitted it with what must have been the first-ever electric starter, a dynamotor bolted to the crank carrier of its rear-mounted engine. In its primitive way, it had been the first hybrid, for Dowsing claimed that 'in the dense traffic of streets like Cheapside, it might be preferable to drive on the electric motor alone'.

When the 1927 Brighton Run aroused interest in veteran cars, Dowsing asked Turner to get the old car, which was lying in a damp shed, running. A somewhat cavalier attitude towards authenticity prevailed at the time, and Turner thought nothing of throwing away the car's primitive surface carburettor and replacing it with a modern motorcycle carburettor. However, the machine failed to run properly, and the goal of entering it for the Brighton Run had not been achieved by the time Dowsing died, in 1930, the year in which the Veteran Car Club was formed.

Among the first enthusiasts to join the VCC was Edward de W.S. Colver, who was anxious to find a car similar to the early Benz in which he had first ridden. Dowsing's old 'Adam' was, according to the club's Secretary, just what he was looking for. Colver bought 'Adam' from Dowsing's widow. 'The car was sold to me as a Benz,' he recalled, 'but when I began to overhaul it I found so many discrepancies from the Benz design, notably in the engine, that I began to fear that I had bought a "dud" and even wondered whether Dowsing's garage had scrapped the whole engine and substituted another.'

Nevertheless, Colver managed to make the car run and entered it as a Benz in a veteran car race at Brooklands on August Bank Holiday 1931 and the September 1931 Croydon-Eastbourne Rally of the Veteran Car Club. These revealed several defects; the modern carburettor in particular proving 'most unsatisfactory… vigorous pushing being required on the slightest up-grade'. Colver used a drawing of a surface carburettor in *Motor Vehicles and Motors*, a classic book on early car design, to make a replica of the original fitting and its controls. 'The improvement effected was considerable,' he recorded. 'It enabled me satisfactorily to complete the 1931 Commemoration Run from London to Brighton, but the functioning was not perfect.'

Colver took the opportunity to discuss the differences between his car and standard Benz design, and Montague Grahame-White suggested that it might be an Arnold Benz, but could remember nothing beyond the name. Then came a real stroke of luck. In those days, veteran car owners used to drive home from

This 1899 6hp Panhard & Levassor was entered in early Veteran Car Club events, such as the 1933 Maidstone Rally, by J.M. Turner; his brother J.A. (Jack) Turner entered another Panhard, a 1902 7hp model, which remained in the family care from 1902 to 2003.

RIGHT: From 1889 the Turner family ran the Walton Cycle Works in Walton-on-Thames, Surrey. In this 1900 photograph, J.M. Turner is on the right in the doorway, with a Royal Enfield quadricycle behind him and the Darracq tricycle that he first rode in August 1897 in the roadway.

BELOW: Edward de W.S. Colver acquired 'Adam' from Dowsing's widow in 1930 and restored it to original condition.

ABOVE: Miss Victoria Arnold drove the centenarian car in the November 1996 celebration of the 100th anniversary of the first Brighton Run.

LEFT: In 1996, at Lord Montagu's invitation, my wife tried her hand at driving 'Adam', which was then on display in the National Motor Museum by courtesy of her then owner, granddaughter of his builder.

rallies, and the morning after the run Colver set off for Hampshire. He had only got as far as Worthing when a chain broke and the connecting bolt was lost. His companion trudged off to find a spare bolt and, while Colver was waiting with the car, the inevitable crowd of onlookers gathered round. All of a sudden Colver heard an old countryman, 'who looked like a jobbing gardener', say to a friend in a broad dialect, 'That's one o' them there Arnolds!'

He quickly asked the old man what he knew about the car, and was told that it was obviously an Arnold Motor Carriage, and that the informant 'frequently saw young Mr Arnold driving them years ago. They were made in Kent.'

Colver wrote to the *Kent Messenger*, who gave him the name and address of the firm, which was still in existence. Moreover, several employees had been with the firm when the cars were built. He found that not only was the firm being run by the widow of 'young Mr Arnold', but its general manager George Mercy and chief engineer W.A. Gladwin had both been with the firm since the car-building period. They confirmed that Colver's 'Benz' was actually an Arnold Motor Carriage; indeed, it was the very first car that the company had built, and had actually been driven in the 1896 Emancipation Day Run.

Colver visited the Arnold company, founded as engineers in East Peckham, Kent, in 1844, as soon as he could:

Following Miss Arnold's untimely death, 'Adam' was acquired by Tim Scott, here seen successfully finishing the 2004 Brighton Run.

> I was delighted, not to mention astounded, when they promptly produced from store replacements for all the parts and components scrapped and wrecked by Dowsing's garage, together with others needed to replace worn items and a variety of contemporary accessories and even a handbook on 'Care and Maintenance'.
>
> The information I obtained was invaluable, and the possession of all the necessary parts enabled me to complete the restoration with the added satisfaction of knowing that the car was now original in every detail. At a later date, in the course of a rally, I called at the works and Adam was housed in the original erecting shop and inspected by many of the older employees, who took a great delight in pointing out the various items for which they had been responsible.

CHAPTER SEVENTEEN

Fit for a King – Daimler

Although the Daimler Motor Company did not put its first vehicle on the road until early in 1897, the fact that it was incorporated on 14 January 1896 makes it without question Britain's oldest motor manufacturer. The company, which was acquired by Jaguar in 1960 (and thus is now part of Ford's group of prestige marques), has been unobtrusive to the point of invisibility of late, but it should not be forgotten that since 1900 Daimler has supplied more than 100 cars to the British Royal Family. In 2004 I was told by a source high within Ford that the Daimler name was set for a high-profile revival in the not too distant future. In July 2005, 'the most advanced Daimler ever', the supercharged 4.2-litre Super Eight, was announced. It is encouraging to think that a name which has always been synonymous with cars of the highest quality really has returned to the road.

Fittingly, one of the very first production Daimlers is today a prized possession of the Jaguar-Daimler Heritage Trust, which preserves a large number of historic vehicles of both makes. For many years this phaeton-bodied 1897 4 hp twin-cylinder car, which bears the appropriate registration index 'AD-1897', belonged to a dedicated Veteran Car Club member named Ted Woolley. He believed firmly in using it on the road, tiller steering, tube ignition, and all. Perhaps his most famous exploit came in 1961 when the Daimler followed in the tracks of Hannibal and crossed the 6834-ft high Mont Cenis pass unaided.

Intriguingly, thistle emblems are cast in this car's steps, suggesting that it may have been one of the early Coventry-built chassis shipped north to be bodied by John Stirling's Hamilton Carriage, Motor Car & Cycle Works. The order, worth £13,000, for fifty 'machines with motor covers', was placed shortly after the Daimler company's formation, before the first Daimler car had been completed. An old-established Scottish coachbuilder, Stirling claimed that they could deliver a car a fortnight and had actually completed their first body – a double phaeton with a varnished walnut body and vermilion chassis and wheels – on a chassis shipped from Coventry in January 1897. However, this was only partly a Daimler, for it had a Paris-built twin-

In the tracks of Hannibal: in 1961 the indefatigable Ted Woolley climbed the Col du Mont-Cenis unaided on his 1897 Daimler, whose hood, appropriately, was covered in elephant hide!

How to start your Daimler

These were the instructions given in 1897 for starting your new Daimler.

> The first operation necessary is to charge the motor, that is, to fill in a supply of petrol, lubricating oil, and water for cooling the cylinders. The water is passed in through the aperture (1), and should be allowed to run until it escapes from the perforated pipe (2) on the underside of the tank (3). The petrol is then filled into the tank (4), and the lubricating oil put into the lubricators on the dashboard. The lubricator (33) inside the engine cover, which supplies oil to the crank chamber, must also be filled. Next close the escape pressure cock (16) ... The burner (36) must next be heated, which is done by pouring a small quantity of methylated spirit into the cups under the burners, and igniting same. In about half a minute these will be sufficiently heated to vaporize the petrol. Pressure must now be forced into the tank by means of a small inflator (40), which is attached to the pressure pipe (5) connected to the tank. This causes a flow of petrol through the pipe (6), which not only supplies the lamps, but also fills the float chamber, (7). A small gauze filter, or strainer (8) is provided, so that any dirt or solid matter is arrested and prevented from choking the small orifices of the lamps and jets. When the lamps have heated the ignition tubes to a bright, clear red, the motor is ready for starting, but before proceeding to start the engine, the hand brake (26) should be applied, and the starting lever (19) be in the notch. The speed lever (20) should also be in the first (or slowest) speed notch. The lamp flames should be an intense pale blue, almost transparent. If the flames are yellow and smoky the lamps are not burning properly, and should be examined to see if they require cleaning, or if the wick needs changing.

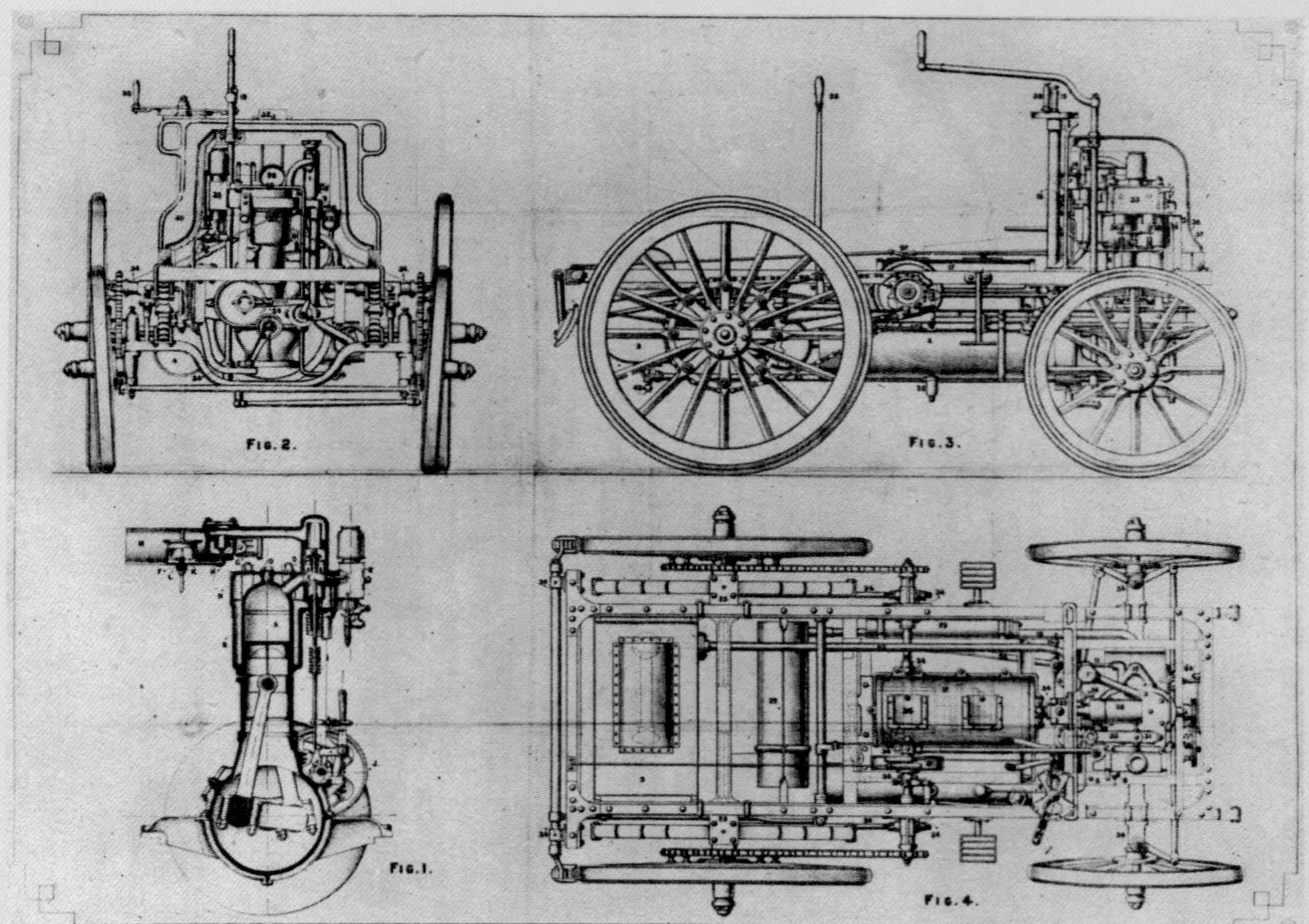

This chart explained the workings of the 1897 Daimler to its proud owner.

Lord Montagu's Daimler, bought new by his father in 1899, heads a gathering of Victorian Daimlers in front of his family home, Palace House, Beaulieu.

cylinder Panhard engine. The first Daimler chassis entirely built in Coventry reached the Hamilton Motor Car & Cycle Works at the beginning of March 1897.

Although of basic Panhard design, Daimler's own engine was obviously an improvement. In a postscript to the British motor industry's very first unsolicited testimonial, Stirling declared, 'We have just returned from a twelve miles' run and we are highly pleased with the behaviour of the car. We got a much higher speed than ever we obtained on the first car and we anticipate still better results over dry roads.'

Trying the 1897 Daimler on for size!

Ten days later, after the car had spent several days running about the city of Glasgow, Stirling delivered a second testimonial:

> We find the car is astonishingly easy to manipulate in the traffic. It is quite a revelation to the public to see it picking its way through the densest traffic. It gives us very great pleasure to write thus and we are pleased to learn that each subsequent motor sent down will be to some extent an improvement on the previous ones.

From the start, Daimler pursued what the industry likes to call a 'policy of continuous improvement'. In a bid to match the products of the leading Continental factories, the company appointed a gifted engineer named Sidney Straker as 'advisor on matters of design' and instructed him to create a new and more powerful car, which appeared during 1899. It was the British industry's first four-cylinder model, and one of the first customers was the Hon. John Scott-Montagu, Conservative MP for the New Forest, who would succeed his father as Lord Montagu of Beaulieu in November 1905.

John Montagu's new four-cylinder phaeton was ready for him in May, and he quickly became Britain's first commuter by car, using his new Daimler to travel between his home at Beaulieu and the Palace of Westminster. He was soon claiming a speed record from his seat in the New Forest to Clapham Common. In 1928 he spoke in an early wireless broadcast about the reaction the car caused:

> I well remember driving from the New Forest to London in those days on several occasions and not meeting one motor car the whole way in the 90 miles. When driving into the House of Commons one day in my 12hp Daimler, I was stopped by the policeman on duty and refused entrance on the grounds that 'them things is excluded by the order of the Speaker'.
>
> On my appeal to Mr Speaker Peel, then in the Chair, and reminding him of the Sessional Order which guaranteed 'free ingress and egress' to Members of the House of Commons, he at once gave orders that my car was to be admitted, and I drove proudly into the inner recesses of Palace Yard. The drivers of hansoms and four-wheelers who were there on the cabstand gazed wonderingly, for I expect in the back of their minds they knew that their doom was coming.

In September 1899, Montagu took his car to France and competed in the Paris-Ostend Race, the first entry by a British-built car in an international motor race. Unintentionally, he created a precedent, for the Daimler was painted dark green – which was to become Britain's international racing colour. Moreover, his third place won the British industry's first motor-racing prize. Restored to its original condition in the late 1960s, after languishing for many years in the stores of the Science Museum, the 1899 Daimler is today one of the most treasured exhibits in the National Motor Museum founded in 1952 by John Montagu's son and heir.

In December 2004, I was given an unforgettable experience when I rode through the gates of the Palace of Westminster aboard this significant early vehicle. The Daimler was returning from delivering to 10 Downing Street a petition signed by over 50,000 enthusiasts protesting against a proposed DVLA levy on stored historic vehicles. John Montagu would have been amazed to see that below the spot where he had been the first MP to park a horseless carriage there is now a huge underground car park to accommodate Members' motor cars!

Not long before, I had ridden on another historic 1898 Daimler, the famous 'Jane' owned by Peter Thompson and originally owned by Sir Oswald Mosley, baronet and father of another Sir Oswald, the Blackshirt leader of the 1930s. Early in its career, 'Jane' had been burnt out – a not uncommon fate for cars with tube ignition – and was bought for £1 by Daimler works manager Percy Martin, who gave it to his foremen to rebuild in their own time.

Rebuilt and updated with wheel steering to replace the tiller, electric ignition and a smart new brass radiator, 'Jane' served for many years as the transport of Mr Wormald, the Daimler erecting shop foreman. In the 1920s the car was acquired by Doug Copley of the 'Wagon and Horses' filling station in Birmingham, who used it for delivering petrol. Copley won first prize with the car in the Coventry Hospital Carnival in 1926 and '27, and in the latter year entered it in the first *Daily Sketch* London to Brighton Run, offering to race it against any car of its age with ten people aboard over a distance of 200 miles. Faced in 1931 with being asked to pay rates on the shed in which he kept the old Daimler, Copley threatened to bury the car, and was even photographed with a block and tackle ready to drop 'Jane' in a deep pit that he had dug. (Oddly enough, 'Jane' was absent from the Brighton Run

Originally built for Sir Oswald Mosley, 'Jane' was burnt out early in her career and rebuilt and updated. For many years she was owned by Daimler foreman Wormald, seen here at the wheel in 1909, at a time when driving a ten-year-old car was a newsworthy eccentricity.

'Jane' on parade outside the Royal Automobile Club in 2004. She has hardly changed in over a century; and is one of the exclusive band of veterans that took part in the first 'modern' Brighton Run in 1927.

King Edward VII at the wheel of John Montagu's Daimler at Beaulieu in 1902.

Autocar*'s first editor Henry Sturmey's Daimler arrives at Land's End in October 1897 to complete the first end-to-end journey from John O'Groats by a motor vehicle.*

for some years, while Copley drove what he claimed was an '1898 Renault', although the Renault company was not founded until 1899.)

In the 1950s, 'Jane' was resurrected and acquired by Arthur James of Aylesbury. I first made her acquaintance a decade later when I went to photograph James's other car, a 10.5-litre Fiat of 1910 vintage that had once raced at Brooklands and which is now part of Fiat's enviable collection of historic vehicles. 'Jane', on the other hand, has stayed in the family, for Peter Thompson is Arthur James's son-in-law, and continues to enter the Brighton Run just as she first did nearly eighty years ago.

Perhaps the most distinguished of all those early Daimlers is the 6hp tonneau bought by the Prince of Wales (later King Edward VII) in 1900, after a Daimler 'Mail Phaeton' – a handsome leather-hooded two-seater with an occasional bench seat behind – had been demonstrated to him in the grounds of Buckingham Palace in January 1900.

As Montague Grahame-White commented in 1943, 'The Prince was of portly build, and comfortable seating was of first importance.' One special feature incorporated, it seems, to accommodate the Prince's impressive rotundity was a steering column 'pivoted at the bottom so that it may instantly be placed in a vertical position to facilitate mounting and dismounting'.

The Prince's car was bodied by Royal coachbuilders Hooper of St James's and painted in the Royal colours of chocolate and black, picked out in red, to create a 'quiet and stylish appearance'. It was delivered to Sandringham for the Prince's approval on 28 March 1900 by a Daimler employee and part-time dancing teacher named Sydney Letzer, who was soon after appointed 'mechanician to the Prince of Wales', in other words, the first Royal chauffeur.

Visiting Daimler shortly before the Second World War, King George VI rode in Edward VII's 1900 Daimler.

The Prince requested some modifications to the coachwork, and the car was subsequently returned to him during a house party at the Royal Stables at Ascot, on Monday 11 June. The Prince, who had been 'fully instructed in the art of motor management', took his first ride in the car two days later, preceded by a groom on horseback to act as pilot. After less than a mile, the Prince became bored of having to hold back the car to match the horse's pace and sent the groom back to Ascot.

The Prince ('a fearless automobilist... although he does not drive himself') soon tired of his 6hp Daimler and wanted something more powerful, and three weeks after taking delivery the first Royal Daimler found a new owner, Lord Suffield, who bought the car on 'easy terms of payment' of four six-monthly instalments of £103, 'the price to include motor and frame only and Lord Suffield to make his own arrangements with the builders of the body'. Suffield only kept the car for four months before selling it to Lord Hastings for £700. Hastings had the Mail Phaeton bodywork converted into a four-seat tonneau by Mr Prentice of the Eagle Carriage Works, Lambeth.

In 1924 Ernest Instone of Stratton-Instone, the company that supplied Daimler cars to the Royal Mews, discovered that first Royal Daimler in a junk yard and bought it for £10. It was a star exhibit in Daimler's collection of historic cars – the first such collection made by a British motor manufacturer – and when King George VI visited the Daimler Radford No 1 'shadow factory' in March 1938, he was shown his grandfather's first car. When the King jokingly asked whether the 38-year-old veteran still worked, he was given a ride in the 1900 car, driven by chauffeur George Street, who had often driven Edward VII.

Although the old Daimler had been modified over the years, most notably with an anachronistic radiator and bonnet, Daimler would not part with it for any price, even when an American made an offer of £2000 for it – a sum far in excess of anything paid for any veteran car pre-war.

Eventually, the old Daimler was presented to Queen Elizabeth II by the Daimler Company, along with three other former Royal Daimlers in their possession, to form the nucleus of the Royal Motor Museum. It was put back into running order by members of the Veteran Car Club in 1968–71, although with the incorrect radiator and other anachronistic features. It was eventually restored to its 1900 condition by the National Motor Museum to celebrate the Queen's Silver Jubilee in 1977 and is now a star exhibit in the Royal Motor Museum at Sandringham.

Perhaps the most historic Daimler of all, this 1900 car was the first of over 100 Daimlers bought by the Royal Family.

CHAPTER EIGHTEEN

'The Car of My Dreams'

Buying a car in the very early days of motoring was a very different experience from what it is today. Apart from a very few isolated examples, there were no showrooms full of shiny new vehicles, handy finance packages were a thing of the future, items such as lamps and a horn were classed as extras, advertising was sporadic and uninformative, and there was not even a sufficient band of experienced motorists whose opinions could be sought.

When cycle-racer Oscar Bickford accompanied his friend the Hon. C.S. Rolls to the 1898 Paris Salon de l'Automobile, he discovered that the sale was only a minor part of the transaction:

> The Paris Salon was a wonderful show, at which Rolls bought a two-cylinder Panhard. We both took it out, up the celebrated Cote de Suresnes, to lunch at the Chateau de Versailles. The bicyclists waited for us on the way and some sprinted past us shouting 'Oop-oop, Cocky!' but we caught them up nicely going down the other side.
>
> Following a perfect lunch, C.S. took delivery of the car and went back to London with it; but I was now myself bitten with the fever for a motor car, so back I went to the Salon. Looking around, I found at last the car of my dreams, a beautiful little two-seater painted fire-engine red, with very shiny nickel plate and a red velvet cushion. It was called a 'Voiturette Parisienne', and although there was a big crowd round the stand, at last I managed to edge my way in. I found it was for sale after the show for £100.
>
> Like everyone else in those days, I knew nothing about motor cars, but the salesman, who spoke English, assured me that it really would go and made a date at the Automobile Club. He said that it had a 2.25hp air-cooled Dion-Bouton engine, that it would run all day and that it would beat a bicycle, which impressed me because that was the fastest transport I had known up then.
>
> The next day I went to a wonderful club in the Place de la Concorde, where I met Count De Dion. The waiters were dressed in claret and purple; gold-lace knee breeches, white stockings, patent-leather dancing pumps, yellow and black striped shirts and tail coats. A lot of the old French aristocracy were taking their midday meal there.

Oscar Bickford and his 'beautiful little two-seater'.

Although the Voiturette Parisienne – also marketed as the 'Victoria Combination' – was not actually built in De Dion's factory in the Rue Ernest in Puteaux, De Dion-Bouton did supply its engine and power train, which were identical to those used on the motor tricycles that were being turned out at the rate of 200 a month, a phenomenal output for 1898. In addition, the factory built 300 engines every month, which were supplied to other manufacturers such as the makers of the Voiturette Parisienne, E. Couturier & Cie. At that point, the De Dion-Bouton company had not introduced the small cars for which it was to become famous. Although the firm had just built 'a magnificent depot' in the fashionable Avenue de la Grand Armée, 'fitted up in the most luxurious manner with true Parisian taste, the machines being shown up on carpets among ferns like diamonds at the jewellers in the Rue de la Paix', its opening had been delayed by several weeks as 'at the moment orders for the automobiles of the house of De Dion & Bouton exceed production'.

The Automobile Club de France, where Bickford met De Dion, had been founded over a dinner at the Count's home on the Quai d'Orsay in October 1895. The organization was just moving into the building that it had acquired for a million and a half francs on the Place de la Concorde – a magnificent palace that was like a second home to the Count and which the Automobile Club de France continues to occupy today.

> Early in the afternoon a message was sent up that the car was outside, so down we went, the Count taking the tiller with myself beside him. Bouton, engineer of the partnership, walked around checking things up; then he got behind and pushed, whereat the engine, out in front, started spitting fire from the compression tap, which caused Bouton to run round and turn it off. The cracking noise then ceased and off we went while the Count skilfully steered the little car round the Place de la Concorde.

Halfway round the square, the engine began to misfire and then stopped. Bouton, who was running behind, was called in to diagnose the problem. De Dion and Bickford stepped out of the little car and watched while Bouton took a screwdriver and prodded around the exposed engine. He glanced meaningfully at the Count, who took Bickford gently by the arm. 'Supposing,' he said, 'we go back to the Club for tea whilst this small contretemps is attended to. Bouton does not like being watched when at work.'

While Bickford and the Count were taking a leisurely tea in the palatial surroundings of the Automobile Club, Bouton entered the room. 'The car will have to go back to the works,' he informed them. 'It is a show model just off the stand, and is not exactly *au point*.'

The Count and Georges Bouton met Bickford again the following day for lunch – for which Bickford paid – before a second attempt was made to give the hopeful purchaser a demonstration run. It was obviously not a success, as Bickford recalled:

> To make a long story short, I stayed a week in Paris and we spent most of our time in the Bois de Boulogne. We found it quite impossible to get up the Champs Elysées to the Etoile with both driver and passenger. The latter always had to jump out and walk to the top. Whilst all this was going on, I went out to the factory to see some of the engines being made and asked De Dion if there were any that just would not go at all. 'Oh, yes,' he said, 'those we take to pieces and use for spares. It is much quicker than trying to find out what is wrong with them!'

This poster for the Société Parisienne discreetly places the voiturette well in the background.

The De Dion-Bouton factory – 'magnificently fitted up regardless of expense' – was in the process of a rapid expansion, having increased its workforce from 250 to over 600 in the space of a year. 'Loads of new machinery of French, English, German, Belgian or American origin are daily being brought into the works. The large proportion of these machines are from America, these possessing the advantage of being constructed on automatic labour-saving principles.'

The company was far ahead of the rest of the industry in the way it tested its engines, which were bench-tested in batches of thirty, running continuously at 1800–2000rpm 'sometimes for twenty-four hours, a week, or even more,' until each engine gave the required power output and was passed as 'efficient'.

The Voiturette Parisienne was marketed in Britain as the 'Victoria Combination'.

In a confidential tone Bouton explained the 'mysterious workings of the Otto cycle' to Bickford. 'Only two things can go wrong, the vapour or the spark,' he declared. 'To test the latter you put your finger on the *bougie* [spark plug] and if you get a shock, well and good; if not, heaven help you! It must then be in the electric box underneath the front axle,' he said, adding as a by-the-way, that 'there is no instruction book, although we are getting them printed'.

Despite the difficulties of the protracted test-drive session, Bickford bought the Voiturette Parisienne and took it back to the Hotel de Jena where he was staying, to give its trusting owner, Miss Schofields, her first car ride. He stayed on in Paris, frequently driving out to the Bois de Boulogne and to the Sunday races at Longchamps. Having heard that horses were frightened by motor cars, Bickford put sugar on the petrol tank, which was out in front above the cylinder, in just the right place to make a merry blaze in the event of a leak, 'for some local horses so as to get them trained to seeing the novel motor car'. He was astonished to find that French horses, evidently more sensible than their English counterparts, took not the least notice.

Finally, said Bickford, 'As the car seldom broke down now, I felt competent enough to attempt the trip to England. All my Paris friends turned out to wave *au revoir*, and I slipped up the Avenue de Jena into the Bois and was stopped at the Octroi [a customs post that controlled imports of dutiable goods into Paris, which included petrol].'

When the customs agent asked Bickford for his papers, he cheerfully replied, 'No such thing – no number plates, no driving licence, no insurance, no lamps. Oh yes, I have a horn!' And he blew it to prove that it worked.

'Where are you going?'

'To England!'

'*Eh bien, allez vite, mon vieux!*' And the official dropped his papers and pushed the little car forward.

Bickford recalled the continuation of his journey:

> I was clear of Paris at last. Along the Route de Calais there was the usual crowd of urchins on bicycles who joined in pursuit, but rather to my astonishment they fell back one by one. Either the engine was well run-in by now or it had got its second wind. Anyway, I easily outdistanced them. Not till then did I remember the guarantee: 'Faster than a bicycle, keeps it up all day.' The former was proved; what about the latter?
>
> It was a wonderful hot summer day and to sit in a comfortable chair and watch the road disappearing under the wheels instead of working hard, bent over and watching the white rim on the back of a tandem, seemed like riding on a magic carpet. Being king of the road. I could pass anything. It was just like a dream and I dozed happily until I nearly ran off the road! This brought back reality with a start and I remembered the instructions to stop every hour and put in a measureful of oil.
>
> This was my first stop, and I had covered nearly 20 miles. Placing a match on the cylinder fins showed there was no overheating, whilst the tank was still three-quarters full. Inspection showed that nothing had come adrift (that I could see), so on I went, forgetting all about lunch, until in the evening I drove to a little hotel, had a meal, went to bed and slept the sleep of the just.

CHAPTER NINETEEN

On the Orient Express

Back in the early 1960s my lunchtime strolls often took me – when I wasn't searching for vintage spares and accessories in the treasure houses of automotive incunabula that still existed round the Elephant and Castle in South London – to the roadside book market outside Farringdon Underground station.

It was there that I acquired for a few pence the first book in what has since become a sizeable collection of early motoring novels: *The Lightning Conductor* by C.N. and A.M.Williamson, first published in 1902. My new acquisition was the Colonial Edition ('Printed on antique paper and bound tastefully in cloth'), and it introduced me to the Orient Express ('high and dignified like a chariot'), a tiller-steered horseless carriage purchased by the book's heroine, which turns out to be a 'German monstrosity… the most confounded thing ever designed; a kind of ironmonger's shop on wheels'. Fortunately, she is rescued from this mechanical horror by the hero, a young nobleman pretending to be a chauffeur, and his splendid Napier motor car.

The Orient Express goes up in flames early on in the book, after exhibiting just about every kind of mechanical vice a horseless carriage is heir to, so I was more than a little amazed to make the acquaintance not long after of one of the rare survivors of the marque. According to the Veteran Car Club, there are just three left in existence. This particular Orient Express was in Crowborough, where it was being restored by a remarkable character in his mid-twenties named Paul Foulkes-Halbard. Even at that age, he told me, had already owned 157 different cars!

His house, Smuggler's Cottage, was a treasure-house of automobilia. Brass lamps and horns were hung from just about every beam, a flat-tank Triumph motorcycle wrapped in a polythene sheet lay on the spare bed, and a famous Brooklands racer named 'Nanette' with a Parry Thomas-designed Hooker engine stood under a lean-to in the garden. In a nearby shed was a curious 'faux veteran', confected from a horse carriage as a publicity stunt in the 1920s by the 'West End Garage' (their name was painted on to its sides in Gothic lettering) and powered by a single-cylinder Fafnir motorcycle engine mounted in the rear of its boxy body. In the garage was the part-restored Orient Express, at the time believed to be the sole survivor of a long-dead marque.

Designed in the mid-1890s by a gifted twenty-something engineer named Joseph Vollmer, the Orient Express had been built by Bergmann's Industriewerke of Gaggenau in Germany. Similar in concept to the contemporary Benz, but altogether more heavily built, the Orient Express had a thumping 1.9-litre single-cylinder rear engine and multiple belt drive.

It is said that Carl Benz and Gottlieb Daimler never met, even though their workshops were only 90 miles apart; however, young Joseph Vollmer, who had qualified as an electrician before training as an engineer, kept a close watch on the developments achieved by both men, as his home in Baden-Baden was about equidistant (by about 70 miles) from Cannstatt and Mannheim. He soon came to the conclusion that he could design a better automobile.

Early in 1894, armed with drawings of a prototype three-wheeled car he had built, the 23-year-old Vollmer made the two-hour journey to Gaggenau to call on industrialist Theodor Bergmann.

This was the first sight of the 'high and dignified' Orient Express for Molly Randolph, the heroine of The Lighting Conductor.

Bergmann approved the design but suggested that the addition of a fourth wheel would create a more saleable vehicle.

Vollmer's revised design, named 'Orient Express' in honour of the new luxury trans-European train that had made its first journey in 1894, went into production in Gaggenau in 1895. In an era when most factories were powered by overhead pulley-and-belt drives and car engines ran at more or less constant speed, the three-speed and reverse belt transmission may have seemed a logical choice, but it had a number of practical drawbacks. For a start, it was impossible to maintain an even tension between the belts. In an attempt to overcome this, Vollmer fitted the Orient Express with a device known as a 'jockey pulley' to tighten the belt that was in use against its pulleys, thus combining the functions of clutch and gear shift. It was only a partial solution, however, and the Orient Express became notorious for its appetite for belts.

Mending broken belts was, according to the hero of *The Lightning Conductor*, 'disgustingly tedious… To begin with, to get at the pulleys I had to open the back of the car, and that meant lifting down all the carefully strapped luggage and depositing it by the roadside. Then the wire and tools were either in a cupboard under the floor of the car or in a box under the ladies' seats, which meant disturbing them every time one wanted anything.'

But in real life, as I discovered by chance one day in the 1970s, Charlie Williamson – the technical member of the husband and wife team who had written *The Lightning Conductor* – had actually been so impressed with the Orient Express on first acquaintance that he had bought one. I was junk-shopping in North London: I'd been proofreading at a printer somewhere in the hinterland of the North Circular Road – in those happy days when bargains could still be had for a few pence – when I struck lucky. On top of a crowded display case were three bound volumes of an obscure magazine called *The Traveller (for whom the World is a Playground)*, dating from 1901–2. *The Traveller*'s 'Own Chauffeur' was Charlie Williamson, who had used his Orient Express as transport when writing a series of articles entitled 'Days out of Town on a Motor'.

From mid-1901, 'C.N.W.' wrote a regular column entitled 'On a Motor Car – notes and news from a Travelled Chauffeur', and in August that year he described a run in the Orient Express in glowing terms:

> Last week I was taken for a ride in an Orient Express, an extremely comfortable car to carry four. It is built high, so that the passengers are well out of the dust, and the car proved itself a powerful hill-climber. With five persons aboard, it went up the steepest pitches of the Hog's Back at not less than seven miles an hour, and owing to the high carriage everyone on board could see over the hedges and enjoy the magnificent views north and south, which would have been impossible with a low car. The Orient Express is a belt-driven car with a jockey pulley, and it is well suited for driving in traffic, as the speed can be quickly and easily changed by pressure on the belt, even when driving on the high speed.

Motoring Novels

The success of *The Lightning Conductor* inspired numerous other authors, including Rudyard Kipling and Arthur Conan Doyle, to write motoring fiction. These are some of the many motoring novels that appeared during the veteran era.

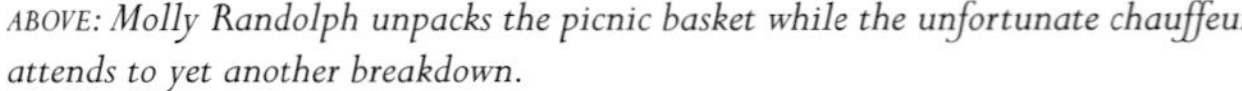
ABOVE: Molly Randolph unpacks the picnic basket while the unfortunate chauffeur attends to yet another breakdown.

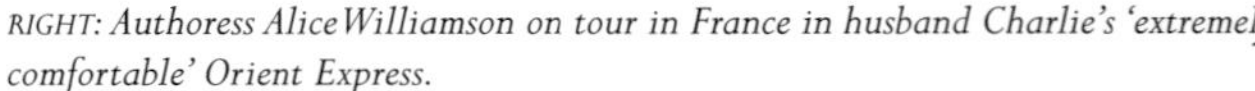
RIGHT: Authoress Alice Williamson on tour in France in husband Charlie's 'extremely comfortable' Orient Express.

Charlie Williamson, unlike the hero of his first and most famous novel (even King Edward VII had a copy), really enjoyed breakdowns:

> Failures in the mechanism of the car interest and excite me. One pits one's brains and hands against the perverse spirit in the engine and there is a delightful sense of elation in compelling a refractory car to carry one home against its will.
>
> I look back with a very cheerful sense of pleasure to certain wayside halts for repairs by the Loire or the Garonne and I remember with keen joy a long struggle with a De Dion at two in the morning when I had no proper tools with me and used the edge of a sixpence instead of a screwdriver.

Despite certain eccentricities of design – it had ten hand controls and only one pedal (which operated a brake on the countershaft), while the main hand brake was under the control of the passenger in the left-hand seat – the Orient Express proved relatively popular. It was initially sold in England by the Automobile Association, a company that had absolutely no connection with the well-known motoring organization, which was founded in 1905.

The car that Paul Foulkes-Halbard was restoring when I first met him in 1964 had been built in Gaggenau in June 1898 and delivered to its first owner, J. Powell of Smeeth Paddocks, Kent, on a horse-drawn cart. In January 1904 Powell sold the Orient Express to George Ward, a Buckinghamshire cycle manufacturer, for £35. It had cost around £200 five-and-a-half years earlier; savage depreciation in a car's value is nothing new. Under the new act that required all cars to carry number plates, the Orient Express was registered 'BH-260' on 31 March 1904, and for the next five years it served as a runabout before being dismantled and put into storage in the loft.

Ward's Wizard Works, which built bicycles between 1880 and 1910, later became a garage and cycle works run by George Ward's sons George and Corry. It was Corry Ward who presented the dismantled remains of the Orient Express to his cycling companion Paul Foulkes-Halbard, in gratitude for Paul's having repainted the works during a fortnight's holiday in 1959. The components were loaded aboard a lorry and transported to Foulkes-Halbard's home in Brighton, where rust-proofing and restoration began in the best bedroom.

After three days' soaking in penetrating oil, the engine was freed, and found to be in remarkably good condition, and assembly of the lower chassis began.

When Paul Foulkes-Halbard moved to Crowborough in 1962, the restoration had to be put on hold, and the part-assembled car was stored in the coal shed. Soon, however, a local character named Dan Bassett – a mechanic who worked at the Southdown bus garage – offered to help with the rebuild, and work could begin again, once the garage had been repaired. Using the axles and reach bars as a guide, the dimensions of the chassis were determined, and the frame was reconstructed by the local blacksmith. Dan Bassett happened to have a distant relative, Charlie Bassett, who was a retired carriage builder from nearby Wadhurst. Charlie provided oak chassis inserts and gave much valuable help in restoring the bodywork, including the mahogany side panels, which were taken from a 200-year-old Dutch bed.

At this point it was discovered that several vital components – the carburettor and its controls, half the countershaft, the flywheel, pulleys and one of the water tanks – were missing. A return visit to the Wizard Works uncovered the missing flywheel, incorporated in an enormous home-made treadle lathe. To undo the flywheel bolt, Paul Foulkes-Halbard had to lie underneath the lathe in semi-darkness. Inevitably, the bolt dropped out and fell into the bottom box of a large pile on the floor. When the pile was pulled out to search for the missing bolt, the missing carburettor and its organ-stop controls came to light, a countershaft pulley was discovered and the missing water tank was found being used as a nest by a jack-

ABOVE: The restored 1898 Orient Express photographed in 1964.

LEFT: Forty years on, and Karl Foulkes-Halbard sets off for Brighton at the tiller of the Orient Express.

daw. George Ward remembered having stored the countershaft under a workbench, and then other major parts, including body framing, upholstery and the foot-operated clarion bell, were unearthed.

Returning home with his treasures, Paul Foulkes-Halbard found that Dan Bassett had fitted the tiller and begun installing the engine in the rebuilt chassis. A local craftsman made new pulleys, which were keyed to the countershaft, and when it was discovered that the flywheel would not stay tight on the crankshaft, a replica had to be cast and machined using the curly-spoked original as a pattern.

With the car nearing completion, an attempt was made to start the engine for the first time since 1909. The Orient Express, unlike the Benz that it resembled, is started with a detachable handle rather than by pulling the flywheel over compression; the snag is that the handle has to be inserted between the spokes of a rear wheel.

Journey's end: safely arrived on Madeira Drive.

Amazingly, the engine started after a few turns of the handle, but then – as is the way of ancient engines – it died, and two hours of frantic cranking failed to revive it. Attention was then given to the magneto and, after some adjustment, the engine ran steadily for twenty minutes. Its preferred diet was volatile SPB1 spirit (also useful for dry cleaning), but nevertheless it ran reliably, and a few months later the Orient Express took part in its first Brighton Run.

That year I drove down to Brighton in the 1927 Clyno that was my everyday transport to watch the veterans arrive on Madeira Drive. I had hoped to see the 1894 Bremer complete its first run, but it had broken its crankshaft in Redhill and only got to Brighton on the back of a lorry. Fortunately, the maiden appearance of the huge 1903 De Dietrich, loaned to the National Motor Museum by Count Lucio Labia, which had originally been bought by his uncle Sir Joseph Robinson and spent some fifty years in a London furniture depository, compensated for the Bremer's failure.

Shortly before the 4pm deadline, Paul Foulkes-Halbard arrived in Brighton on the Orient Express. It had been, he said, a good run down, with no mechanical bother whatever.

There were certainly some problem in subsequent years but, once the quirks and eccentricities of Herr Vollmer's belt transmission had been tamed, the Orient Express became a regular finisher in the run for four decades. Today she is handled by Paul Foulkes-Halbard's son Karl, who was still a baby in his pram when I first saw the car at Smugglers Cottage!

CHAPTER TWENTY

Playing Fast and Loose with an 1898 Georges-Richard

One of the very first veterans I ever drove was a real first-generation motor car, an 1898 Georges-Richard, based uncompromisingly on the first popular mass-production motor, the Benz. Those who accuse modern cars of all looking alike forget that in the early years of motoring plagiarism was rife, and the Benz was the most widely-copied design of all time. Makers such as Arnold, Hurtu, Marshall, International, Star and L'Hollier all copied or adapted the Benz and sold their version of this basic but well-proven design under their own name.

The Georges-Richard was typical of this – and a true horseless carriage into the bargain. It had been built just one year after the Georges Richard factory at 13 Rue Théophile Gautier, Paris, had started production and was powered by a genuine Benz engine, which was basically a stationary gas engine that made few concessions to the task of powering a motor car. Under the lid of what would normally be the luggage boot, the rear-mounted engine was quite visible, with its conrod and crankshaft exposed to the open air – it was actually possible to see the piston going up and down in the cylinder!

There was no sump containing oil to lubricate the engine bearings; instead, the owner had to stop every few miles to check the glass oil cups that supplied those bearings and squirt a little oil up the cylinder. The engine compartment was a real plumber's nightmare, with copper piping everywhere. There were copper water tanks on either side of the body, and their levels needed checking every time the car was stopped. Instead of a radiator the car had a crude water condenser behind the driver's seat that looked rather like an exhaust silencer.

A big brass cistern above the cylinder that looked like the automatic flushing mechanism from a Victorian public lavatory was actually a surface carburettor, in effect, a small fuel tank in which air was passed over volatile motor spirit to create combustible fumes, which were sucked in through the inlet valve. The motor spirit was more akin to dry-cleaning fluid than to modern petrol.

There was no throttle pedal, as the engine ran at a virtually constant speed, although some variation could grudgingly be coaxed out of the unit by varying the mixture strength. This was done by moving a little lever across a brass quadrant behind the driver's left leg. It was a very inflexible system of control, and it felt as though the engine took half an hour to respond.

Starting was, in theory, simple. The Benz engine was blessed with electric ignition, so – wearing a pair of stout gloves and making sure that the ignition was switched off – the driver pulled the engine over compression a few times with the rim of the ornately spoked flywheel to fill the cylinder with that crucial fuel/air mixture, then switched on and pulled again.

These primitive machines rely on the petrol giving off inflammable vapour, so if

Mechanically speaking, the Georges-Richard was based closely on the Benz Velo, although with a certain individual Gallic style.

the car has been standing awhile, it is important to empty the fuel tank and put in fresh fuel. Fortunately, the petrol in the Georges-Richard had not gone stale and the ignition batteries were charged, so it only took a few minutes' energetic heaving before we were rewarded with a lethargic chuff from the engine. It fired; it began to turn over so slowly that you could actually count the spokes on the turning flywheel.

After the engine had warmed up a little, I climbed up into the driver's seat, which was on the left – surprisingly, in an age when most vehicles, motorized and horse-drawn, were controlled from the right-hand side. The steering standard rose vertically between the occupants in the centre of the car, topped by a wood-rimmed five-spoked steering wheel the size of a modest dinner plate. At the bottom end of the steering column a small horizontal sprocket with a short chain running round it pulled on a sprung bell-crank linkage to the front wheels. Happily for my peace of mind, the chains were wired on to the sprocket to prevent them falling off under the influence of gravity, with a consequent loss of steering.

Of the two pedals, one was apparently just for show, for it had no visible effect that I could discover, while the other tightened narrow brake bands around the rear hubs. The handbrake, on the left of the body, forced wooden brake shoes against the solid rubber rear tyres. Originally solid-tyred, the front wheels were fitted with pneumatic tyres. This anachronistic feature was probably added when the wheels were rebuilt with tangent spokes instead of the original radial spoking.

I soon discovered that the most effective way of regulating the car's speed was with a handle beneath the steering wheel, which was pushed forward to select low speed and pulled back for high. It moved a double stirrup device transversely across the car's two driving belts, shifting them from a free-running 'loose' pulley on to 'fast' pulleys of different diameters – one for high speed, one for low – keyed to the countershaft. The fast pulleys were slightly tapered, to give the effect of letting in a clutch, but I found that it was essential to feed the power in slowly with the engine running at a preset constant speed, otherwise the front wheels reared up off the road like the front hooves of a frightened horse.

Low speed was good for about 8mph (13km/h), at which point the lever was pulled gently back to slacken the drive and ease in the high speed. The engine briefly ran free, then settled back as the belt gripped, and the car began to nod along at the gait of a trotting horse. These little cars were, after all, intended to replace a pony and trap.

Despite the car's minimal performance, the poor steering and brakes meant that it would be all too easy for it to run away if it was given its head. Indeed, going downhill on the top speed, the car could easily begin to travel faster than was safe, for the steering was so high-geared that a moment's inattention could land the whole thing in the ditch.

Going uphill was quite a different matter. The best idea was to plug away on the low speed until the engine began to falter, then, the Georges-Richard owner faced a number of options. First, the passenger could jump overboard to lighten the car. If that did not do the trick, the passenger had to start pushing. When that began to fail, the driver had to jump out as well, and run alongside, steering. Finally, on gradients of more than 1 in 8 or so, both driver and passenger had to push the car to the top, with the engine running, praying that it would not run away as it topped the rise.

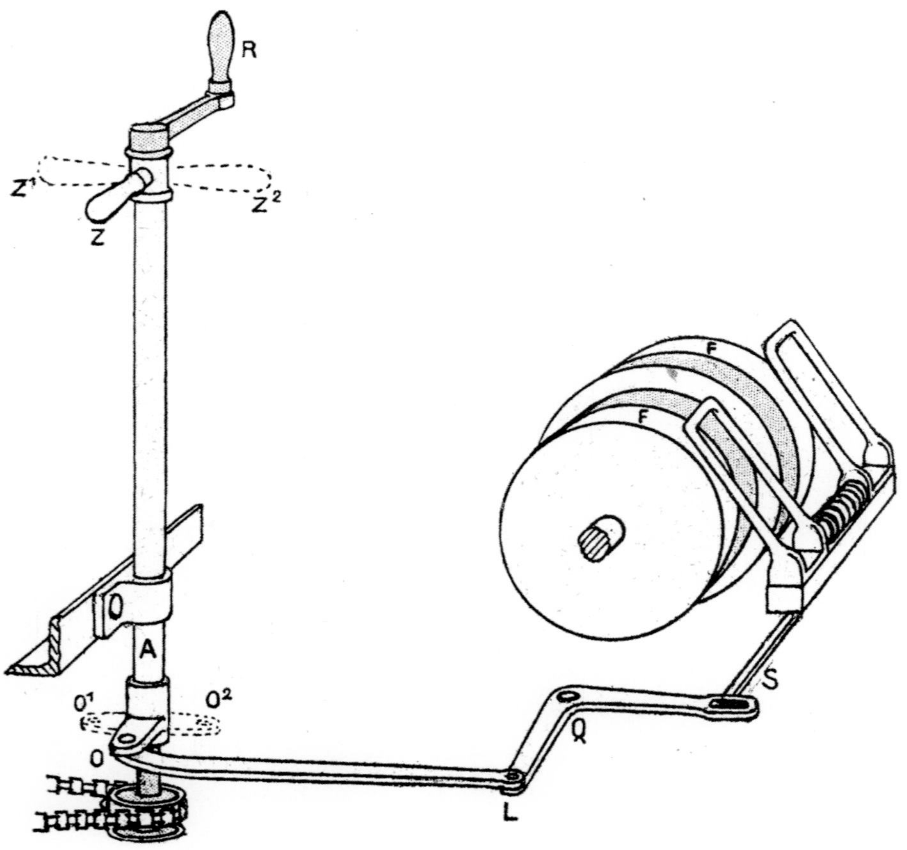

A complex linkage controlled the shifting of the belts from loose to fast pulleys; the diagram also shows the dubious horizontal chain and sprocket steering linkage.

Brighton Belles: the crew of this 1903 10hp twin-cylinder Wolseley are dressed in period elegance for any eventuality.

The 1904 Rothschild-bodied Mors Landaulet entered by the Louwman Collection has an unusual forward control layout.

LEFT: This 1902 Darracq, found in America with a lengthened chassis and body, has been carefully restored to its original configuration.

Careful attention to the engine of the oldest known Napier, a 1900 Double Phaeton.

The George Hotel at Crawley is the midway staging point for the Brighton Run. In the foreground are a 1904 Bayard and a 1902 Siddeley.

This 1902 Panhard & Levassor once belonged to Sir John Prestige, who had loaned his 1904 Rolls-Royce to Land Speed Record holder Sir Malcolm Campbell for the 1930 Brighton Run. Afterwards Sir Henry Royce asked to see the veteran Rolls-Royce, which was acquired by the Rolls-Royce company. Sir John was given the Panhard in exchange as he had worked on this car when serving his apprenticeship with the French company. In 1935 Sir John sold the Panhard to E. P. Boorman for £35, and it has remained in the Boorman family ever since.

Dating from 1903, this 9hp Léon Buat was built in Senlis, France.

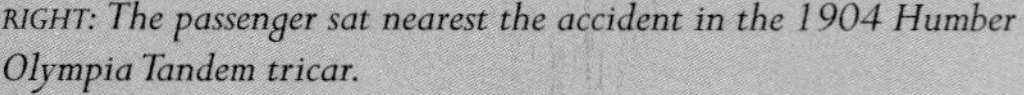
RIGHT: The passenger sat nearest the accident in the 1904 Humber Olympia Tandem tricar.

CHAPTER TWENTY-ONE

Let It Be!

Although today many think of Italy as being the country with the biggest love affair with the motor car, its motor industry was relatively slow to get off the ground. The first real attempt to begin production was made only in July 1899, when a little group of car-mad youngsters met in a Turin cafe run by one Signora Burelli and decided to found a company to make motor cars. The name they coined – 'Fabbrica Italiana d'Automobili di Torino' ('Italian Car Manufacturing Company of Turin') – was hardly imaginative, but they quickly abbreviated it to 'F.I.A.T.'. In 1907, they dropped the full stops and the company became 'Fiat', which just happens to be Latin for 'Let It Be!'.

They had no problem in deciding on their first model; they simply took over an existing, if commercially unsuccessful design, the 'Welleyes'. There was nothing wrong with the concept of the Welleyes, a prize-winning design by Bolognese engineer Aristide Faccioli, which was being built in the newly opened bicycle works of one of the group, Giovanni Battista Ceirano. Indeed, it had won a silver medal at the May 1899 Turin Fair. The main reason for its lack of success seems to have been its curious name, which had apparently been chosen with a hopeful eye on the profitable export market, for there is no letter 'W' in the Italian alphabet. (There are only a half-dozen or so 'W' words in the Italian dictionary, and they are all foreign imports such as '*il water-closet*'.)

Initially, a change of name did not seem to make much difference, and only eight examples of the 3½hp F.I.A.T. Tipo-A – a Welleyes redesigned to incorporate chain final drive rather than leather belts – were built in 1899 and 1900. Amazingly, half of those still survive, two in Italy, one in the USA and the pristine example owned by Fiat (UK), which has been displayed at the National Motor Museum at Beaulieu for some years.

It was not until the most dynamic member of the founding group, a young cavalry lieutenant named Giovanni Agnelli, was elected managing director of the company, in 1902, that the spectacular growth of F.I.A.T. began. A member of a well-off family of landowners, Agnelli had been a keen experimenter with the primitive internal combustion, and, indeed, his batman Scotto had become Italy's first casualty of the petrol engine. The poor man's shoulder had been broken when the driving belt flew off an aged Daimler engine, which his master had rescued from the scrap man, and adapted to drive a dynamo to power his workshop.

By 1906 the original Corso Dante factory had quadrupled in size and the workforce had grown from 150 to 2500. By the end of 1904, F.I.A.T. had built fewer than 500 cars in four years; in 1905–06 alone, the company built 1500. An industrial giant had been born!

The 1899 F.I.A.T. at Beaulieu was restored in the National Motor Museum's workshops some twenty years ago, after its purchase by Fiat in 1988 from veteran car enthusiast Geoffrey Willis. Almost sixty years earlier, it had been found on a Devon farm, where its engine had powered a sheep-shearing machine. The rest of the car was scattered round the farmyard, and the only clue to its identity was the maker's name on the hubcaps. Reassembled, it first took part in the Brighton Run in 1930. During the 1930s and 1940s the veteran F.I.A.T. had belonged to racing driver Antony Powys-Lybbe who, like many Brooklands racers, enjoyed the sporting atmosphere of the

A proud family out for a spin in their 1899 F.I.A.T., one of just eight built that year.

Despite the low production, F.I.A.T. proudly advertised their new model with a charming poster.

In 1994 Giovanni Alberto Agnelli, great-grandson of Fiat's founder, drove the 1899 F.I.A.T. in the Brighton Run.

The distinctive bodywork of the F.I.A.T. is by Alessi, nineteenth-century Turin's most fashionable carrozziera.

Brighton Run, which came as a welcome diversion at the close of the racing season.

The car has pretty 'Duc' coachwork by Turin's most fashionable coachmaker, Marcello Alessio, whose company had been one of the first Italian bodyshops to build coachwork for motor cars. His premises on the Via Orto Botanico were a meeting-place for Torinese high society, who would call between 5 and 6 in the evening to take a glass of vermouth with Alessio. The F.I.A.T. Duc is only 7ft 6in long, yet it is a full three-seater, although somewhat lacking in practicality for long journeys. Its seating arrangement is more suited to a horse-carriage than a motor car, with the driver and one passenger side by side on a forward-facing bench seat, and the third passenger on a little seat facing them with his back to the accident. It is all very cosy, although the close-coupled seating arrangement means that the car's three occupants end up playing footsie on the limited floor space.

The little F.I.A.T. is a remarkably competent design for 1899, powered by a 650cc horizontal twin engine with its cylinders cast in a single block – something that did not occur to most manufacturers until at least a decade later. It also has wet liners (another advanced feature) and a detachable cylinder head, an innovation normally (and erroneously) attributed to the 1908 Model T Ford. The engine cranks anticlockwise – this was thought to give less risk of injury if the car kicked back when it was started – has exhaust valves operated by external cams and levers, and automatic inlet valves sucked open by the descending pistons.

Its chassis has the odd feature of full elliptic front springs and semi-elliptic rear suspension and could basically be described as bicycle maker meets blacksmith, with a lightweight tubular frame hung about with over-engineered brackets and levers.

Capable of around 20mph (32km/h), the F.I.A.T. has controls that for a veteran are almost conventional, for they have been designed for a person with the normal complement of hands and feet! The left foot clutch and right hand brake are operated by vertical pedals with about a half-inch of in-out movement, while two hands are sufficient to operate the gear change, sudden-death handbrake, throttle and steering, as the ignition and mixture controls – mounted on the seat base under the driver's right knee – can be left alone once the engine is running.

The one big snag is that the controls the driver needs most – the steering handle on the transverse tiller and the hand throttle – are both on the left. Moreover, the steering is direct – about 45 degrees of movement from lock to lock – and alarmingly sensitive.

Gear-changing is by a fore-and-aft lever operating against a notched quadrant, with right back for first, forward one notch for second, then neutral and right forward for top. For reverse, it is a question of getting off and pushing....

Pausing in front of Palace House with the 1899 F.I.A.T. that is displayed in the National Motor Museum.

I discovered a hidden hazard when I stalled the engine while turning the car around at the end of its run. I tried to bump-start it under its forward momentum, and all I got was a worrying whirring sound from the transmission and no drive. Had I destroyed the transmission? It was a few weeks before the 1999 Brighton Run, and I was under strict instructions from Beaulieu engineer Ian Stanfield not to break the car. I was more than a little worried.

'It's all right,' Ian assured me. 'It catches everyone out. There's a freewheel incorporated in the final drive. We nearly broke our teeth when we tried to push-start the F.I.A.T. when we first restored it; it just ran away.'

Although the little F.I.A.T. had set Italy's largest car manufacturer on the path to total market domination, design moved fast in those days, and it was soon obsolete, although engineer Faccioli refused to accept the fact. Two years later Giovanni Agnelli asked him to design a new model with the engine at the front, as fashion dictated. Faccioli resigned in a huff and went off to follow his dreams of designing flying machines.

Ironically, when Fiat introduced its first model with a rear-mounted parallel-twin engine since 1901, the 1957 Nuova 500 proved one of the company's biggest successes, with sales of over three million by 1973. Somewhere in automotive heaven, old Faccioli must have been looking down and saying, 'You see, Signor Agnelli, I was right after all!'

CHAPTER TWENTY-TWO

Do It Yourself – The English Mechanic

Just imagine: it is the end of the first week of 1900, the dawn of a new century, and you are a keen, young amateur mechanic, fascinated by the new pastime of motoring. You dream of owning a motor car – they have been around long enough for people to have stopped calling them 'horseless carriages' – but they are impossibly expensive to buy. You are, perhaps, one of the many thousands who catch the train up to work in London every day and, since it is Friday, you buy the latest number of the tuppenny magazine *English Mechanic* to read on the journey.

There, on the first page, is the answer to your impossible dream of motoring: the first article of a series entitled 'A Small Motor-Car and How to Build It'. The schematic shows a simple rear-engined two-seater with belt and chain drive looking rather like a Benz. The anonymous author explains the philosophy behind his choice of this already rather old-fashioned design:

> I have adopted the single-cylinder horizontal motor and belt transmission gear as the most simple arrangement. The use of belts makes a much more silent car than gearing; the starting is more gradual than with the usual friction clutch as used with gear wheels, and with quite a moderate amount of attention they will be found to work extremely well... While fully recognizing the desirability of having plenty of power, yet it must not be forgotten that a very powerful motor mounted in a light car gives rise to unpleasant vibrations, and tends to shake the carriage to pieces very rapidly.
>
> Therefore, for our carriage, which is intended to carry two persons only, I believe the happy medium will be a three-brake horsepower engine.

This was hardly do-it-yourself for the faint-hearted. The following week came general arrangement drawings of the engine, while week three's article offered instructions on how to make the pattern from which the iron cylinder would be cast; and, having cast it, how to bore out the cylinder on a home lathe.

The series went on for thirty-one weeks, the specification subtly changing as, presumably, the author updated his design as he himself built a car and discovered the practical flaws. Finally, at the beginning of August, provided that you had kept pace with the weekly instructions, you had a chassis complete and running and were just starting to build the body along the lines suggested by the author, who now partly revealed himself as 'T.H.W. (care of Mr D.J. Smith, Great Arthur Street, Goswell Road, London)'.

'T.H.W.' was, in fact, a 29-year-old engineer named Thomas Hyler White. The address he gave was that of the engineering company that supplied castings for the home-build motor car for those unadventurous (or sensible) enough not to attempt to set up an iron foundry in their back garden. Despite his indifferent health (he suffered from consumption), Hyler White had been a pioneer of the motor industry, having worked for the Daimler Motor Company in Coventry in 1896–98, and had taken part in the 1896 Emancipation Day Run.

Still believed at that time to be a 'Hurtu', the English Mechanic took part in several pre-war Brighton Runs.

The 1900 'English Mechanic' design was not Hyler White's first design for a

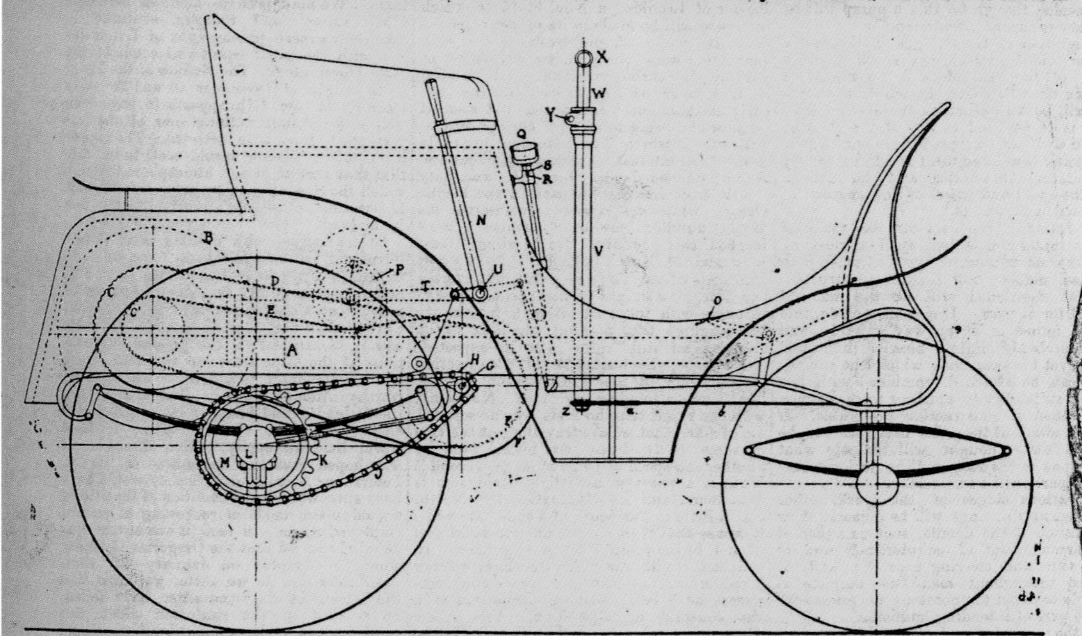

The English Mechanic

AND WORLD OF SCIENCE AND ART.

FRIDAY, JANUARY 5, 1900.

A SMALL MOTOR-CAR, AND HOW TO BUILD IT.—I.

IN introducing this design of motor-carriage to the readers of the ENGLISH MECHANIC, I would point out that there are no startling innovations; but I have endeavoured to make it as simple and cheap to build as is consistent with efficiency and strength. To this end, I have adopted the single-cylinder horizontal motor and belt transmission gear as the most simple

the engine are based, I give them here. Bore of cylinder, 4in.; stroke, 5in.; compression, 50lb. per square inch above atmosphere—i.e., 65lb. per square inch absolute. Now it may be taken that the mean effective pressure in the cylinder is roughly 75lb. per square inch. The engine is designed for a normal speed of 700 revolutions per minute, and using the ordinary formula—

$$\frac{P \times L \times A \times E}{33{,}000},$$

where P = mean effective pressure in pounds per square inch.
L = length of stroke in feet.
A = area of cylinder in square inches.
E = number of explosions per minute.

we get— $$\frac{75 \times {\cdot}416 \times 12{\cdot}56 \times 350}{33{,}000} = 4{\cdot}17 \text{ I.H.P.}$$

Allowing an efficiency of 75 per cent. makes

by the hand-lever N. Another band brake-drum is keyed on the countershaft, but not shown in Fig. 1. This brake is put into action by depressing the pedal O with the foot. When either brake is used, the engine is put out of gear with the countershaft in this manner. The belts normally run slack over their pulleys. The jockey-pulley P is arranged in such a manner that it can readily be brought vertically over either belt and depressed into contact with it. Hence the belt is tightened, and the car propelled at a slow or high speed, according to the belt in use. When, however, the brakes are used the jockey-pulley is raised, thus cutting off the power from the road wheels and allowing the motor to continue running although the car is stationary.

Change of speed is effected by means of the spade handle Q, which is first raised till

Realizing the impossible dream – this was how English Mechanic *beguiled 1900 readers with the vision of building their own motor car.*

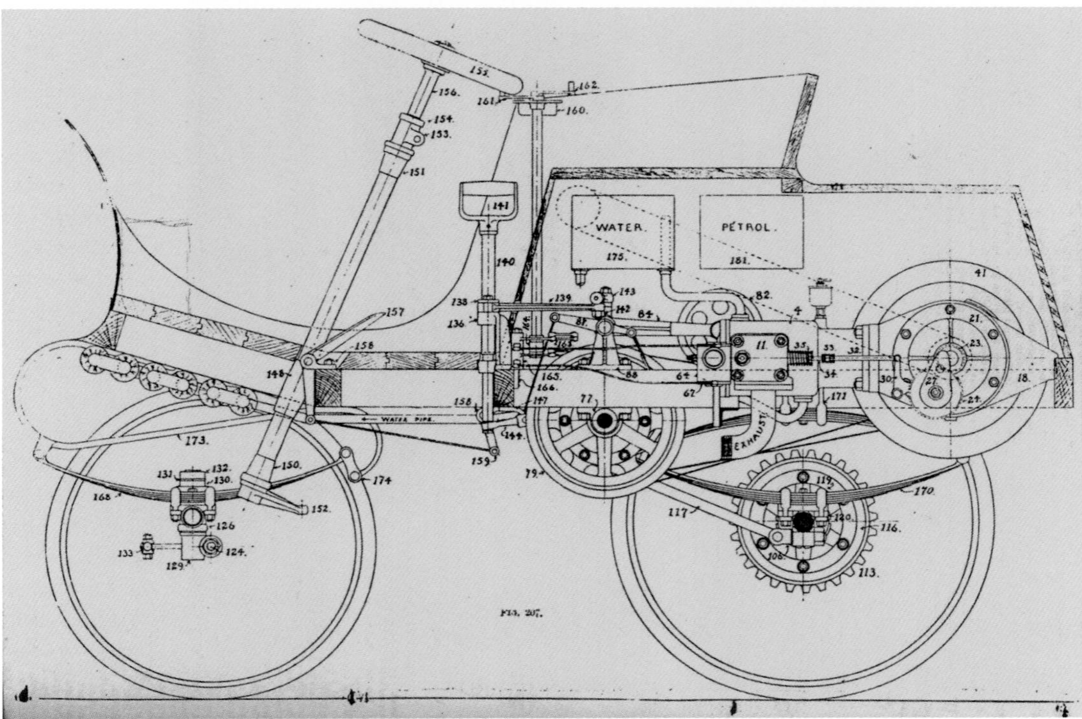

By the end of the series, the design of Hyler White's build-it-yourself car had changed in several significant respects.

The Dorrington English Mechanic conforms with the final 1900 specification.

home-build motor vehicle. He had published instructions on building a petrol tricycle in the *English Mechanic* in 1899. Neither was it his last, for he would continue to produce articles on the building of steam and petrol vehicles of varying degrees of viability until 1913, when he outlined a home-build cyclecar in the magazine. He died in 1920, aged just 48.

Amazingly, several 'English Mechanic' cars were built, and a number survive today. One of these belongs to my near-neighbour George Dorrington, although for many years nobody was quite sure what it was. It first came to light in 1921 when the redoubtable C.A. 'Bath Road' Smith, ex-record-breaking cyclist and landlord of the White Lion at Cobham in Surrey, came across a curious veteran in a field in Kent. The little car had been lying there so long that a tree had grown through the back end of its chassis and had to be chopped down before the car could be moved.

The unknown amateur mechanic who built the English Mechanic made an excellent job of interpreting Hyler White's instructions.

The car had a single-cylinder engine under a lid in its tail and two-speed belt drive, so Smith thought it might be a Benz. That is what it was called when it first took part in the Brighton Run in 1928, driven by E.G.Blake of the Fair Green Engineering Works of Mitcham. Dating was a black art in those days, with one man's guess as good as another's, so a date of 1897 was plucked from the air.

While most of the thirty-four veterans entered in that year's run managed to reach the finish at Brighton, the '1897 Benz' was one of the four cars that fell by the wayside. It did much better in 1929, when *The Autocar* recorded that it arrived at Brighton at ten minutes past one, 'under the gradually increasing rain'. It arrived safely in 1930, too, at the creditable – amazing, even – average of just over 16mph (26km/h) – Hyler White had designed the car for a top speed of 14mph (23km/h)! After missing the 1931 run, the so-called Benz ran again in 1932, driven by H.J.F. Parsons, who had previously taken part with a 1900 De Dion, but in that year its elaborate water pump packed up near Reigate and the car retired in a cloud of steam.

With increasing numbers of Benzes around for comparisons to be made, Parsons decided that his veteran probably was not of that make. In 1933, he entered it for the run as an 1897 'Hurtu', on the basis that this French company had built copies of the Benz in the late 1890s (although nobody was quite sure what they looked like).

This seemed a good enough explanation, and the car continued to be entered as an '1897 Hurtu' by successive various owners until well after the war. Then a car that was quite definitely a Hurtu of similar vintage was unearthed, and the pundits had to guess again. In the end, it was probably well-known Veteran Car Club member Reg Taverner from Essex who solved the puzzle, identifying the mystery car that he acquired in the 1950s as an 'English Mechanic' built from those 1900 partwork instructions.

At the end of the 1950s Reg Taverner sold the English Mechanic to Louis

Holland, a VCC member who was well known as a dealer in lamps and horns (and as the owner of a vociferous parrot that regaled visitors to his London home with a rendition of the 'Ding Dong Song', an Edwardian ditty on the joys of De Dion ownership). Holland was the son of a horse trader, and, after hours of haggling, agreed a deal at 1.00am, on condition that the vendor – who lived in mid-Essex – could deliver the car to the Holland homestead near the Crystal Palace before daybreak!

Although Louis Holland did not keep the English Mechanic long, he did give it a thorough restoration and replaced its 1920s registration with the more appropriate 'A-166'. (In those days, the old London County Council would happily issue the few early 'A' registrations that remained unissued, against a payment of £5.) In November 1959 Louis Holland drove the English Mechanic in its first Brighton Run under its own name.

In the mid-1960s the English Mechanic was acquired by George Dorrington and a member of his family drives it down to Brighton every November. A chance meeting during the 1972 Brighton Run threw further light on the history of the car, when George Dorrington halted at a garage in Redhill. There, he encountered an 85-year-old gentleman named Mortlock, who had been a boyhood friend of Thomas Hyler White. 'We built our own bicycles before the turn of the century,' he recalled. 'Hyler White then built a steam engine for his bicycle. Around 1898 he became an engineer with Smiths of Carshalton in Surrey, who specialized in making water pumps.'

And still had time to write articles on making motor cars and musical instruments for the *English Mechanic*....

Remarkably, several home-built English Mechanic cars – both petrol and steam-driven – still survive today as a tribute to Hyler White's design skills.

The simple one-cylinder engine of the English Mechanic is built on gas-engine lines.

Another surviving English Mechanic car, the 1904 twin-cylinder 8hp tonneau version.

CHAPTER TWENTY-THREE

Meet the Automobile – The Thousand Miles Trial

The event that really established motoring in Britain was not Harry Lawson's 1896 Emancipation Day Run but the 1900 Thousand Miles Trial, organized by the infant Automobile Club of Great Britain & Ireland (which became the Royal Automobile Club in 1907). In the words of *The Autocar*, 'To the man in the street, automobiles prior to 1900 were as a sealed book. They merely served as pegs on which to hang some comic allusion in the lighter journals, and as butts for the sarcasm of many serious writers in the lay press, and, on their appearance in the streets, as objects on which the passer-by might exercise his wit. The Thousand Miles Trial marked the end of this period.'

The concept was simple: a demonstration run that passed through most of the major cities of Britain and Scotland to show the practicality and reliability of the motor car.

Symbolically, the Thousand Miles Trial started from London on the morning of St George's Day 1900. It proved a resounding success. Of the sixty-five cars that started, forty-eight completed the course. That might seem today like a high 'drop-out' rate, but by the standards of 1900 it was a remarkable demonstration of reliability, and the lessons learned made a considerable contribution to the development of the British motor industry as well as making the public realize that the motor car had come to stay.

The event would never have happened without the dedication of the Secretary of the ACGBI, Claude Johnson, whose idea it had largely been. He carried out a detailed survey of the route between 19 December 1899 and 5 January 1900. He began by covering the initial westward leg of the 1000-mile route on an 8hp Panhard belonging to newspaper magnate Alfred Harmsworth, who had underwritten the trial to the tune of £500. For the northern section of the run, he picked up a Daimler at the Coventry works, designed by the company's works manager James Critchley.

On the twenty-first anniversary of the trial, Montague Grahame-White, who accompanied Johnson on his survey of the route, painted a vivid picture of the hazards regularly faced by the motorist of 1900:

> In December 1899, Mr Critchley detailed me off from the Daimler works at Coventry

Participants in the Thousand Miles Trial line up outside Buckingham Palace on St George's Day 1900, headed by Henry Edmunds' 6hp Daimler.

to drive Claude Johnson, the then secretary of the Automobile Club, round the proposed course of the 1000 Miles Trial, which was to take place the following year. My delight knew no bounds, as a motor tour with all expenses paid, and a good fee in the bargain, was something quite new to me.

The car selected was one of Critchley's own design, a voiturette having a Daimler motor, tube ignition, and belt transmission. There were two speeds forward and one reverse, reputed to be eight, sixteen, and four miles per hour respectively, but which experience subsequently showed were in reality slow, damned slow, and stop!

The car was got ready by Mr Alfred Bush at the works – a man who initiated me, more than anyone else whilst with the Daimler Co, into the secrets of the Daimler engine of those days – and; having pestered the storekeeper for a miniature 'spares stores' of my own to take on the car, everything was ready for a start when Claude Johnson arrived at the works some days later.

The first run was from Coventry to Birmingham, and Critchley's parting words to me were, 'Take it easy, and drive slowly.' The latter advice was more than easy to follow; the former must have been sarcasm on his part!

We reached Birmingham, averaging about 15mph, without incident, and the following morning started at 6.30 for Manchester, where we arrived after a day's run in a high wind necessitating several stops to relight the pressure burners and take up slackness in the belt. Johnson, being an enthusiast and also an early riser, suggested leaving for Kendal early, so I got the car ready by 5.30am. I found he was already about but rather undecided about starting, as snow was falling and we had to negotiate Shap to reach the end of the day's programme.

Well, we started, it being quite dark and very dismal through the streets of Manchester, the Lancashire cobble stones proving a heavy test for the belt-driven car, which waltzed all over the greasy roads, the latter frequently causing the car to make an involuntary semi-circle, as though it had had enough and intended being off home.

Windscreens and side doors not having come into fashion, and the car not being

This 1899 Wolseley performed with honour in the Thousand Miles Trial and repeated the run in 1970 driven by the octogenarian St John Nixon, who had ridden in the 1900 event aboard the prototype Napier.

fitted with a hood, Johnson suggested getting some veiling to place under our caps to keep the snow out of our eyes, and this we purchased in a village some miles from Manchester, after covering thirty miles in a little over three hours.

Having donned our veils, our troubles started in earnest. Belt fasteners either broke or tore through the Gandy belting every ten or twelve miles. Having experienced troubles of this description with a three-wheeled Leon Bollée car purchased from Charles Jarrott in 1898, I had taken the precaution to bring a good-sized box of fasteners with me from the works, and goodness knows we wanted them!

From the foot of Shap to the summit I must have fitted over two dozen, and renewed many feet of belting, with Johnson aiding me, lying on my back under the car in the snow, with the light of two ordinary carriage candle lamps with which the car was fitted. Climbing at a speed of about 5mph, the summit was reached at 12.30am, having used up all my stock of belt fasteners, spare belting, and a quarter of a. pound of powdered resin.

The run down into Kendal with the road well frozen was something to remember, and when writing to Critchley the following day I told him he had underestimated the speed of the Critchley car in the Daimler Co's printed catalogue!

Reaching Kendal on Christmas morning, Johnson got out of the car to rouse the landlord of the best local inn, and the hospitality of that man and his wife to two half-frozen and famished strangers I am sure neither of us will ever forget. Big fires going, hot water to wash in, a good hot meal, and two feather beds well warmed, within an hour, at two o'clock in the morning! Rising at ten o'clock the following day, we had a splendid breakfast, were greeted like a couple of princes, and the bill for the two of us was under a half-sovereign!

Having crossed Shap, the little Critchley Daimler would go no further – its axles were twisted by its exertions – and Johnson continued on a borrowed Daimler to Newcastle via Edinburgh. Young Grahame-White took over again at the helm of a more reliable 5½hp gear-driven Daimler to transport Johnson back to London.

Nearly seventy years after the Trial, I had the opportunity to interview G.F. Hodgkinson, a stalwart of the Veteran Car Club, who had vivid memories of the event:

> In November 1899, Claude Johnson arrived at our works in Buxton with a Daimler. He was making a survey of the route, and arranging for the marshals, etc. He was in trouble with the car, and my father gave it some attention. By that time we had got a

I followed the 1970 event and rode part of the way aboard the 1902 8hp Dennis belonging to John Dennis, which was taken back by his company in 1904 in part exchange for a new car and has remained in the family ever since.

supply of petrol from Carless, Capel & Leonard, which used to arrive four two-gallon tins in a case, and come by rail. Claude Johnson stayed the night with us and then proceeded on his journey, and my father was appointed chief marshal and timekeeper for that section of the Trial.

These 'engines of death' were not permitted to come through the main street of Buxton, because Buxton was a town which catered for ailing people – rheumatism, arthritis, sciatica and all the other complaints – so it was my job to marshal the cars at the entrance to Buxton by a secondary road so that they didn't come through the main part of the town. This I was doing with a ¾hp Werner motor cycle, the engine mounted on the handlebars, and driven with a flat belt to the front wheel. Very high and very liable to skid, and you could quite easily come off, and when this went out of commission, then it was my duty to pilot them on a pedal cycle, and that was my part in the Thousand Miles Trial.

The route chosen was a real test of the machines, for it included many hills, and points were given for performance on several of these. However, Percy Richardson, who drove a 6hp 'Parisienne' Daimler, felt he had legitimate cause for complaint about an unacknowledged additional handicap.

I had with me, as passengers, two then familiar figures in the motor world, Sir John Macdonald and Colonel McGrath, who travelled with me throughout the whole journey, and very cheery companions they were, too. At the outset, I rather jibbed at taking Sir John Macdonald, owing to his enormous size and weight, for cars in those days were not over-efficient. The allowance for weight per passenger, as laid down by the conditions of the trial, was, I believe, ten and a half stone. I pointed this out repeatedly to Mr Claude Johnson (the then secretary of the Club), and suggested that Sir John should be counted as two passengers.

After arguing this matter out the whole way up to Edinburgh, Sir John then consented to be officially weighed at the Waverley Market, Edinburgh, which was done on a penny-in-the-slot machine there. This machine only weighed up to twenty-one stone, and when Sir John stood on it, the indicating finger on the dial immediately swung round to the full extent of the capacity of the machine with a jerk, indicating that he weighed even more than two passengers, after which my claim was admitted, and Sir John assumed a dual personality for the remainder of the trial!

One of the test hills was near 'Uncle Fred' Hodgkinson's home in Buxton, as he recalled in the late 1960s: 'Taddington, which was five miles out from Buxton, had been the first test hill, and I think it was the Ariel that made the fastest time, and the second was the Hon C.S. Rolls on a Panhard. The fastest car averaged about 17mph, and today you're very fortunate if you can get up Taddington Dale at 17mph because there has been no improvement to the road except a bit of tar put on and a long double line probably for over a mile.'

Another pioneer I interviewed in the 1960s was George Lanchester, who had helped his brother Fred build one of Britain's first petrol cars in 1895. He also had memories of the trial:

> One of the regulations of the tour was that competitors received penalties if they had to refuel at other than specified points. One competitor, hoping to escape a bad mark, stole a two-gallon can from another car, and it was not until he had decanted its contents into the tank that he discovered that it did not contain petrol. The can contained water for the boiler, for the car from which he had taken it was a steamer.

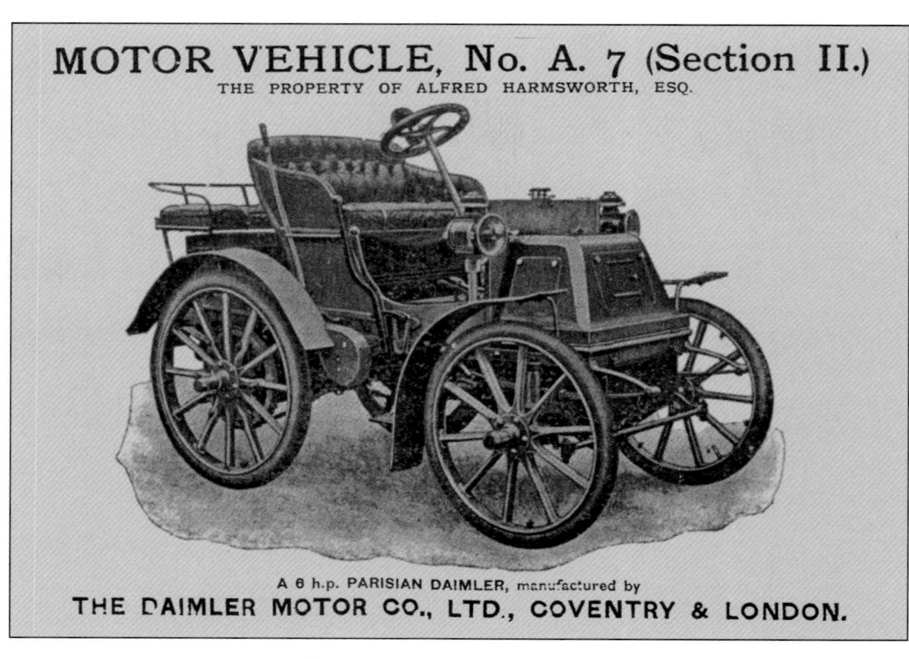

The event's catalogue illustrated Alfred Harmsworth's Parisian Daimler, on which E.A. Rose acted as mechanic.

Instead of a trifling penalty for a brief unofficial stop, it took him several hours to get going again, and he was heavily penalized for arriving late at that day's destination.

Colonel E.A. Rose, who had gone through the event as a riding mechanic, gave me an overall picture of the Thousand Miles Trial:

Roger Wallace QC was chairman of the Automobile Club that year. It was a very small affair: it just had two rooms in Whitehall Court.

Mechanics were in great demand on the Trial: very few people had any mechanical knowledge of cars in 1900. I was on two cars in the Trial; for most of the time I was on the Marshall dog-cart driven by J.J. Mann – we had enough trouble, I can tell you! – and then, as Mann had arranged for someone else to come on the car, transferred to Alfred Harmsworth's Daimler Parisian Phaeton, driven by Sir Hercules Langrishe. It had two cylinders, four seats and six horsepower. It was listed as weighing 16 cwt, but it felt more like two tons when you were pushing it!

It was an unusual car: it had about ten lubricators on the dashboard, and the mechanic had to sit on the floor, with his feet just off the ground, ready to jump out if the car stopped on a hill. It was his job to see that the drip-feed lubricators did their work – so many drops a minute to each bearing.

Charles Cordingley of the *Motor Car Journal* – I knew him very well – had a 6hp MMC. It was practically the same as the Daimler; only the change gear mechanism was slightly different, that was all. It was a brute to drive – even if you double declutched, you used to make crashing noises.

Those Daimler and MMC cars were devils. For ignition, they had a platinum tube inserted into the cylinder head, and below the part protruding from the cylinder was a sort of metal cup which you filled with methylated spirits or petrol, put a lighted match to, and when the tube became red-hot you then started your car. People often used to set the damned things on fire!

I recall some of the competitors. There was Frank Butler, of Hedges & Butler, the wine merchants, on his Panhard – that was a lovely car – who had his daughter Vera with him. She was one of the first women to go up in a balloon. There was old Freddie Simms on the Simms Motor Wheel – that was an extraordinary thing! He was a great character. I remember he built a terrific armoured car, which was shown at the Crystal Palace. C.S. Rolls had a 12hp Panhard. This was the first big Panhard: earlier models had been between five and seven horsepower. Moffat Ford, who drove a Decauville, afterwards became the

Henry Edmunds lost control of his Daimler near Keswick and punched a hole in a drystone wall, breaking a front spring; he rejoined the rally at Newcastle after repairs.

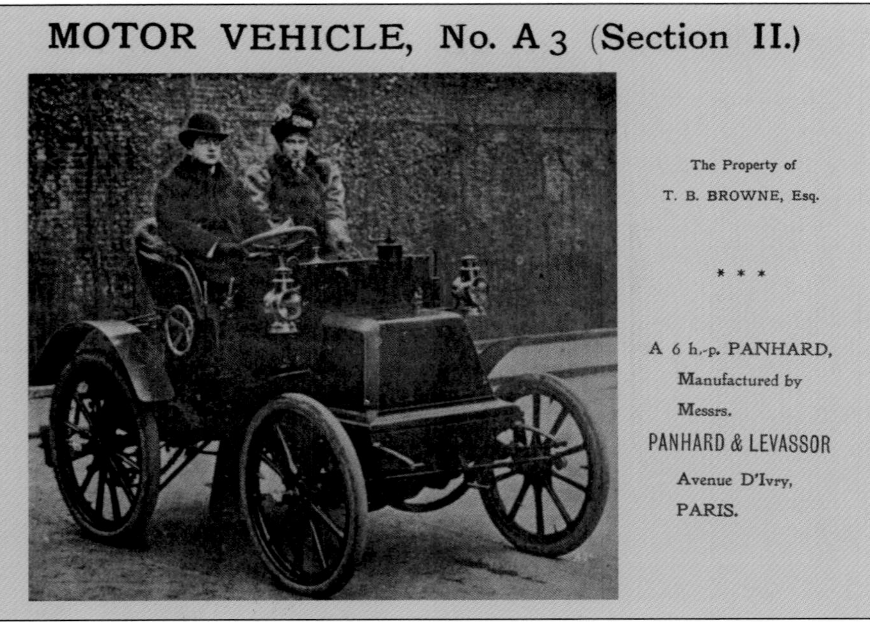

T.B. Browne, who later built the James & Browne cars, urged his Panhard on as though it were a horse!

The contestants put their cars on show in Edinburgh.

Darracq concessionaire. S.F. Edge was on the first Napier car.

Holder of Birmingham had a big Daimler, and there was very great rivalry between him and John Scott-Montagu, who became Lord Montagu of Beaulieu, who was also a Daimler owner. T.B. Browne, on a Panhard, had a most peculiar way of driving – he used to urge his car on as though he was driving a horse!

Young Iliffe, who was riding an Enfield Quadricycle, eventually became Lord Iliffe – he was the son of Iliffe of *The Autocar*.

The exhibitions in the towns en route were terrific – the interest they aroused! Even if you broke down on a remote road, while you were doing a repair, crowds of people would appear apparently from nowhere and gather round you so closely that you couldn't get on with the job. The interest was great because cars hadn't been seen much at all previously, though around 1899 S.F. Edge had sent his cousin, Cecil Edge, around the country to try and take magistrates and people like that for short runs to get them interested in motoring, so that they would not be so hostile. Cecil Edge came down to Chelmsford, where I was at Crompton's works; I knew an awful lot of the people round there, and we used to take them for these demonstration runs.

One of the most remarkable incidents of the 1000 Miles Trial occurred on the run from Edinburgh, when Montague Grahame-White, who was driving a Daimler car, was involved in a collision, which bent his steering gear. He then drove the car sitting on the offside foot-step, and steering the wheel with his foot on the hub.

I remember one of the last halts on the Trial, at Sheffield; we had a great evening with Montague Grahame-White, his cousin Claude, and one or two others. Montague Grahame-White used to play the violin very well, and we had a tremendous sing-song with him playing for us.

The other really vivid recollection I have is of an incident in Lincoln. Mrs Edward Kennard, the authoress, was driving a De Dion voiturette across a level crossing. We were two cars behind her. Her wheel apparently caught in the road and the car overturned. She wasn't hurt, the car was righted, and she drove on. Mrs Kennard was a very well-known woman; she used to write these sporting and hunting stories – the only one I can remember was called *The Girl in the Brown Habit*.

Just before the speed trials in Welbeck Park, the car I was on as mechanic – the Marshall dog-cart driven by J.J. Mann – broke the drive to the water pump. It was driven by friction from the flywheel, and we carried out a wonderful repair. We got a cork and two pennies, drilled a hole through the cork and the pennies, wired them together, shoved them on the spindle in some way and were able to get drive from the pump. We were hours getting the pump going, and we did a rotten time in the speed trials. I don't think we even got up to 30mph!

The Marshall was a belt-driven car, and you got this terrible slip on the belts. They stretched when they got wet, and you spent your time cutting and riveting and putting resin on them to make them grip. The Marshall was a Benz copy – there were a lot of Benz cars and Benz copies in the Trial.

These were outstanding incidents: of course you had the ordinary stoppages and running back on hills when the mechanic had to jump out and push the car, which I did once or twice. All sorts of funny things happened: we were under the cars as much as on them, but we did get round and finish the Trial.

I wanted to get one of the number plates after the event but the drivers held on to them.

Asked many years later about the beneficial results of the Thousand Miles Trial Trial, Lord Montagu of Beaulieu – the former John Scott-Montagu – was happy to give his views:

I often think the pioneers of the early days of motoring were a remarkable set of men – vivid and alert humans – very typical of the new spirit which was just beginning to wake up in England, a spirit of enterprise awakening after a somewhat long period of lethargic years at the end of the Victorian era. A most desirable change.

Think how many things have happened as a consequence of the growth of automobilism. We have now, as direct results, dustless roads, smooth in surface and strong in foundation; an immense amount of extra employment in connection with roads; greatly increased facilities in transport for passengers and goods all over the Kingdom; the livening up of country life; a great increase in the value of land and houses in districts then remote from railways and therefore from transport; an immense reduction in the number of horses used in towns, to the great improvement of the public health.

And last, we are gaining year by year an intimate knowledge of other countries; travellers from other countries, in the meantime, getting to know us better and better; a knowledge much more intimate and correct than that gained merely from a knowledge of boulevards, of the inside of a restaurant or from a seat in a railway train. Finally, the light and powerful motor-car engine made flying possible. A fine record indeed!

The Georges-Richard was one of the marques taking part in the Thousand Miles Trial.

RIGHT: The Hon. John Scott-Montagu's Daimler at the Haddington control in 1900…

BELOW: … and, driven by his son, Lord Montagu of Beaulieu, at the St Mary's Loch control in the 1970 re-enactment, in which it was the only car from the 1900 event to take part.

Postcards

The general public was not completely sure what to make of the new mode of transport. Motor cars, with their masked and goggled occupants, often seemed alien to the old-established ways. These postcards reflect some contemporary attitudes to the automobile in an era when speeds of more than 12mph (19km/h) were regarded as excessive and dangerous.

Motoring. A nerve tonic.
JWS 2567

In haste for the post.

EXCEEDING THE SPEED LIMIT.
Hi! Hi! there! clear the way!
We're both out for fun to-day.

A Friend in need is a friend indeed.

CHAPTER TWENTY-FOUR

A Lost Opportunity

In many ways, Frederick Lanchester was his own worst enemy. A brilliant, unconventional engineer, whose ideas were years ahead of his time, he did not suffer fools gladly – and made it quite obvious. Once, when told that the members of his board had changed their mind over some business matter, Lanchester is said to have remarked loudly that if he had minds like theirs, he would change them for something better at the earliest opportunity.

As early as 1894 Frederick Lanchester had proposed developing an aeroengine – nine years before the Wright brothers made their first powered flight, at the end of 1903 – but had been dissuaded because his ideas were too far ahead of what the scientific establishment would accept.

Lanchester had formed a private syndicate to acquire the rights to his patents with the backing of friends James and Allan Whitfield, and began designing a motor car, which was first road-tested in the spring of 1896. The original single-cylinder 'balanced' engine was not powerful enough, so he rebuilt the car with a twin-cylinder power unit. Helped from 1897 by his younger brother George, Lanchester's refusal to compromise in any way in the design or construction of his car meant that it did not go into production until 1901. By that time, car design had settled into a broadly established pattern in which the engine was in front, driving the rear wheels through a multi-ratio gearbox in which the cogs slid into engagement, and a wheel was used for steering.

Against this, Lanchester's idiosyncratic but logical layout looked like eccentricity, even though the 'balanced' flat-twin engine mounted between the front seats with twin crankshafts and six connecting rods was remarkably smooth-running, the side-lever steering was said to be more natural to use than a wheel and the preselector epicyclic gear change was easier to use than a conventional gearbox. While the Lanchester marque had a dedicated and exclusive clientele – novelist Rudyard Kipling even immortalized his Lanchester in some of his short stories – many potential customers found the Lanchester too unorthodox and bought more conventional cars.

The irony is that Frederick Lanchester had devised a system of jigs and limit gauges that guaranteed complete interchangeability in production, which could have been used to produce cars in great numbers. One motoring pioneer who appreciated Lanchester's pioneering work in the manufacture of interchangeable components was Henry Ford, who bought a Lanchester to study in his early years of assembly-line production.

Rudyard Kipling immortalized this 1902 Lanchester, converted from air- to water-cooling in 1903, as 'The Octopod' in his short story Steam Tactics, *inspired by the real-life 'kidnapping' of a policeman who had wrongly accused Fred Lanchester of speeding. This picture was taken on the 1937 Brighton Run.*

ABOVE: Lanchester's 8hp 'Spirit Passenger Phaeton', seen here on test at Petersham Hill, won the Gold Medal for Excellence in the Automobile Club's 1899 Richmond Trials.

RIGHT: This 1903 12hp Lanchester Tonneau had already covered some 100,000 miles by 1923, having been used for towing broken-down Army vehicles during the Great War.

CHAPTER TWENTY-FIVE

Life in the Motor Mills

Around 1966 I interviewed an elderly gentleman named H.P. Small, who had been mechanic to Charles Jarrott, a great motor racer of the veteran period. Jarrott was a founder member of the Automobile Association, which was formed in 1905 with the principal aim of preventing motorists from being caught in speed traps. Mr Small had actually fitted the first-ever AA badge to the front of Jarrott's car.

A few years earlier, Small had served his apprenticeship with the Motor Manufacturing Company in the legendary Motor Mills in Coventry. 'MMC occupied the main part of the building,' he told me, 'and Daimler was in a lesser building round the back. But there was very little difference between the two companies except for the manufacturer's plate fitted to each vehicle. The Motor Manufacturing Company concentrated on bodybuilding, while the Daimler Company was concerned with the mechanical components of the vehicles.'

This distinction was hardly made clear in a contemporary account of the Motor Manufacturing Company written in March 1902, when Mr Small was still working in the Motor Mills. (In fairness, at that time MMC was fast running out of money and had begun a prolonged separation from Daimler. Attempts to amalgamate the two companies had failed after Daimler had expressed its refusal to pick up more than £6000-worth of MMC's debts.)

A correspondent to *Motoring Illustrated*, signing himself 'Petrol', had the following remarks to make:

> To go down to Coventry without taking a run over the Motor Mills of the Motor Manufacturing Company, Limited, would be like paying a visit to Paris without having a look at the boulevards.
>
> To some extent, I found the works of the Motor Manufacturing Company unique. All parts of a motor car, excepting tyres, are made on the company's premises. The wisdom of this practice is demonstrated, so the company's managers say, by every car they sell.
>
> In any case, the policy of home manufacture of every portion enables the company to dispose of its cars with confidence, and to undertake, if any of the working parts fail within the first three months of actual use, renewal of such parts gratuitously.

Even though the company had already been threatened with closure and had spent all but £400 of the £37,300 it had raised to settle its outstanding

ABOVE: H.P. Small (left) and Charles Jarrott working on the latter's De Dietrich at Brooklands race track in 1907.

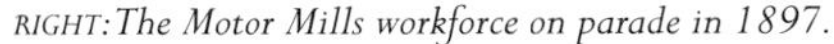

RIGHT: The Motor Mills workforce on parade in 1897.

commitments, it seemed to be working flat out. 'Petrol' was impressed:

> From the manager downward the staff was in a whirl of activity. 'We start work in the early morning, soon after six o'clock,' said Mr George Iden, the manager, 'and some of us on the administrative staff are here until ten and eleven o'clock at night.'
>
> They believe extensively in automatic machine tools at the Motor Mills, and some of the cutest ideas in the machinery line emanating from the United States, Germany, France, and our own little country, are represented in the tool shops. There are automatic gear-wheel cutting tools, which cut the teeth on, say, eight wheels at once, thus ensuring absolute accuracy and relative precision in each set of gear wheels, a matter of considerable importance for the efficient and easy changing of the gearing. One man can supervise the running of six of these machines, an item of great consideration in these days of excessive cost of production, high wages, and dear fuel.

This 1900 MMC is virtually indistinguishable from the Daimlers also built in the Motor Mills.

That impression of 'absolute accuracy' did not quite fit with the experience of MMC owners, one of whom complained bitterly, 'I have never yet got the smallest spare part that would fit properly, and all other MMC owners I have come across seem to have had the same trouble: no two cars were exactly alike… things were done in a haphazard fashion by individually good workmen.'

MMC devoted the entire top floor of the Motor Mills to bodybuilding, with an automatic woodturning machine to produce the hickory spokes for the wheels. It must have been like the automatic wood lathes used to make gunstocks for the American Civil War, which are featured in the restored Armoury at Harper's Ferry in West Virginia: 'It is a French invention, and almost human in its action; indeed, it is much more than human in its mechanical exactitude. Four spokes are simultaneously turned according to any given pattern, and there is not the hundredth part of an inch difference in the dimensions of any of the four.'

'It is,' continued the industrious scribe known to his readers as 'Petrol', 'by the use of labour and time-saving appliances

This 1900 1527cc twin-cylinder MMC 6hp Albany Concave Dog Cart was rescued from a scrapheap in 1930 by Edmund Gonville Bromhead of Birmingham. In 1942 it was bought by George Milligen for the then considerable sum of £100.

By 1903, when this 12hp car was built, MMC design had diverged from the Daimler pattern – but financial crisis loomed…

such as I have instanced that the Motor Manufacturing Company is able to supply the public with efficient cars at reasonable prices, for it is not everyone with motoring tastes who possesses a millionaire's bank book.'

The split with Daimler meant that MMC had to turn out its own power units, although these were mostly copies of established designs:

> In their voiturettes the company are now fitting an eight-horse De Dion type engine of their own manufacture, but similar engines of much greater power are now made not only for the cars built at the Motor Mills, but for those turned out by several other makers, who, understanding the difficulties connected with the manufacture of engines, find those of the Motor Manufacturing Company admirable for their purpose. All the engines are separately tested before being fitted into cars or delivered to buyers.
>
> There is accommodation in the testing shop for ten or twelve engines on the benches at one time; and every engine is run for seven hours before the test-is considered complete.

'Petrol' anticipated a great expansion of the company: 'Large as are the four extensive floors at present occupied to the full by the Company's machinery and men, they are proving insufficient for working needs. To provide the additional floor-space which the company's business renders absolutely necessary, an important addition to the factory has been arranged for. A plot of land facing the front of the main works has been acquired, and thereon the Directors intend erecting a big one-floor workshop on the most modern lines. It will have north lights in the roof, and be connected by a bridge with the main block.'

The truth was less palatable. By the end of 1905 the receivers had been called in, and, although MMC survived a little longer, it was forced to leave the Motor Mills and move into smaller premises in the Parkside district of Coventry. The happy days when MMC was 'so much sought after by people who want to enjoy the pleasures of motoring' were over.

CHAPTER TWENTY-FOUR

The Giant that was Born in a Garden Shed

Although his schoolmates regarded Louis Renault, the son of a rich manufacturer of buttons, as a dunce, he was fascinated by machinery. In 1890, when he was just thirteen, he used to hang about outside the workshop of steam-car pioneer Leon Serpollet, who had just set up in business in the Rue des Cloys in the Montmartre district of Paris, in the hope of seeing a car come out on test. Serpollet noticed the lad and gave Renault his first drive, which ended abruptly when a wheel fell off the car!

In 1898 the 21-year-old Renault built his first voiturette, powered by a 273cc De Dion engine, in a shed in the garden of his parents' house, at Billancourt, Seine. It featured direct drive by shaft to a live rear axle. Renault did decide to patent this novel idea, but he had no plans to put his little vehicle into production. However, when he demonstrated the little car to a number of friends on Christmas Eve, 1898, a dozen of them were sufficiently interested to ask him to build replicas. With financial backing from his two elder brothers Fernand and Marcel, Louis was able to found the company of Renault Frères.

The little Renault cars proved popular, and production in 1899 totalled seventy-one cars, which more than doubled in 1900, to 179. More importantly, turn-over soared from 117,600 Francs to 569,000 Francs, while in 1901, when 500 cars were made, turnover exceeded 1.7 million Francs. The first Renault cars had De Dion and Aster single-cylinder engines, then in 1902 Renault began fitting single-, twin- and four-cylinder engines of their own manufacture, the largest having a capacity of 5 litres.

Then, as now, an active racing policy and racing success were powerful selling points that boosted business. When the Renault team won the voiturette class in the 1900 Paris-Toulouse race, the company received 350 orders. Marcel Renault's most famous victory came in 1902 when, thanks to a 'job's-worth' customs man who delayed the Mercedes of the favourite, Count Elliott Zborowski, at the Austrian border, he finished a surprise first in the Paris-Vienna Race. He had covered 808 miles at an average of 39mph 63km/h) on appalling Alpine roads at the wheel of a prototype Type K 5-litre racer. He arrived so early – two hours early, in fact – that the judges, who had not expected anyone to finish before they had enjoyed their lunch, had to be prised away from the table!

Louis Renault's first workshop was the garden shed of his father's house at Billancourt. An army comrade, Edouard Richet, was his first employee.

This 1899 3hp Renault displayed at Beaulieu is claimed to be the oldest surviving example of the marque. It was once owned by Doug Copley.

By the time this Type C Renault was built, in 1900, the marque had adopted its trademark lateral radiators, which were used until 1904, when an equally distinctive dashboard radiator layout was adopted.

Marcel Renault's win resulted in a flood of orders for Renault cars, and represented a turning point in the history of this famous French marque.

To celebrate the victory, the Renault factory produced a special 'limited edition' of Paris-Vienna replicas, Types N-A (2.6-litres) and N-B (3.8-litres), which were sold with touring coachwork. It seems that, while the racer had the primitive feature of overhead automatic inlet valves, which were sucked open as the piston descended in the cylinder, the production cars were the first to have what became known as an 'L-head' engine, with both inlet and exhaust valves mechanically operated and arranged stem down, head up ('side valves') in line down one side of the engine. It was a pattern that would become almost universal in popular cars well into the 1930s and beyond.

Amazingly, three examples of this first 'same-as-you-can-buy' replica racer model survive. Renault itself also claims to have Marcel Renault's Paris-Vienna victor, although the chassis manifestly is not the same as that used on the 1902 racer.

George Dorrington's 1903 Type N-A was discovered in Peterborough in the late 1960s, missing many important components, not least the chassis, front axle, steering gear and radiators. The chassis and other parts were later discovered on a farm in Normandy; amazingly, they proved to have come from the same car. However, the complex lateral radiators were missing, and George Dorrington had to make these himself. The job involved the manufacture of over 3200 cooling fins, all of which had to be cut, crimped and soldered into place on the vertical water tubes.

The restored car was fitted with an exact replica of Marcel Renault's racing bodywork, and later, George made a four-seat body so that more passengers could be carried on the Brighton Run and other touring events.

In 1977, fitted with its racing bodywork, George Dorrington's Renault successfully completed a 1000-mile rally following the route of the 1902 Paris-Vienna Race.

LEFT: This 8hp twin-cylinder Renault dates from 1903.

OPPOSITE, TOP: Grand Prix driver Jenson Button on an unfamiliar mount – the Paris-Vienna racer preserved in Renault's own collection, which has automatic inlet valves.

OPPOSITE, BOTTOM: The Type N of 1903 was a touring derivative of the Paris-Vienna racer; this tonneau-bodied example took part in the 2005 rally to commemorate the centenary of the final Gordon Bennett Trophy race.

On its way to Brighton in the 1970s is George Dorrington's 1903 Type N, bodied as a replica of the Paris-Vienna winner.

'Catharine', the 1903 10hp Renault, gets her name from the amazing spring-spoked road wheels, each one containing 413 separate parts!

I have driven George's replica racer and it is a lively performer. Like many veterans, it has a quadrant gear change, in which the lever simply moves fore-and-aft, with reverse in line with the forward gears and a neutral between each gear notch.

The robust construction of the early Renaults means that good number of cars survive from the veteran era, and for many years I have been fascinated by the 10hp 1903 model known as 'Catharine', distinguished by the unusual red-and-black pyjama-striped livery of its coachwork and its unusual wheels. Catharine was originally owned by successful conjuror Charles Bertram, a member of the Magic Circle who had given twenty-one command performances before the Royal Family, and a member of the Savage Club. Fellow member Henry Vander Weyde had invented a folding car that could be stored in a passageway or pass through a narrow gateway. He had persuaded Bertram that there was money to be made from marketing his invention, but inevitably, the venture failed and Bertram lost his investment.

Despite this setback, Bertram retained his enthusiasm for motoring, and bought a 10hp two-cylinder Renault with an elegant three-quarter landaulette body by the Parisian coachbuilder Verheyden. Because the pneumatic tyres of the day were short-lived and unreliable, Bertram had his new Renault fitted with a set of ingenious solid-tyred spring wheels – another of Vander Weyde's clever inventions. Each wheel incorporated several hundred separate parts, had eight tangential telescopic spokes that contained coil springs working both in compression and tension, and weighed a sturdy 175lb.

Poor Bertram contracted cancer and died in February 1907, aged only 53, leaving his widow Clara in straitened circumstances. Reluctant to sell her husband's car, she had it bricked up behind a wall in the garage of their home in Streatham, South London. When in 1925 she decided to move, she asked a local mechanic, C.W. 'Ebb' Rowe, to take the Renault away. As he had no particular interest in the old-fashioned car, apart from its curiosity value, he paid nothing for it. However, as he would say later, he did not charge for taking it away, either.

A couple of years later, the first veteran car run to Brighton was organized and – as the route passed within a hundred yards of Rowe's workshop – he was inspired to put the old Renault back into running order and enter it. He worked on the Renault on and off for several years, but, although he drove the old car on trade plates, it took several years to get it running properly. Finally, he entered it for the November 1936 Brighton Run, re-registering it as 'DLH 202'.

Rowe realized that the unique and ingenious sprung wheels were part of the car's remarkable originality, and determined not to replace them. It seems that he took them on trust, even though he had calculated that between London and Brighton the thirty-two telescopic spokes made a combined total of 2,851,200 compressions, a severe test of the complex design. Eventually, reported *The Autocar* in 1936, 'C.W. Rowe's Renault's wonderful spring wheels had had enough. One collapsed and the energetic crew spent nearly two hours adapting the wheel of a Morris to the ancient car.' Inevitably, the Renault finished late.

The 1937 and '38 runs were completed without serious incident, but in the first post-war Brighton Run, in 1946, another wheel collapsed and Rowe had to lash a modern wheel to the spokes in order to finish. He decided to rebuild all the wheels, in a mammoth project that took an enormous amount of time. Rowe used fabricated rims instead of the original cast-steel units in order to save money, although this called for a complex arrangement of welded plates and wooden spacers in the rims. Fortunately, he kept one of the original cast rims as a souvenir.

After spending many hours working on the wheels, Rowe gave the car – its date of birth now confirmed by the Veteran Car Club as 1903 – the name 'Catharine', finding it a huge joke to ask unsuspecting garage attendants to pump up Catharine's solid tyres!

There was no Brighton Run in 1947 because of fuel rationing, but Catharine was back in action when the run was revived in 1948.

In November 1953, 'Ebb' Rowe retired to Sussex and sold his Renault to Philip Watters Westbrook, a tobacco wholesaler from Adlington in Cheshire. After the new owner died suddenly, aged 59, in August 1967, Catharine – which had twenty-three Brighton Run finishers' medals to her credit – was driven in the 1967–68 Brighton Runs by his son Peter. Soon afterwards, Peter emigrated to Canada (where he still lives), so his mother stored the car for him at the family home.

In March 1977 a near neighbour, Veteran Car Club President Frank Smith, persuaded Mrs Watters Westbrook to let him get Catharine running again. He took the car to his home in Wilmslow, Cheshire, and, after working on her, entered the old Renault for the 1978 Brighton Run. This time, the wheels had become noisy and had poor directional stability; one of them collapsed on the way to Brighton and Catharine only just finished the run.

Frank Smith's company, Ollerton Engineering Services of Preston, began restoration work in November 1981. Some of the body panels were in poor repair, and the original trim and hood had become brittle, so it was decided to strip the body paint, replace damaged body panels and remove the trim and hood. Work began on the wheels in 1983, but sadly Frank Smith died the same year, and for years Catharine sat on blocks in the corner of the workshop, with little progress being made. In February 1992 Peter Watters Westbrook asked his nephew Michael Bithell to see the restoration through to completion. By July 1994 the major task – rebuilding the wheels – was complete, after more than 1600 hours of work, during which 'Ebb' Rowe's fabricated rims were discarded and new rims cast from the surviving example. Nevertheless, many 1904 parts, including the springs and hub and spoke components, were retained.

Repainted and retrimmed, Catharine is now back on the road to Brighton with a new spring in her step, seemingly as unstoppable as the early growth of Renault. By 1904 the company was turning out 1800 cars a year, had a turnover of more than 11.4 million Francs and employed 700 workers in a factory that was doubling in size year on year. It was a far cry from the garden shed where the story had begun. At the very end of the veteran years, in December 1904, the magazine *La France Automobile* reported on the Renault exhibit at the Paris Salon:

> All its cars... are only delivered after meticulous preparation, which sets them apart from their fellows. But what is to be praised about the Renault brothers is that they only standardize new features after having tried and tested them for reliability on the road.
>
> This concern has been taken to such a degree that only recently M Louis Renault undertook a journey of some 6000 kilometres through Austria, Germany and Holland over all kinds of roads, which allowed him to modify certain fittings and improve certain details with that confidence that only lessons learnt in the school of the road can give.

A proud mechanic working on a twin-cylinder Renault, newly registered under the Act that introduced number plates (and an increase in the speed limit to 20mph) in January 1904.

CHAPTER TWENTY-SEVEN

Prelude to a Legend

One of the hoariest legends in motoring history was, sadly, repeated by Rolls-Royce in the lavish press pack that celebrated the centenary of the 'Best Car in the World', in 2004. The luxury-car maker claimed that 'Royce ... bought, second-hand, a 10hp two-cylinder French Decauville ... but its standard of construction and workmanship was not good and Royce wanted to improve its unreliable electrical system, general rough running and vibration that was the norm for vehicles of the time'.

That slur on the Decauville, which was actually one of the better light cars of its day, was quite unjustified. The old-established firm of Decauville was a well-known maker of narrow-gauge steam locomotives, which had also built Serpollet steam cars, commercial vehicles and tramcars since the beginning of the 1890s. Its engineers Pierre and Yves Guédon had designed a perfectly viable independent front suspension system for Decauville's first petrol car, the 1898 'Voiturelle' (although it had no rear suspension except for the air in the tyres). They had also written one of the first practical books on motoring as early as 1897.

When researching in the library of the Royal Automobile Club in London's Pall Mall in the 1990s, I found a fascinating article in a 1902 issue of *Motoring Illustrated*, a rare magazine produced by the industrious Kenealey brothers. Henry Royce's friend 'the well-known electrician' W.J. Crampton, a motorist since 'the old days of tube-ignition tricycles', had been interviewed and had nothing but praise for the Decauville: 'I have had three tricycles, two small cars and now own a ten-horse Decauville which has given me every satisfaction. To my mind no make equals the Decauville. I have driven this car over 3000 miles and have much increased its engine efficiency by certain modified and electrical ignition arrangements of my own.'

It seems that Crampton's experience impressed Royce, who had just taken up motoring for his health, and persuaded him to buy a new 10hp Decauville. While Royce certainly tinkered with his new car – he was, after all, a leading manufacturer of electrical equipment, and had his own ideas on electrical ignition – it was not the undesirable machine that the Rolls-Royce press release implied. Indeed, Decauville had been one of the very first manufacturers to fit a dynamo as standard to keep the accumulators that provided the current for the ignition system's trembler coils fully charged. This electrical novelty may have been the particular feature that commended the Decauville to both Crampton and Royce.

Certainly, leading Rolls-Royce expert Paul Wood, who with his twin brother

LEFT: Decauville was already famous as a maker of narrow-gauge railway locomotives when it ventured into the motor world with the little 'Voiturelle', whose independent front suspension was offset by the fact that the rear axle had no suspension at all!

OPPOSITE, TOP: Spanish nobility venture out in a 1902 10hp Decauville.

OPPOSITE, BOTTOM: Ownership of a Decauville inspired Henry Royce to build a car of his own design; this 1904 10hp model is the oldest known Rolls-Royce motor car.

V.C.C.
1904
ROLLS-ROYCE
228
U 44

ABOVE AND RIGHT: 'Quite remarkable for 1901' is Paul Wood's verdict on his 10hp Decauville, which once belonged to aviation pioneer Sir Geoffrey de Havilland.

Andrew runs the highly-respected Rolls-Royce and Bentley specialists P & A Wood, of Great Easton, Essex, has a high opinion of the Decauville. Paul owns a 1901 10hp twin-cylinder Decauville, which is identical to Royce's first car and was once owned by aviation pioneer Geoffrey de Havilland, who drove it on its first Brighton Run in 1930.

Paul Wood is probably the first man since Henry Royce a century earlier to drive both a 10hp Decauville and an example of the first production Rolls-Royce, also a 10hp twin-cylinder car, on the same day. Does he agree that the Decauville deserves the bad press it is given by over-enthusiastic supporters of Henry Royce? It seems not: 'The Rolls-Royce is certainly smoother-running, but the Decauville is quite remarkable for 1901. I'm just amazed how good it is and I'm so pleased I own it.'

Maybe the true measure of Royce's achievement is that he improved on a car that was already good. After all, any fool can improve on something bad; it takes real skill to improve on the best!

CHAPTER TWENTY-EIGHT

The Magnificent Mercedes

'We have entered the Mercedes era!' gasped leading French journalist Paul Meyan, who declared himself 'struck with terror' at the workmanship, design and performance of the astounding new car from the Daimler factory at Cannstatt. It had just swept the board at the 1901 Nice Automobile Week, astounding onlookers with its speed, capability and its many technical innovations: 'the stamped nickel-steel frame, which appears to give wonderful hill-climbing powers to the car'; the 'H' gate gear change, the honeycomb radiator, the mechanically operated inlet valves and magneto ignition, which had at a stride moved car design out of the horseless carriage era and rendered just about everything else on the road obsolete.

The new-born Edwardian age greeted with a sense of amazement the marque that had replaced the elephantine Cannstatt-Daimler, launched at the end of the 19th century. More than a century later, it is still possible to experience something of that amazement as the big 60hp Mercedes thread their way effortlessly through the pack of slower Brighton Run cars, to the accompaniment of their unique 'gobble-gobble' exhaust note. In 1903 the sheer arrogance of the Mercedes' power inspired the one-legged poet W.E. Henley to celebrate the

Cannstatt Daimler

Wealthy Austrian Emil Jellinek loved power and speed, and in 1899 he ordered five powerful front-engined cars from the Cannstatt Daimler company and set to work to sell them to his equally rich acquaintances. The resulting 'Phoenix' racing car was certainly quick, but its short wheelbase made it dangerous to handle, and its appearance led Baron Henri de Rothschild to remark that it 'had more the characteristics of an elephant than a gazelle'. (He still bought one for himself, though.) Jellinek was not satisfied; he commissioned Daimler designer Wilhelm Maybach to create 'the car of the day after tomorrow' and committed to buy a whole series of thirty-six cars, provided they proved satisfactory. There was one other condition: they were to be named after his teenaged daughter Mercedes.

This 1899 Cannstatt Daimler racer originally belonged to Count Zborowski.

ABOVE: Driver Wilhelm Werner on the Mercedes with which he won the Nice-Aix-Salon-Nice race and the Nice-La Turbie hillclimb in 1901.

LEFT: Competing in the Brighton Run at the age of 100, this 1902 40hp Mercedes, originally owned by American millionaire William Kissem Vanderbilt, is the oldest known example of the marque.

Mercedes in verse as 'The Angel of Speed'.

The Mercedes was effectively the first 'supercar', even though the first use of that now overworked term lay thirty-five years in the future. In a world in which few cars were capable of significantly exceeding the blanket 12mph (19km/h) speed limit to which an ignorant legislature had condemned law-abiding British motorists, the Mercedes came like a bolt from the blue. Sadly, Gottlieb Daimler never saw the revolution created by the Mercedes, for he had died in 1900, and the success of the new marque – which took its name from the eldest daughter of Emil Jellinek, the flamboyant agent for Daimler cars in Nice – was due to its designer Wilhelm Maybach. Despite his achievements, Maybach resigned in 1907 to build Zeppelin engines, and was replaced by Gottlieb Daimler's eldest son Paul.

The 60hp model first seen early in 1903 offered a top speed of 80mph (129km/h). Even when Britain's pusillanimous Parliament raised the nationwide speed limit at the beginning of 1904 to 20mph (32km/h), in deference to improving performance, the top speed of the Mercedes was still four times greater. It is perhaps the only veteran car whose performance is still staggering by modern standards. Writing in the *Badminton Magazine* in 1904, Claude Johnson – soon to become the commercial genius behind the Rolls-Royce marque – described a truly epic journey, undertaken at a time when the roads were poor and a blanket 20mph speed limit prevailed across Great Britain, with widespread police traps to enforce the law: 'Mr Ernest Hutton, in the early hours of a fine summer's morning, drove his 60hp Mercedes car from London to Holyhead, 270 miles, in 5½ hours. He was at Holyhead by 8.15am. His average speed was 49 miles per hour. Such a performance would be impossible in this country except when the road, as in the case mentioned, is quite clear of traffic and foot-passengers.'

When Johnson took the wheel himself, he was seduced by the charms of Miss Mercedes: 'When the road is clear and her lover sees no reason why she

The 12mph speed limit

In 1896 the speed limit had been raised to 14mph (23km/h), but was quickly revised down to 12mph (19km/h) to keep these 'engines of death' in check. Progress meant that the limit quickly became an onerous burden on the motorist, with the police in many counties over-zealous in setting up speed traps, often gaining their evidence in a Heath Robinson fashion, using a cheap stopwatch. This led to much bad feeling between motorists and the police, who often used speed trapping as a route to quick promotion; Sergeant Jarrett of the Surrey Police rose to the rank of Inspector within a year because of the great number of speeding convictions he secured. Pioneer accessory provider Alfred Dunhill was so incensed at what he felt was an unfair conviction in Surrey that he added these wonderful 'Bobby Finders' to his 'Motorities' range in 1903. An increase in the blanket speed limit to 20mph (32km/h) in 1904 – coupled with compulsory number plates – did little to ease the situation.

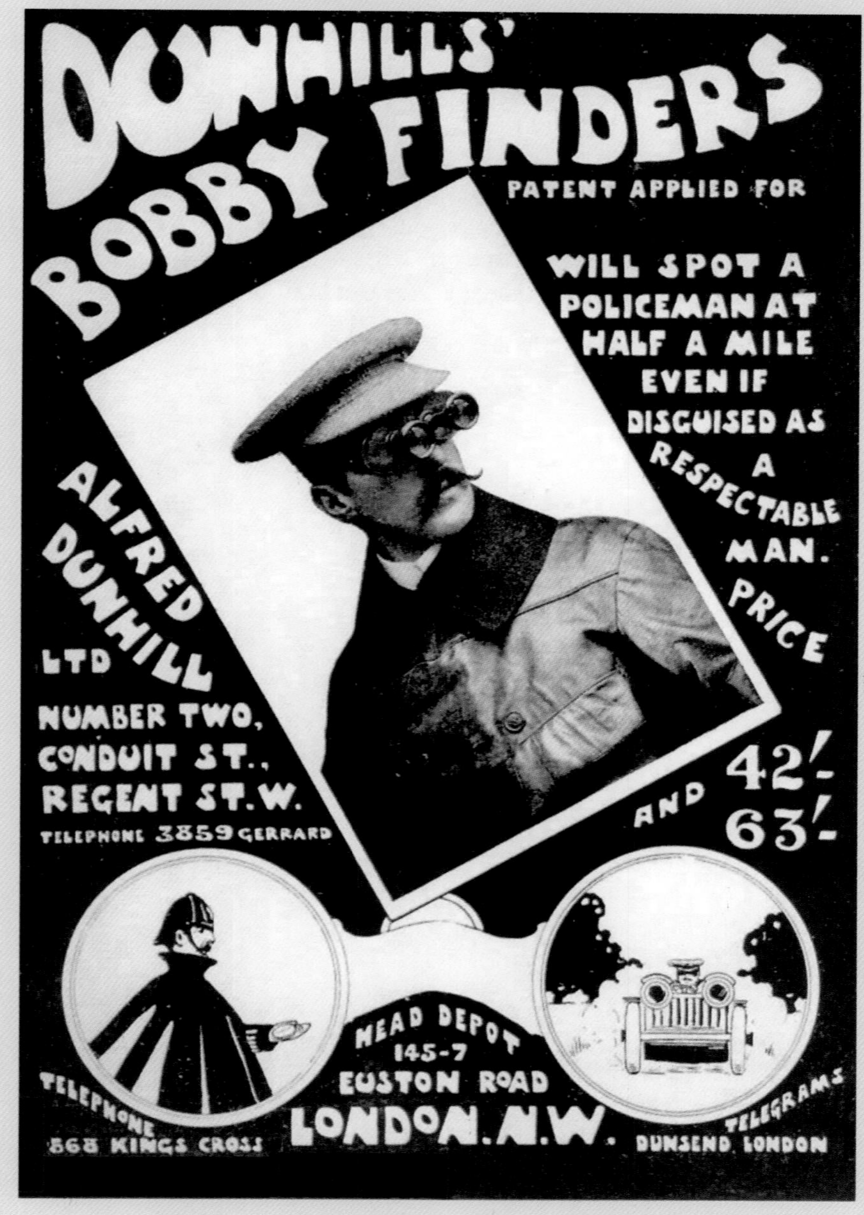

This 1903 60hp Mercedes cared for by the National Motor Museum was originally owned by press baron Alfred Harmsworth and still belongs to his family. In the 1960s it was regularly driven to Brighton by top racing drivers such as Stirling Moss, seen here finishing the run in 1968.

At the wheel of the 1903 60hp Mercedes, formerly the property of Peter Hampton, which made a record £1.6 million when auctioned by Robert Brooks in 1992.

should not be indulged, the throttle is gently opened, and, with unparalleled rapidity of acceleration, the speed increases, the wind is split in twain by her fair form and rushes by the driver's ears, and when the inexperienced passenger thinks the utmost possible pace has been reached the fourth speed is suddenly slipped in, she bounds forward and is skimming the road surface at nearly 80 miles an hour.'

It was the sort of performance that might normally have been expected of a racing car rather than a road-going four-seater, but then the 60hp Mercedes had already proved its worth on the race track. After a disastrous fire at the Mercedes factory, which destroyed the 90hp racers that the factory had built to contest the 1903 Gordon Bennett Race in Ireland, the factory had to fall back on 60hp cars borrowed from private owners. An elderly American named Clarence Gray Dinsmore loaned the Mercedes company his 60hp touring car. That vehicle, with no more tuning than the replacement of its everyday body-work with a two-seat racing shell, carried the Belgian driver Camille 'Red Devil' Jenatzy to a famous victory against the finest purpose-built racers in the world.

Back in the 1980s, when I wrote an anniversary supplement for *Autocar*, the world's oldest motoring magazine, we photographed a 60hp Mercedes, then owned by Roger Collings, in London's Regent's Park. The sight of that potent red veteran hurtling round the park's Inner Circle at speed while we took tracking shots was an absolute joy.

It was around that time that I drove Paul Foulkes-Halbard's veteran 70hp Mercedes, a car whose adventurous career had included a spell as a mission bus in Argentina. I was entranced. Paul easily swung the 9230cc four-cylinder engine into life on the starting handle, aided by a half-compression device operated by a lever in front of the radiator that caused the exhaust valves to open on the first half of the compression stroke. The huge engine ticked over at a leisurely 200rpm as I clambered into the driving seat – a bit of an acrobatic exercise, for the floor of the car was high off the ground and there was no step.

RIGHT: *This 1904 18/28 Mercedes was originally delivered to Samuel White (later head of the Bristol Aeroplane Company) and in the 1930s belonged to Sir Roy Fedden, the main force behind the development of the powerful radial engines that played a key role in the Second World War.*

BELOW: *This 1904 18/28 Mercedes had a successful racing career at Brooklands in 1907–08 in the hands of its then owner Tom Faulkner.*

Song of Speed

Hence the Mercedes!
Look at her. Shapeless?
Unhandsome? Unpaintable?
Yes; but the strength,
Of some seventy-five horses.
Seventy-five puissant,
Superb fellow creatures,
Is summed and contained,
In her pipes and her cylinders.

* * *

Yet ask but a sign,
But a proof of her quality,
Handle her valves,
Her essentials, her secrets,
And she runs down the birds,
(You can catch them like flies,
As, poor wretches, they race from you!);
Ay, and become,
As the Spirit and Mind,
Of God's nearest approach.
To Himself hath so willed it.
The Angel of Speed –
Speed in the Laugh of the Lord.

* * *.

Thus the Mercedes,
Comes, lo, she comes.
This astonishing device,
This amazing Mercedes,
With Speed –
Speed in the Fear of the Lord.

W.E.Henley, 1903

The late Paul Foulkes-Halbard in full flight on his way to Brighton aboard his 70hp Mercedes.

Since the tight-fitting seat was not adjustable, I had to stretch to operate the car's toggle clutch, which operated two shoes acting inside a drum. This was a change from the early Mercedes cars, which more usually had a powerful coil spring clutch, in which a flat spiral spring coiled round a drum on the flywheel centre like a python crushing its prey.

'You really need to let the car rev in the gears,' Paul told me. Although the engine peaked at a mere 1100rpm, the car accelerated rapidly as I shifted gear through the H-gate. Although drivers would have to wait almost another thirty years for synchromesh after the Mercedes was built, the car had an amazingly sweet down-change. I only had to dip the clutch and slide the massive straight-cut gear-wheels gently into engagement as the revs rose imperceptibly. There was no crash of protesting gears, for the relative tooth speeds were so slow that the gears went home easily.

The steering was positive and very high-geared, with less than a turn lock-to-lock, and I found it easy to place the car precisely where I wanted, for there were no mudguards and I could see exactly what each front wheel was doing. It was easy to hold the car at speed with one hand on the 20-inch steering wheel while I changed gear or pulled on the outside handbrake, which acted on massive drums on the rear wheels. It was, however, advisable to leave the handbrake 'notched on' slightly when going down a twisty hill to leave both my hands free to hold the car and change gear.

The right-hand pedal operated drum brakes on the drive shaft and counter-shaft, which were cooled on long descents by water fed by exhaust pressure from a brass tank on the nearside of the chassis. The exhaust pressure also fed oil to the engine bearings through an impressive array of drip feed lubricators on the dashboard and forced petrol from the rear-mounted fuel tank to the massive carburettor once the car was on the move.

The car was so quiet – all I was aware of was the low boom of the exhaust and the rhythmic swish of the driving chains over the massive sprockets – that I was

The ex-Peter Hampton Mercedes in racing guise, driven by current custodian Tim Scott in the 2005 Gordon Bennett centenary rally.

glad that the Mercedes had a powerful 'warning device' in the shape of a plunger-operated Swan & Stuart 'Bugle Motor Horn', which played a strangled four-note call. This was a car of which Mr Toad would have been proud!

Because the engine turned so slowly and smoothly, I felt less actual impression of speed than with many a slower veteran. Indeed, I had felt more sense of danger in the 15mph rear-engined 1898 Georges Richard than I did when driving the Mercedes at 60mph, although the speed with which corners came up, and the fact that the car only had rear-wheel brakes, made me realize how easy it had been for the first Mercedes drivers to have horrific accidents when they let their cars go all-out. Most notorious of these accidents was the fatal crash of Count Elliott Zborowski in the Nice-La Turbie hill-climb in April 1903, when he tried to take a corner too fast: 'His death was instantaneous; his 60hp Mercedes a ruin. His end should be a warning to the millionaires who may woo and acquire one of these fair, but to the unskilful terrible, mistresses!'

A 1902 7-hp Panhard & Levassor speeds through Crawley on the 2005 Brighton Run.

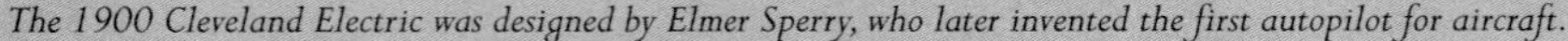

The 1900 Cleveland Electric was designed by Elmer Sperry, who later invented the first autopilot for aircraft.

The number plate records the fact that this primitive 1900 motor car is powered by an engine built by Frederick Simms, who founded the Royal Automobile Club.

The 1898 Fisson from the Loder Collection has a 3-litre engine and three gear levers controlling five speeds!

ABOVE: The National Motor Museum's 1903 22hp Daimler is a movie star – it appeared in the film Half a Sixpence.

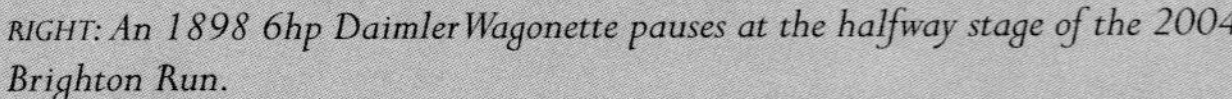

RIGHT: An 1898 6hp Daimler Wagonette pauses at the halfway stage of the 2004 Brighton Run.

This 1904 28–35hp Mercedes was originally ordered from the marque's Paris agent C. L. Charley in July 1903 by wealthy New York banker William Burden. It was updated in appearance in 1907, with Daimler of Long Island altering the chassis to accommodate a larger body by coachbuilders Healey & Co. of New York. In 1915 Mr Burden gave the car to his German chauffeur Otto Hammer as a retirement present, and in 1928 Hammer sold the car to renowned motoring artist Peter Helck.

CHAPTER TWENTY-NINE

The Great Races

Today, the term 'road racing' is most closely associated with classic Italian events such as the Mille Miglia and the Targa Florio, but in fact road racing was born in France in the earliest days of motoring, with marathon events that started from Paris. For eight crowded years, from 1895, these events dominated the sporting calendar.

The winner of one of the very first motor races, an 1896 Panhard & Levassor *dos-à-dos* owned by Daniel and Toby Ward, is nowadays a regular entrant in the Brighton Run. Back in 1896 this Panhard, first owned by Emile Levassor, won the Paris-Marseilles-Paris race, driven by Mayade. It then took part in the 1896 Motor Car Tour to Brighton, again driven by Mayade, and 'carrying a party of Parisian automobilists', and was bought from Levassor (at a considerable premium) by Harry Lawson, who sold it on to the Hon. C.S. Rolls late in 1896. The following year, Rolls, known as the 'man of speed', fitted the car with a four-speed gearbox to improve its performance. He kept the car, which he displayed on his stand at the 1903 Crystal Palace Show, as 'a relic of the past', until his death in a flying accident at Bournemouth in 1910. The Panhard was discovered in derelict condition on the Rolls family estate near Monmouth in the 1970s.

City-to-city races grew ever more ambitious, and in 1899 the eccentric American newspaper proprietor James Gordon Bennett (the man who had sent Stanley to find Doctor Livingstone) conceived the idea of a challenge cup for motor racing while he was cruising the Mediterranean in his luxury steam yacht *Lysistrata*. The high-living Bennett, reputedly 'a notorious indulger in the demon drink and women', had gone into self-imposed exile in Paris after bringing a New Year's party at his future in-laws to an abrupt end by relieving himself in front of the guests. Some say it was the grand piano that he chose as the all-too-public convenience, while others declare that it was the fireplace. Either way, Bennett suddenly became *persona non grata* in polite New York society, which anyway had become more than a little shocked by his habit of riding through the countryside on his four-in-hand coach stark naked and screaming.

Despite a continued enthusiasm for carriage driving, Gordon Bennett had been a motoring enthusiast since 1893 and had done much to further the cause of motoring through his editorial columns in the Paris edition of the *New York Herald*, which he ran like a real-life Citizen Kane. In consultation with the Automobile Club de France, Gordon Bennett drew up the rules for a race series that would encourage international competition. The *International Motor Review*, an English-language magazine published in Paris, explained the thinking behind Gordon Bennett's new race:

> France had so completely monopolized the industry that other countries seemed to be incapable of building satisfactory cars, to say nothing of competing with the French in their own races.
>
> Mr Bennett was well aware that the time was not far distant when France would find her monopoly threatened. He wanted to encourage foreign countries to enter upon this struggle, and also provide a means of showing the progress they were making by instituting an annual contest.
>
> To make the comparison a fair one, he offered the cup with the stipulation that the vehicles competing were to be built throughout in the countries they represented. He also desired that the trophy

The first-ever true motor race was the 1895 Paris-Bordeaux-Paris, won by Emile Levassor, who drove solo for 48 hours 48 minutes, sustained merely by weak beef broth and champagne.

should be known as the 'International Challenge Cup'. Needless to say, it soon became known as the 'Gordon Bennett Cup'.

A contemporary cartoon of millionaire newspaper magnate James Gordon Bennett and his elaborate trophy.

Entry in the race was strictly controlled. Only official representatives of clubs recognized by the ACF could compete, so the Automobile Clubs of America, Austria, Belgium, Germany, Great Britain and Ireland, Switzerland and Turin were all eligible to enter teams consisting of three cars and three drivers. However, the first Gordon Bennett race, held on 14 June 1900, was a fiasco; while France fielded a team of three Panhards, there were only single entries from America, Belgium and Germany. The three French drivers – De Knyff, Charron and Girardot – had been chosen by ballot rather than ability, causing a great deal of ill-feeling, while it proved extremely difficult to obtain official permission to hold the 354-mile race from Paris to Lyon on the public highway.

Suddenly, with just twenty-four hours' notice, the race was on! The German entrant, Eugen Benz, refused to start because his Benz car was not ready, and the Belgian entrant Camille Jenatzy (Bolide) had to be persuaded to take part. Because of the uncertainty, fewer than 200 people turned up to watch the start on the Versailles road.

An further element of confusion was introduced when the ace Mors driver Levegh turned up as an unofficial entrant in the hope of reaching Lyon first to register his protest against not having been chosen for the French team. 'If the start was inauspicious,' complained *International Motor Review*, 'the race itself was utterly devoid of interest.'

The American entrant Alexander Winton retired when a wheel of his Winton racer collapsed, while 'Red Devil' Jenatzy lost his way because the race was so badly organized, and wandered about the countryside for a while before giving up. 'What with car troubles, obstreperous gendarmes, dogs and flocks of sheep, I have never in my life driven such a race!' he complained.

The farce continued: De Knyff stripped the teeth off top gear and Girardot lost his way and damaged his steering; Charron bent his back axle and was about to retire when he was told that he was the only official driver still in the race, so he carried on, with his mechanic pouring oil over the straining driving chains to keep them from snapping.

Ten miles from the finish, Charron hit a St Bernard and skidded off the road, across a ditch, through a field and back on to the road facing back the way he had come. Nevertheless he finished, watched by a handful of sightseers and the five members of the official reception committee who had bothered to turn up. Charron, his mechanic and the officials adjourned to the nearest bar, along with Levegh, the unofficial second, and Girardot, who had managed to repair his steering and limp home.

The second Gordon Bennett race proved an absolute disaster, with little interest from the French manufacturers and even less from the rest of the world. The French team consisted of Charron

The magnificent Gordon Bennett Trophy, showing the Goddess of Victory on a Panhard car, was created by Parisian silversmith Aucoc.

They called Girardot 'the eternal second', but he actually won the second Gordon Bennett race in 1901 by being the only contestant to finish!

and Girardot on 24hp Panhards and Levegh on a 50hp Mors, 'the most powerful car that had ever taken part in a race'. The only foreign challenge was a last-minute entry from the English firm of Napier, which had built a huge 50hp car for S.F. Edge. The new Mercedes marque decided to concentrate its efforts on the Paris-Berlin race.

There were so few entries that the Gordon Bennett was combined with the Paris-Bordeaux race. Then Edge was disqualified from the Gordon Bennett before the race began because the Dunlop tyres fitted to his Napier had burst so many times that he had been forced to change them for French tyres. He took part in the Paris-Bordeaux race anyway, but retired with a broken clutch. Of the remaining Gordon Bennett racers, Charron crashed, Levegh retired, and only Girardot finished: he was ninth in the Paris-Bordeaux.

The great race of 1901, the Paris-Berlin, was the last major event organized under a total *formula libre*, with no restrictions on engine capacity or overall weight. The lack of crowd control in the villages through which the course passed resulted in several accidents, while Panhard driver Pinson wrapped his 40hp racer around a tram in a German town.

The other hazards were stray dogs and blinding clouds of road dust. The Mercedes driver Degrais thought he had found the answer to the lack of forward vision by steering by the treetops above the dust cloud... and then he arrived at high speed at a point where the trees went straight on and the road turned sharp left!

The winner was Fournier's Mors, which averaged 44.1mph 71km/h) over the difficult 687-mile course. He had led most of the way, and so kept ahead of the dust cloud.

In 1902, the Gordon Bennett was combined with the Paris-Vienna race, and Edge was once again the only foreign competitor. The French team was arbitrarily chosen as De Knyff (Panhard),

Driven by S.F. Edge, this Napier was a surprise winner of the 1902 Gordon Bennett race.

This 9.2-litre 60hp Mors Type Z was one of six works entries for the 615-mile 1902 Paris-Vienna race that also encompassed that year's Gordon Bennett Trophy. Driven by the Baron de Caters, it placed ninth after three days of brutal racing, which included crossing the Alps.

ABOVE: *The victor of the Paris-Vienna Race was Marcel Renault, who arrived so early that the judges were still at lunch!*

The little monoposto Renault racer driven by Pol Sonet from Belgium in the 2004 Brighton Run was the mount of works driver Oury in the 1902 Paris-Vienna event.

Leading French artist Montaut depicted the amazing victory of Fernand Gabriel on his Mors Dauphine in the 1903 Paris-Madrid 'Race to Death', halted at Bordeaux because of the number of accidents.

Fournier (Mors) and Girardot (CGV). On the first day Fournier broke his gearbox racing an express train carrying spectators and Girardot retired with clutch trouble; on the third and last day, De Knyff broke his differential crossing the Alps and dropped out 30 miles from the finish of the Gordon Bennett at Innsbruck, making Edge the winner and giving Britain, a country where racing on the public highway was forbidden, the problem of arranging the event on home soil.

Competing vehicles in the 1902 Paris-Vienna race were limited to a maximum weight of 1000kg (plus an allowance of 7kg for a magneto), which inspired manufacturers to seek the maximum power-to-weight ratio by cramming huge engines into flimsy frames. The Panhard entries were typical, with monstrous 13,672cc engines in wooden chassis strengthened with steel 'flitch plates'. These had to be reinforced, and the Panhards then took first, third, fourth and fifth places in the heavy-car class. British driver Charles Jarrott's Panhard had not been reinforced, and he had to patch his cracked chassis with string and wood purloined from a bedside table, smuggled out of the hotel in his trousers, to come 23rd overall.

However, the monstrous Panhards

The Darracq team for the 1903 Paris-Madrid race.

were not the outright winners. The first car home was the relatively small 5.5-litre Renault driven by Marcel Renault, while the main challenger, Count Zborowski had been held up at the Austrian border by an over-officious customs officer. Edge's Gordon Bennett-winning 40hp Napier came 15th overall.

The route control for the Paris-Vienna had been carefully organized, with flag-waving marshals positioned at every dangerous bend, but the lessons of that event were not applied to the great race of 1903, the Paris-Madrid, which was organized against a background of French Government disapproval. The dangers of racing on public highways were already evident, and the French Government had expressed its disapproval of the Paris-Madrid. However, the young King Alfonso XIII of Spain, a keen motorist, had enthusiastically given permission for the Spanish section of the event (which also included a touring class for normal road cars).

The Automobile Club de France decided to start the race at 3.30am on Sunday 24 May so that the maximum number of spectators could watch the competitors pass through France.

Because there were only weight limits, without restrictions on engine size, the designers of the racing cars went all-out for sheer power, fitting engines that were as large as possible in chassis often lightened to the point where they became dangerously flimsy. There were three classes: large cars weighing over 650kg (1433lb), light cars weighing 400–600kg (880–1433lb) and voiturettes of 250–400kg (550–880lb). The ACF received a huge number of entries, and eventually 170 cars and 53 motor cycles assembled at the start outside the Palace of Versailles, following scrutineering in the Tuileries Gardens in Paris. They were watched by a huge crowd of spectators who had arrived during the night on foot, on bicycles, in horse-drawn carriages and on motor cars.

The *Motor-Car Journal* was in ecstasy:

> Versailles has not known such a night since the King of France lived there. In all directions there were illuminations, as if the Great King had been coming back to take possession of his palace. All the shops were open, and the footpaths were impassable on account of the supper tables that had been installed everywhere.
>
> It is estimated that fully one hundred thousand visitors crowded around the starting place. The cars were lined up at the side of the road, numbers being hung on the trees to indicate to each competitor where he should take his place. It is said that 25,000 litres of petrol – equal to nearly 6000 gallons – was supplied by one firm alone.
>
> The Fifth Regiment of the Engineers lined up the road and kept order, and soon after daybreak began to colour the sky, two rockets announced that the competition had begun.

Charles Jarrott was first away in the Paris-Madrid with this De Dietrich racer.

First away was Charles Jarrott on his De Dietrich. 'It seemed impossible that my swaying, bounding car could miss the reckless spectators,' he recalled. 'A wedge-shaped space opened out in the crowd as I approached, and so fine was the calculation made that at times it seemed impossible for the car not to overtake the apex of the human triangle and deal death and destruction.

'I tried slowing down, but quickly realized that the danger was as great at 40 miles an hour as at 80. It merely meant that the crowd waited a longer time in the road; and the remembrance of those hundreds of cars behind me, the realization that the hunt had commenced, made me put on top speed, and hope that Providence would be kind to the weak intellects which allowed their possessors to run such risks so callously.'

Inevitably, there were dreadful accidents as the competitors hurtled between a 'double line of human hedges scarcely two metres apart' at up to 80mph (129km/h), leaving the route strewn with wrecked cars, 'some in ditches, some in fields, some mere tangled and smoking heaps of scrap iron'. Among the fatalities was car maker Louis Renault's brother Marcel, who left the road at speed and crashed into a ditch at Couhe-Verac, about halfway to Bordeaux, prompting the Renault company's temporary withdrawal from racing. Three-quarters of a century later I followed the route of the Paris-Madrid race and found the roadside memorial that marked the spot where Marcel Renault's car had overturned.

In 1913 a British owner acquired the sister car driven in the race by Louis Renault: 'It was beautifully made, the chief feature being its very high gear. It took a long time before top could be engaged, but if the speed of the car could be kept up, the engine would pull this high gear. During the Paris-Madrid race Marcel's car was timed to do a stretch of several kilometres near Chartres at over 90 miles per hour. It was a dangerous car because of the temptation not to slow down. One can understand Marcel Renault in the excitement of the race,

A rare survivor of the Paris-Madrid carnage is the little Motobloc of Mike Timms, which for many years was in the little-known Bonnal-Renaulac collection in Bordeaux.

Another survivor of Paris-Madrid, this Serpollet steam car is now in France's National Motor Museum (the former Schlumpf Collection).

having got his car going, refusing to lose its rhythm of speed and in consequence meeting his death.'

Charles Jarrott's racing mechanic Arthur Bray described the roadside carnage:

> We came upon car after car smashed and abandoned on the roadside. A De Dietrich lay upside down on a heap of stones with a Panhard on top of it. Again another De Dietrich upside down with, this time, a Napier on top of it.
>
> The most terrible sight of all, however, was the wreck of Lorraine Barrow's car. It was the most complete wreck ever known. When doing over 80 miles an hour he struck a dog. The body of the dog had jammed the steering and the car went end-on into a tree. One of the front dumb irons was driven up to the hilt into the tree. The leather strap holding the starting handle cut its way into the solid wood.
>
> The car, as a car, just did not exist. The motor was wrenched out of the frame and hurled yards away with the flywheel and crankshaft torn out of the engine. Even the pistons came adrift and were found nearly 20 yards farther on. The frame, gearbox and road wheels (from which the tyres had come off) were in fragments scattered round the grass verge.

Ironically, dining with other members of the De Dietrich team the previous night, Lorraine Barrow is reputed to have exclaimed, 'Cheer up, you chaps. Why so glum? Come, eat, drink and be merry for to-morrow we die!'

A second De Dietrich driver, Stead, had hit another competitor at 80mph (129km/h) and been crushed under his car, while Porter's Wolseley 'Beetle' had caught fire, killing the mechanic, when it hit a wall in swerving to avoid a closed level-crossing gate. Tourand had skidded his Brouhot into the crowd, trying to avoid a soldier chasing a child who had run out into the road, with the sad result that the child, the soldier and Tourand's mechanic had all been killed.

The first car to reach Bordeaux was Gabriel's streamlined Mors 'Dauphine', which had started eighth and carved its way through the field, averaging over 65 miles an hour. It would be difficult to match that time in a modern car on today's well-surfaced highways.

The unprecedented casualty level caused the French Government to halt the 'Race to Death' when the 99 surviving cars reached Bordeaux. They were ignominiously hauled to the railway station behind horses so they could do no more harm, and put on trains to be shipped back to Paris. It was the end of the age of the great city-to-city races.

Lamented Charles Jarrott, 'To my mind, it was a fitting end to an inevitable happening that the curtain should have been rung down on the Paris-Bordeaux road, the scene of many a Titanic struggle, and the road on which Levassor himself showed to the world at large, in the first great motor race in history, the vast and far-reaching possibilities of the motor-propelled vehicle.'

At least three Paris-Madrid racers survive today: a private French owner, M. Ville, has a de Dion-Bouton that has appeared on the Brighton Run; a Serpollet steam car is on show in the Mulhouse Museum; and in England Mike Timms owns one of the Bordeaux-built Motobloc racers.

At least one of the touring-class cars (which did make it all the way to Madrid) survives in England, too: a 24hp four-cylinder Darracq driven in 1903 by one Albert Arvengas as No 41 in the tourist class. It too is in the remarkable collection of Mike Timms, alongside the Motobloc.

Soon after the Paris-Madrid disasters, the Automobile Club of Great Britain and Ireland organized an event that many considered to be the best of the Gordon Bennett races. Permission for the race to take place was given via a special bill through Parliament, and the course was a figure-of-eight shape, centred on Athy and Carlow, in Ireland.

It was the first time that the Gordon Bennett race had attracted a worthwhile entry list, with Britain fielding Edge, Jarrott and Stocks on Napiers; France entering De Knyff and Henry Farman on Panhards, and Gabriel on a Mors; and America putting forward Winton and Owen on Wintons, and Mooers on a Peerless. Mercedes had built six 90hp racers especially for the event, but five of these were destroyed in a fire at the Cannstatt factory, forcing the Germans to borrow three 60hp touring cars. Since the 60hp Mercedes was superior to the 90, this was a fortunate disaster!

Jenatzy won the race at the wheel of Clarence Gray Dinsmore's Mercedes,

'Red Devil' Camille Jenatzy is congratulated for his victory with a borrowed 60hp Mercedes in the 1903 Gordon Bennett race.

ABOVE LEFT AND RIGHT: *Another competitor in the 1903 Gordon Bennett race was the Napier driven by Charles Jarrott. It crashed, and the unconscious Jarrott and his mechanic Bianchi were taken for dead, only to recover under sheets in a temporary morgue!*

and the massive trophy passed to Germany, who organized the 1904 Gordon Bennett race over a 79.5-mile course in the Taunus mountains. Teams were selected from the finest drivers and cars of Britain, Germany, France, Belgium and Italy, although the Swiss Dufaux did not start. The race was highly successful, with victory going to the Frenchman Léon Théry's Richard-Brasier at an average of 54.5mph (87.7km/h). His lap-times were almost unbelievably consistent: he covered three out of the four laps in 1 hour 26 minutes with only a few seconds' variation, and took just three minutes more to complete the longest lap.

However, the regulations of the Gordon Bennett Trophy, drawn up to ensure that no nation had the advantage of numbers over its rivals, were proving too restrictive, and the 1905 Gordon Bennett race, held over a course near Clermont-Ferrand in central France, would prove to be the last of the series.

Low-slung Winton Bullets representing America in the 1903 Gordon Bennett race.

This 11.1-litre four-cylinder 100hp Napier was the first British car to be built for the 1904 Gordon Bennett race. It was potentially the fastest British car, but crashed during practice and failed to qualify. It was selected for the 1905 Gordon Bennett team, but withdrawn in favour of the new 90hp Napier 'Samson'.

RIGHT: *Now owned by the Dutch National Motor Museum, the 100hp Napier car was shipped to Napier's American branch in 1906 and fitted with the strong front wheels still on the car for hillclimbing. Work was never completed, and it lay in a barn until it was rescued in 1950 by collector George Waterman.*

BELOW: *The 100hp Napier competed in the 1904 Circuit des Ardennes in Belgium, finishing ninth.*

ABOVE: The 1903 Spyker owned by the Dutch National Motor Museum was the first successful motor car powered by a six-cylinder engine, and the first petrol car with four-wheel-drive and front-wheel braking.

LEFT: Designed by 20-year-old Joseph-Valentin Laviolette, the 8.8-litre engine of the 1903 Spyker had six separate cylinders and was mounted in a pressed-steel chassis.

CHAPTER THIRTY

'The Car of Three Firsts'

The 1903 Spyker owned by the Dutch National Motor Museum is arguably one of the most significant cars in motoring history. Not only was it the first motor car to take the road powered by a six-cylinder engine, but it was also the first petrol car with four-wheel-drive and the first with front-wheel braking.

Despite the fact that the car combined three major technical firsts, the four-wheel-drive Spyker never attracted the acclaim it merited. If anyone outside its native Holland still remembers the Spyker marque, it is almost certainly because of the Spyker driven by the rambunctious Ambrose Claverhouse (Kenneth More) in the film *Genevieve* than for any of the firm's remarkable technical achievements.

'Nulla tenaci invia est via' ('No road is impassable to those who are persistent') ran the firm's Latin motto, but ironically it was a lack of persistence by the firm's guiding spirit, Jacobus 'Mr Ko' Spijker, which condemned the four-wheel-drive car – and ultimately the company – to obscurity.

Jacobus and his brother Hendrik-Jan had established a coachbuilding company in Hilversum in 1880, moving to Amsterdam six years later as their business grew. Their clients included the Dutch Royal Family, with the Golden Coach the brothers built in 1886 being used for the wedding of Queen Wilhelmina and Prince Hendrik in 1901.

Jacobus bought his first car – a German Benz– in 1898, and soon the brothers were offering an improved version of the German car under their own name (which means 'nail' in Dutch). With an eye on the export market, they wisely anglicized it to 'Spyker'. Early in 1900 the brothers unveiled the first true Spyker car, a 5hp twin, and put it into production in their magnificent new Trompenburg factory, on the outskirts of Amsterdam. However, sales of the new model never really took, off as the Dutch, perversely, seemed to prefer imported cars. The Spijker brothers decided to fight fire with fire by employing foreign engineers to design their cars, most notably the brilliant 20-year-old Walloon designer Joseph-Valentin Laviolette, who joined the company bearing designs for the world's first six-cylinder car engine.

Laviolette was the ideal foil for the mercurial Mr Ko, who came up with 'a new invention every day'. It was the gifted young Belgian who had to turn his boss's often eccentric ideas into reality.

When the Automobile Clubs of France and Spain announced that they were to hold a road race from Paris to Madrid in May 1903, Mr Ko devised a special car for the event, combining great power with a freedom from skidding. It was the ideal opportunity for Laviolette to make his dream of a six-cylinder engine come true. Only electric cars with hub motors had previously managed to drive on

In 1904 the six-cylinder Spyker came to England, at the time of the 1904 Crystal Palace exhibition. An awe-struck journalist taken up Anerley Hill found it 'more like an ascent in a lift than a run up on wheels'.

all four wheels, but Laviolette drew up plans for a novel transmission that drove all four wheels through fore-and-aft cardan shafts from a power take-off on the side of the gearbox, managing the difficult trick of making the front wheels of his car drive and steer at the same time by using spherical universal joints within the axle ends.

He also fitted a transmission brake on the forward shaft that braked the front wheels and added the final touch of modernity by specifying a pressed-steel chassis rather than the steel-reinforced wooden frame used on the firm's production cars.

Although the 4x4 Spyker appeared on the entry list for Paris-Madrid, to be driven by Emile Hautekeet (another of Spyker's Walloon engineers), however, it was not finished in time to start. Instead, it made its public debut at the Paris Salon in December 1903, where *Motor-Car Journal* called it 'the novelty of the display'. The four-wheel-drive Spyker came to England the following February, and was shown at the Crystal Palace Exhibition. An awe-struck journalist who was given a ride up nearby Anerley Hill wrote breathlessly that it was 'more like an ascent in a lift than a run up on wheels'.

Two four-cylinder production models – the 25/36hp and the 32/40hp – appeared late in 1904, but only sold in very small numbers, mostly to England. The 4x4 Spyker racer lapsed into obscurity as Mr Ko found new rainbows to chase: he was ousted from the bankrupt company when it was reorganized in 1908 after Hendrik-Jan had been drowned in a North Sea ferry wreck.

Ineptly rebuilt with a new radiator and bonnet and crude 'boy-racer' bodywork in the early 1920s, for demonstration runs to uphold Spyker's claims to having built the first six-cylinder car, the 4x4 racer was sold to a former director named Springer in 1926 after the company declared its final bankruptcy. It languished in various museums between 1953 and 1993, when it was acquired by the Dutch National Motor Museum at Raamsdonksveer, near Rotterdam. The museum's enthusiastic owner, Evert Louwman, supervised a five-year restoration of the Spyker by veteran expert Howard Wilson to the form in which it had astounded the British press at the Crystal Palace in 1904.

Ninety years later, the 4x4 Spyker returned to the site of its dramatic hillclimbing demonstration for a re-run of the breathtaking ascent.

CHAPTER THIRTY-ONE

The Not So Merry Oldsmobile

It had always been my ambition to drive a car in the Brighton Run, so when Paul Foulkes-Halbard offered to loan me a 1903 Curved-Dash Oldsmobile for the 1983 event, provided that I paid the entry fee, I grabbed the opportunity with both hands.

The Oldsmobile was a basic single-cylinder buggy that looked rather like a sleigh on wheels, with long fore-and-aft springs forming the basis of its chassis. It was America's first mass-produced automobile and, despite its glacial progress and rudimentary specification, had been one of the first cars reliable and sturdy enough to make the 3000-odd-mile journey from sea to shining sea in the days when America had no coast-to-coast road (nor, indeed, many roads at all in the mid-West). The little Oldsmobile was built by the thousand, and it paved the way for the legendary Model T Ford that came along a few years later to put the world on wheels.

The Oldsmobile that Paul Foulkes-Halbard was offering me had a current MoT certificate and, according to the man who had sold it to him, ran reliably. 'But,' he warned me, 'I make no guarantees – you'll have to take it as you find it!' With a borrowed trailer and towing vehicle, I collected the Olds from Paul's home in Crowborough and towed it home to Essex.

The little black car had an interesting history; it had apparently been owned by a missionary in the Australian outback and had steel-spoked wheels instead of the customary wood as a protection against white ants! At some stage, the original carburettor – a primitive 'mixer valve' of the most basic kind – had been replaced by a 1920s Smith multi-jet carburettor, ostensibly in the interests of reliability. Although Paul had the original unit on a shelf, I thought there was no need to take it home with me. After all, the previous owner said he had made many successful Brighton Runs, and surely a more modern carburettor would give more flexible running. How wrong I was!

Having got the Oldsmobile home, I checked it over and ensured that fuel was getting through to the carburettor and that the ignition system – which used the crudest kind of wipe contact imaginable – provided a fierce spark at the plug. All I had to do, it seems, was to crank it over and it would start. Starting an Oldsmobile has much in common with winding up a horn gramophone; a handle is inserted into a hole in the side of the boxy body and turned furiously. Olds claimed that the car could be started from the seat, in an act requiring only a minimum of contortion and involving only the slightest risk of a broken arm. I played it safe and cranked from the side. And cranked. And cranked....

There was not a whisper of an explosion, so I decided to try tougher measures. I hooked the Olds up to the back of my Cortina and my wife towed me up the road as I gently let in top gear (there are only two) in the hope of

The illustration for this advertisement for the Oldsmobile echoes the words of the popular song of the day, 'Come away with me Lucille, in my Merry Oldsmobile'.

ABOVE AND LEFT: *The Curved-Dash Oldsmobile safely away to Brighton. After 'our' run, it was restored and sold to an American who had been a child movie actor. Many Brighton Runs later, he died and eventually the Oldsmobile came back into the ownership of the Foulkes-Halbard family.*

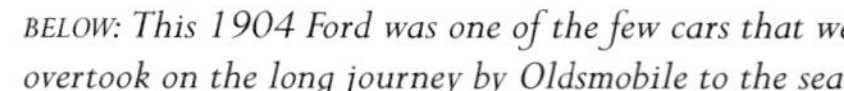

BELOW: *This 1904 Ford was one of the few cars that we overtook on the long journey by Oldsmobile to the sea!*

Brooklands racing driver Vernon Balls discovered this 1902 Oldsmobile derelict in a field in the 1930s and drove it on many Brighton Runs, his passenger ringing its floor-mounted warning bell with a golf club. Originally used for many years by a doctor and later by his wife for shopping, it had a bantam nesting in the accumulator box and sparrows nesting in the hood when found!

bump-starting the car. Some hope. We towed that car for miles and it failed to fire once. I took the carburettor apart and reassembled it. Still no joy.

Since this was now the day before the Brighton Run, I needed help, so I rang Paul and said I was on my way with the Oldsmobile on the trailer. A couple of hours later we were in Crowborough and, despite the fact that final preparation of Paul's Brighton Run entries was in full swing, willing hands helped remove the carburettor and fit the original mixer valve, which basically dribbled petrol into the inlet manifold through an adjustable needle valve.

Amazingly, the engine started at once, and we left it running for a while to show that it was no fluke before heading back home for a brief night's sleep.

The next morning came the 5.30am departure for Hyde Park, where the car was decanted from the trailer, started readily and was driven round to the assembly area for signing on. With my wife Christine as passenger, I set off on the road to Brighton, with the car running steadily at first, although showing a lamentable tendency to slip out of top gear. Since the Oldsmobile had a planetary transmission in which top gear was engaged by a cone clutch, that meant holding the stubby gear lever, which was under my right elbow, in place while steering with my left hand (and full right lock on the tiller-steered Oldsmobile almost meant handing the tiller to the passenger!).

There had been no time to check the water level before leaving home, nor had there been the opportunity at Hyde Park. So I turned into the first filling station we came to that had a sloping exit, down which I could bump-start the car, and asked if they had a receptacle that I could use to fill the Oldsmobile's water tank. 'There are some plastic containers at the side of the garage,' replied the attendant. He failed to mention that the containers had held the concentrated liquid used in the car wash, so, on filling with water, bubbles erupted furiously like some alien life form. It must have done wonders for the inside of the Olds' cooling system.

The first serious hill on the Brighton Road is Brixton, and here the Olds began to lose power. Jumping out to lighten the load, my wife slipped awkwardly, and retired to the towing vehicle, which in those days was allowed to follow in the wake of the veteran. My son Paul, then aged 18, took her place as passenger. The gradual loss of power meant that he had to jump out to lighten ship on every hill (low gear) and push on most hills (bottom gear), while on the worst hills, I had to jump out too (emergency gear) and walk alongside steering and holding bottom gear in place.

We made up for this by putting the Olds in neutral on downgrades and coasting flat out (terrifying!), particularly on

Handcross and Bolney hills, which graphically revealed the shortcomings of tiller steering.

At one point, we were chuntering away happily in the middle lane of a dual carriageway somewhere in the Gatwick area (the inner lane was being used by rubbernecking moderns), when a white van with its rear doors tied together with string began to accelerate past on my nearside. Suddenly the string parted and a large washing machine fell out on to the road, apparently to the detriment of the car behind. As we were running somewhat late, we decided it was definitely time to apply a Nelsonian blind eye to the chaos on the inside lane.

All afternoon we thrashed and cajoled the Oldsmobile down the A23, my foot flat down on the 'speeder' pedal, watching with alarm as the hands on my wristwatch began to approach the 4pm deadline. At that time the official finish was at the Pylons, the two Art Deco monoliths that mark the northern boundary of Brighton. Over the top of Pyecombe Hill at 3.50 we chugged and coasted furiously down towards the Pylons. As we passed the timekeeper, the petrol pipe broke and the Oldsmobile rolled to a halt in the next lay-by, awaiting the arrival of our trailer vehicle.

That year they had to post our finisher's medal on to us!

As a postscript, when we returned the Oldsmobile to Paul Foulkes-Halbard, he stripped it down to rebuild it for sale. A few days later he rang me. 'I have no idea how you got that Olds to Brighton,' he chuckled. 'Both valves are completely worn out, with large chunks missing off their edges. By rights, the engine shouldn't have run at all.'

This Anglo-American team face the slow ride to Brighton in their Oldsmobile with equanimity...

CHAPTER THIRTY-TWO

Leakily to Brighton

For years I had nurtured the ambition that one day I would own a Brighton Runner but, with the pressures of raising a family and restoring a Victorian house, somehow the opportunity seemed to have passed me by. That is, until the day in 1989 when I had a phone call at work – I was then Manager of the Ford Corporate History Office – from my friend John Bonnett, owner of a unique and lofty 1918 Model T Ford Landaulette. 'I know you're looking for a Brighton car,' he said. 'Well, there's one being advertised on the staff notice board at Dunton.'

John Bonnett had just been down to a meeting in the Ford Development and Engineering Centre, where he had seen the ad offering an unrestored De Dion-Bouton, date not guaranteed, for sale. I rang the internal number given and made an appointment to see the car, which was in a large garage with a number of vintage cars and a veteran Panhard two-seater.

It seemed that the vendor had bought the Panhard at an estate sale and had had to take the De Dion as well to secure the car he wanted. The De Dion looked pretty complete, although the central portion of the body and some of the engine accessories were missing; instead of coach bolts, its wings were held in place with the sort of cheap crosshead bolts used to assemble plastic carports; and it had been crudely painted a disgusting shade of mauve, but it looked restorable and I agreed to buy it for the asking price.

Having done my homework before I went to look at the car, I knew that it was a 1903 6hp 'Populaire' model from various distinctive features, but it was only when I got it home and began to clean it that I realized how basically original it was beneath the horrible paint scheme. Our local mechanical guru, a gifted self-taught engineer named Colvin Gunn, came to inspect the little car. He took hold of its starting handle, turned the engine over compression a couple of times and declared, 'That will run!'

He was right, too! My spares box produced a vintage Cox Atmos adjustable jet carburettor that was the right size for the De Dion's long induction manifold, while a splendid chap named Reg Whapham, who restored early cars near Gatwick Airport, provided a brand-new ignition system literally off the shelf. Friends provided a drip-feed lubricator and a petrol tank of the right size and vintage.

Once I had all these auxiliaries in place and had linked up the complex cooling system, I jacked the rear axle – the famous 'De Dion' suspension – on to axle stands, fitted up a petrol pipe, and began

Beneath its horrid paint scheme, the little De Dion was basically original; it had once belonged to a one-legged enthusiast named Slater.

cranking. The engine fired a few times, and then caught and ran, probably for the first time in half a century – and kept on running strongly.

Old shelves and cupboards ousted in the restoration of our Victorian house provided floorboards and panels to restore the missing centre section of the De Dion's bodywork. We used as a model the near-identical sister car at the National Motor Museum, which has been in the Montagu family since it was taken in part payment for a bad debt almost 100 years ago. Interestingly, even though the engine numbers of my De Dion and the Beaulieu car indicate that they were built only four months or so apart, many small but noticeable mechanical differences reveal the pace of development at the time. Clearly, the design was changing by the week as detail improvements were made to what was then the world's most popular car.

Although it was missing carburettor and ignition system, the engine of the De Dion was judged capable of running.

Work in progress: new centre-section woodwork was made from scrap furniture of a similar vintage to the De Dion.

Once my car had proved that it was capable of running, it was entered for that year's Brighton Run. With a target date for the restoration, I was obliged to get up at 5am each morning and spend a couple of hours working in the garage before changing to go to the office. The theory was that the first Brighton Run would be a 'dummy run' to find out the faults, which could then be rectified for the following year. If the car finished, it would be a definite bonus!

Missing parts, such as the brass hubcaps, were copied from other cars; an amazing timewarp ironmonger's shop in Walthamstow provided period pattern brass screws and nuts; while a metal stockist a few doors away provided the right sort of brass angles and beadings. The missing floor panels and sides were small in size but took a lot of cutting and shaping until they looked right; a broken dressing table that had been used as a workbench by the previous owner of our house yielded a nicely weathered mahogany panel that made a handsome toeboard.

Of course, it all took time, but gradually the car came together. The seat was still away being upholstered when the newly painted car went back on its wheels, so I made the first test runs up and down the drive sitting on planks.

Inevitably, the rebuild became a close-run thing; I had booked an MoT test for the day before the Brighton Run, but the first serious test run for the De Dion was the ten-mile drive to the MoT station, from which we were also hiring a 'piggy-back' Transit transporter. Fortunately, the car got there without a hint of trouble, passed its MoT and was loaded aboard the transporter. On the way home I licensed the De Dion, and did not touch it again until very early the following morning, when we unloaded it near Hyde Park Corner.

I had decided to make the run solo in case the weight of a passenger would slow down the car or overload the untried mechanism, but everything seemed to be working correctly – until I felt the vibrations from the single-cylinder engine increase as the car passed the M23 junction at Hooley. (At the same spot, more or less, where the pyromaniac Stanley had burst into flames a few years earlier.) Had I run a bearing? I brought the car to a standstill and lifted its crocodile bonnet, to see the whole cylinder gently moving up and down. The four locating nuts at its base had all loosened off slightly with the constant vibration, so I just tightened them up with a spanner, pausing to wave at my friend John Darlow as he passed in his 1904 Ford Model C, with the amiable Derek Barron, Chairman of Ford-Britain, as passenger. Nothing else seemed to have come loose, so I closed the bonnet and carried on. There is always something quirky to deal with on veteran cars.

A few miles further on, on the steep climb out of Redhill, the De Dion began to falter. Willing bystanders stepped off the pavement and started to push but, as in the film, they dropped out one by one until, as the car breasted the rise, there was just one weary stalwart left, who grinned weakly after me as the De Dion puttered away.

I stopped on the downslope to tighten the ingenious expanding clutches that engage the De Dion's two constant mesh gear ratios. (This is done simply by raising a spring-loaded drawbolt on the hub of the transmission brake drum on the front of the car's transaxle unit and turning a single nut to expand or contract the clutches.) And that, really, was it. It was not a particularly fast run, but it was steady. The car just kept plugging steadily on with me keeping an eye on the drip-feed lubricator that feeds Castrol GP50 to the engine, which runs on an incredibly small amount of oil, and also tops up the transaxle. If the engine is being over-oiled, the surplus is thrown out of the front main bearing, leaving a tell-tale trace on the sidewall of the offside front tyre.

The first test runs were made while the seat was still away being upholstered.

The De Dion ready for its first Brighton Run, November 1990.

Six and a half hours after leaving Hyde Park, the De Dion rolled over the finishing line to earn its first finisher's medal, 'for punctual arrival at Brighton', which is the only reward for sixty of the most gruelling miles in the motoring calendar. That distance in modern traffic for a centenarian motor car is akin to many hundreds for a twenty-first-century motor. It provides a considerable test of components designed for a traffic density of about one car per thousand horses; incidentally, there were around 8 million of the creatures in Edwardian England, producing between them some 52 million tons of exhaust pollution – maybe car-exhaust emissions are not nearly as bad as the 'greens' would have us believe!).

The Brighton Run seeks out the many mysterious ailments to which antique machinery is prone, and, just as the ancients used to mark the passage of time by the occurrence of natural disasters such as flood, fire and famine, so the

A successful arrival at Brighton after a (relatively) trouble-free run.

Burgess-Wise household remembers its Brighton Runs by the mechanical excitements that befall its De Dion-Bouton.

We recall them all: the year that an emergency halt ripped the linings off the brakes; the year that the gravity fuel feed was beset by theoretically impossible air locks; the year of the broken throttle linkage that brought the car to an untimely halt at the top of Brixton Hill; the year of the lost ball-bearings on the road into Burgess Hill; the year of the spectacular water leaks; and the year of the wooden splint....

The water leaks came in 1997, a year in which I had invited David Holland, companion on a number of memorable motoring adventures, to make his Brighton Run debut. I should explain that the cooling system of the De Dion-Bouton reveals a certain Gallic insouciance towards the laws of thermodynamics on the part of its designer, the diminutive Georges-Thadée Bouton. Even though elementary school physics tell us that hot water rises, M. Bouton placed the heavily finned serpentine radiator of his Populaire at the lowest point of the cooling system. To defy the tendency of hot water to rise, the radiator is force-fed from the 2-gallon brass header tank by a powerful pump spring-driven from the timing chest of the 700cc single-cylinder engine, whose vibration sends the radiator into a real dither at tickover speeds.

However, until the centennial year of 1996, when unscheduled roadworks on Brixton Hill caused the biggest veteran traffic jam in history, the water system had not leaked a drop since I had rebuilt the little car in 1989. The congestion on the 1996 run, however, caused it uncharacteristically to boil. I had run out of spare water (many veterans carry a gallon or two in their lockers) and needed a refill by the time we topped Redhill. Looking around, I noticed that one of the roadside houses was obviously holding a Brighton Run drinks party, so I walked up the path, knocked at the door and asked if they had a watering can I could borrow to fill the water tank.

'I've been watching the Brighton Run for years, and you're the first person who's ever asked for water!' said the householder. 'Have as much water as you like!'

By then, however, the congestion had worked its mischief and, when I got home, I discovered a tiny weep from one side of the radiator. This became more noticeable on the De Dion's summer outing to a friend's house in Suffolk, and got worse every time I started the engine after that. Duly repaired by a local mechanic and pressure-tested, the leak seemed cured, although I still put some anti-leak compound in the system as belt and braces.

On the 1997 Brighton Run, the De Dion proved absolutely trouble-free in the initial stages. We lost nothing but a brass thumbscrew through vibration in the heavy London traffic and climbed both Brixton Hill and Redhill two up, which is no mean feat for a 6hp veteran with only two speeds to its transmission. However, when we arrived at the halfway stage at Crawley after a glorious (but bitterly cold) run, the indefatigable commentator Graham Robson announced that we had sprung a spectacular water leak. It took three gallons to refill the system.

We restocked with anti-leak compound, which seemed to cure the radiator of its incontinence, but as we picked up speed towards our cruising speed of 18mph or so, I could see water continuously jetting from the edge of the radiator, forced out by the pressure of that potent little pump. However, apart from needing a little light Land-Rover assistance to restart the engine, after it stalled on a long slow gradient, the car ran perfectly. It even climbed the dreaded Jack and Jill Hill at Clayton – the last hurdle before the long run down to the sea – unaided and two up, although by then we were doing about one mile to the gallon of water.

We tipped our last couple of gallons into the tank for the run down into Brighton, and might even have had some left at the end, had it not been for the long hold-up caused by a policewoman at the entrance to the finishing straight on Madeira Drive, giving priority to modern traffic. We crossed the line in a cloud of steam: the radiator was bone dry, but the engine kept on running, a remarkable tribute to the merits of a cast-iron piston in a cast-iron cylinder, kept well lubricated by a total-loss system that uses about a pint and a half of oil between London and Brighton.

Those proprietary anti-leak jollops for which so much is claimed! We tried them all and the little De Dion defeated the lot.

The modern miracle workers at P & A

Wood of Great Easton, better known for their award-winning restorations of Rolls-Royce and Bentley cars, had the radiator rebuilt by a man who normally rebuilds aircraft radiators. This will hopefully have cured that particular problem for the next century at least.

Two years later, the leaks were all forgotten; that was the Year of the Wooden Splint. The car had been running exceptionally well when we pulled in to give it a check-over and top-up at the marshalling point at Cuckfield Golf Club, at the top of a long and challenging upgrade (which goes practically unnoticed in a modern car). As I lifted the bonnet to check the water level, I happened to glance down at the offside front dumb iron, a stout casting which, unusually, is T-shaped in cross section. Horrified, I saw that it was beginning to resemble an over-ripe banana, as the upright section of the T had developed an alarming split, presumably the opening-up of a long-ago collision scar.

But the car was going well and we were so close to Brighton – we only had to cross the South Downs and, if push came to shove (literally), it was downhill from then on and we could walk the little car to the signing-off control.

I sent my resourceful son-in-law on a scavenging mission to find a suitable block of wood, and he quickly returned with a short piece of firewood from the Golf Club's store. I wired it into place between the dumb iron and spring (soft iron wire is another indispensable item in the veteran tool kit) and, fingers mentally crossed, set off cautiously for Brighton.

Believe me, I watched that dumb iron out of the corner of my eye all the way to Madeira Drive, but the timber chock never moved, although it did restrict the steering lock a bit. When we limped over the finishing line, it was obviously one of the year's better get-you-there stories, for artist Basil Smith immortalized it for the following year's Brighton Run programme!

The dumb iron fractured two-thirds of the way to Brighton in 1999; the temporary repair held all the way to the finish!

With the block of wood still in place, the De Dion reaches Madeira Drive in plenty of time for a finisher's medal.

CHAPTER THIRTY-THREE

The Man on the Stanley Steamer

Fact is so often stranger than fiction, and the story of the Stanley Steamer is certainly a bizarre one. Twin Yankee brothers with a penchant for making violins saw a horseless carriage, decided they could do better (and did), were persuaded to put it into production, sold the business for a quarter of a million dollars and used the money to start making steam cars all over again....

In the 1890s Francis Stanley* and his twin brother Freelan had founded a photographic dry plate business in Lewiston, Maine, which they ultimately sold to George Eastman of Kodak for a handsome profit. They learnt about automobile building from other experimenters, notably George Whitney of Boston, Massachusetts. In 1897 the first of the legendary Stanley Steamers took to the road, built by cycling enthusiast Francis Stanley, with the aid of men hired from Whitney's shop, so that his 14-stone wife Augusta – who kept falling off her bicycle – could ride with him in safety.

Unhampered by prior knowledge of steam engines and steam engineering, the ingenious Stanleys developed a boiler that could withstand extremely high pressures – they worked at 200 to 300lb/sq in, when conventional practice said that 150lb/sq in was excessive – by strengthening the boiler shell with a wound-on 'jacket' of many yards of piano wire.

Francis and Freelan built more steam carriages in 1898, and soon had orders for nearly 200 cars. They sold their automobile business to asphalt tycoon Amzi Lorenzo Barber for $250,000 in 1899, only to return to car manufacture in 1901 with an improved design. In 1903 George Eastman, worried by the competition from the Stanley Dry Plate Company, bought the brothers' photographic business for a rumoured $800,000. The Stanleys converted the old dry-plate factory into an automobile factory, and immediately almost doubled production, from 300 to 550 cars a year. In 1906 a racing Stanley established a land-speed record of 127.659mph, but that was virtually the high point for the marque, which, after reaching an annual output of 775 cars, in 1908, faded away in the mid-1920s. They had built a total of some 5200 cars.

When I first rode on a 1920s Stanley I had been impressed by its silent progress – the only sound audible as it ran around a grassy meadow was the gentle creaking of its wood-spoked wheels. I jumped at Paul Foulkes-Halbard's offer to lend me a Stanley Steamer for the 1985 Brighton Run. It was the usual type of Stanley Runabout, a model built until 1905, which had its boiler directly below the driver and a fold-out front seat that doubled as a luggage locker when it was closed. It was powered by an underfloor twin-cylinder 8/10hp engine mounted in unit with the rear axle, which it drove through bevel gearing. There was no clutch, since with steam when the supply was cut off the engine stopped. It was, I was told, as effective as a normal brake.

The Stanley brothers learned useful lessons from studying the Whitney steamer; this surviving example dates from 1896.

Driving a steam car is unlike driving any kind of petrol vehicle, and so Paul Foulkes-Halbard's friend Peter Watford came along to instruct me in the mysteries of external combustion.

The first step, once the car was unloaded from the transporter, was to light the boiler, which was fired by a ring of jets fuelled by volatile SBP1 spirit fed under air pressure from a tank. A fascinated crowd gathered round to watch the lighting-up ceremony. Peter hauled a big gas torch and its squat red cylinder from the transporter, turned on the fuel supply to the boiler and lit the torch, which he thrust underneath the car. The burner jets caught with a subdued 'wumph!' and I noticed signs of unease among the inner ring of spectators. Then the fun really started, for, as the burner warmed up, it began to emit otherworldly howling sounds that grew in intensity to a banshee wail. The crowd melted away like summer snow....

Asphalt tycoon Amzi Lorenzo Barber bought the original Stanley design for $250,000 and built it as the Locomobile. He split with his partner but kept the company. Rudyard Kipling described his unpredictable Locomobile as a 'wicker-willow lunch basket with a boiler seated on four little paper clips'.

Barber's partner John Brisben Walker built a very similar steam car under the name 'Mobile'; it was celebrated in the song 'My Mobile Gal' from the musical The Belle of Bohemia.

This 1903 7hp Stanley Runabout is typical of the early-pattern Stanleys, with the boiler beneath the driver and a fold-out front seat.

Driving a borrowed veteran is a case of learning on the job. I had had no chance to sample the Stanley beforehand, so the learning curve was rather steep! In fact, the controls were quite simple. Steering was by a curved nickel-plated tiller, slightly offset from the centre-line of the car so that the driver did not have to stretch quite so far across the passenger when turning right. The speed was controlled by a little throttle lever on the right-hand edge of the seat. Legend had it that the speed of the Stanley was so great that any driver who dared to hold the throttle fully open would be given a new car by the factory. It was, of course, untrue, but it is a fact that a runabout similar to Foulkes-Halbard's had been driven by Francis Stanley in a speed contest on the eight-mile 1 in 8 Auto Road, to the summit of the 6288-ft Mount Washington, New Hampshire, the 'most dangerous small mountain in the world', in a time of 28.19 minutes. The Stanley was beaten only by a 60hp Mercedes, which made the climb in 24.35 minutes. The following year, a stock Runabout had made the climb in an amazing 22.17 minutes; only a 60hp Napier was faster, at 20.58 minutes.

I was happy to treat the throttle lever with some caution, for it was immediately apparent that the Stanley possessed a far greater degree of acceleration than veteran petrol cars, and the effect of the brakes appeared to be minimal.

'The secret,' Peter told me, 'is to husband your steam. Always keep something in reserve, particularly on hills, where you should start fairly slow and accelerate as you near the top. And keep an eye on the boiler gauge.'

The great thing about steam engines is that they develop maximum torque from rest, so that acceleration is seamless, something I really appreciated on the hills. It all seemed effortless but, as we passed the M23 junction south of Hooley, I noticed jets of flame shooting up between my knees. Fortunately, I was wearing leather riding boots, so at least my trousers were protected from catching fire! I hurriedly coasted to the side of the road and emptied one of the two fire extinguishers I had put on the car into the blaze that had broken out beneath the seat. It seemed that, as we passed the end of the motorway slip road, a strong cross-draught had been diverted up the horizontal flue that exhausted at the rear of the Stanley by the back number plate and extinguished the burner jets. These had simply continued to emit atomized fuel, which had been ignited when the pilot light had flared up.

When my wife arrived with our support vehicle and saw the grey powder that lay across the road from the extinguisher, she asked whether that was it and

Up from the ashes... this was the aftermath of our first fire with the Stanley!

were we going to load the Stanley on to the transporter.

'No,' I replied. 'We're going to carry on.'

Cautiously, we set off again, conscious that it was fairly urgent to top up the water in the boiler. The Stanley had no condenser to turn exhausted steam back into water and return it to the boiler, therefore the water needed replenishing every twenty-five miles or so. At Horley a big service station conveniently occupied the centre of a major roundabout, and I coasted in to use their water supply. Just as the Stanley passed between the rows of petrol pumps, there was a 'whoosh!', and the flames were licking at my knees again. I had visions of the whole service station going up in flames, but fortunately we managed to empty the second fire extinguisher on the fire before any real disaster ensued. We quietly refilled the water tank and set off again.

That was the last pyromaniac emergency, and the Stanley behaved itself for the rest of the way into Brighton. We arrived about 1.30; it had been the fastest Brighton Run I have ever driven and, as we crossed the finishing line on Madeira Drive, I could not resist sampling that effortless acceleration again.

But I did not open the throttle wide; I did not need a new Stanley that much....

The satisfactory conclusion of a run that was sometimes too warm for comfort!

One last burst of acceleration before the paddock! Sadly, the Stanley, although identical to 1904 models, was later confirmed as having been built in 1905 and was therefore ineligible for the Brighton Run.

CHAPTER THIRTY-FOUR

As She Is Spoke...

Driving veteran cars is an art in itself, but imagine the plight of the hapless owner who, having just taken delivery of his new De Dion-Bouton around 1902, finds himself having to make sense of the instructions that come with it. Clearly, they have been translated into English from a dictionary by a Frenchman whose grasp of the language of *Les Rosbifs* is less than adequate.

'HURL THE MOVER TILL HIS STARTING'

When you received it, put some water in the tank of water which is placed under the capot, see if there is some oil in the mover; put in it one measure with the graisseur of the pump which is fixed at the plank before the capot, inhale with the pump one measure of oil and drive back while you move the pump round with the arrow on mover. See essence, tank under the coachman's box, open the cock.

For Making the Mover Walking.

1° Lean on the pointeau of the carburateur, till the essence unbordes.

2° Put the first manette (Advance of the lighter) close to the tube of direction, that is to say at the left of the lathe.

3° Put the second manette (Admittance of air) completely at the right, that is to say, the contrary of the advance to the lighter.

4° Push thoroughly the handle on, and hurl the mover till his starting.

5° Increase the advance to the lighter with an eighth of lathe forward at the right; then, take sensibly back at left backward the second manette, with a fifth of lathe; just at this moment, the mover must goes regurlarly with 1,500 lathes; for making it slacken without touching the 2 first manettes, put the big manette of the moderator at the last but one notch going at left.

For Making the Carriage Walking at the First Speed.

1° Take back the drag of the wheel backward, crow-bar of the right.

2° Lean on the pedal, so that the mover turns slowly round and take back the big manette of the moderator, at the right.

3° Raise up the pedal with ¾ and take completely and progressively back the crow-bar of embrayage to you, while you keep the direction with your right hand and the crow-bar with the left hand.

For Getting from the First Speed to the Second One.

The carriage beeing drawing along at a superior speed of 10 kilometers, for taking the second speed, push rapidly the crow-bar forward without brutality and take care that the pedal must be raised up again after the embrayage of the first speed which changes between 18 and 45 kilometers, according to the speed of the mover. The mover must be regulated from the pedal of the moderator. When the mover is engaged thoroughly, it turns round slowly: when it is raised up again, it gaves all his strength.

For Making the Carriage Slacken and Making Stopping.

When you are embrayé with the second speed with the advance to the lighter completely at right, and admittance of air completely at left, you must go at 50 kilometres in a hour. For slacken at 15 kilometres in a hour, engage the pedal almost thoroughly without making drag and take the manette of advance of the lighter at half pace.

For making the carriage completely stopped, when it goes at 15 kilometres in a hour, take abruptly the crow-bar of embrayage back in the middle and tighten thoroughly the pedal and so, you must stop in 5 yards.

When you are in first speed push the crow-bar forward at the debrayage and make drag with the pedal.

For Going Backward.

When you are at the thoroughly debrayage push the pedal of backward step with your right wheel and push completely forward the crow-bar of embrayage. For the backward step, take back the crow-bar in little speed and in debrayage if you will stopped.

OPPOSITE: The Comte de Dion at the wheel of a 1902 Populaire, accompanied by his faithful Abyssinian chauffeur Zélélé.

RIGHT: It would take more than an instruction manual to teach these veteran dogs to drive!

London to Brighton Album

ABOVE: An 1899 Peugeot Phaeton (left) and Benz leaving Hyde Park at the start of the 2004 Run. The Benz was in regular use by its original owner until 1907, touring England in connection with geological research.
RIGHT: The crew of this 1901 6_hp Gladiator look cheerful enough, despite the heavy rain that fell on the latter part of the 2005 Brighton Run.

ABOVE: The bar holding the acetylene headlamp has to be swung away in order for this 1903 Panhard & Levassor Detachable Limousine to be crankstarted.

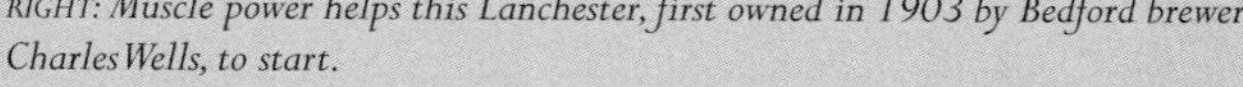

RIGHT: Muscle power helps this Lanchester, first owned in 1903 by Bedford brewer Charles Wells, to start.

Part of the 'Brighton Early' collection from Sussex, this 24hp Model JJ Darracq is a rear-entrance tonneau dating from 1903.

This stately 1897 Delahaye Limousine, one of the earliest cars with enclosed passenger accommodation, is powered by a 6hp twin-cylinder engine.

E: This 1901 Renault Model E is identical to the car that the voiturette class of the 1901 Paris-Bordeaux Race.

T: Originally built for a Belgian Count, the Ward Collection's l 12 hp Gardner-Serpollet Berline de Voyage was once owned nerican collector Cameron Peck.

CHAPTER THIRTY-FIVE

Hooray, Henry!

I have a very soft spot for the earliest Ford cars for I learned much about them from a very good friend, the late Herman Smith, who for many years had been historical consultant to Ford of Canada. Herm had owned the oldest-known Canadian-built Ford, a 1904 Model C built at Ford's first out-of-the-USA plant, at Walkerville, Ontario. (In fact, the two sites, although in different countries, are just a short distance apart, across the Detroit River, since Detroit lies right on the border with Canada.) We had seen Herm's Model C when we visited him and his wife Evelyn at their home in Oakville, Ontario, although by that time he had donated it to the National Museum of Science and Technology in Toronto to ensure its continued preservation for all time.

At the time I was running Ford's European Corporate History Office for that public-relations genius the late Walter Hayes, but a decade earlier, in 1976, I had first ridden in the Brighton Run, aboard a 1904 Canadian-built Model C Ford – like Herm's car, one of just 117 Fords built at Walkerville in 1904 – owned by John Denton. It was one of two veteran Canadian Fords imported into Britain by Ford Motor Company in the 1920s and had been owned for many years by the Bedfordshire Autocar Company, an old-established Ford dealership.

It was a very wet Brighton that year, and I remember the awful discovery that the steady rain had filled the deep buttoning of the Ford's rear cushion with water so that I was sitting on a network of little puddles. It was the first (but not the last) Brighton Run at which I had to change every stitch of clothing on arrival at Madeira Drive.

The Model C passed not long after to a Ford enthusiast named John Darlow and is still a regular participant in the Brighton Run; in a nice historical conjunction, John Darlow also acquired the other Canadian-built Model C brought into Britain in the 1920s by one-time Ford-Britain boss H.S. Jenkins, which stood for many years in the show-rooms of Manchester Garages. The two often make the run together, and for many years one or the other has regularly carried the chief executive of Ford of Britain as passenger.

My first Brighton Run as a passenger was in 1976, aboard a Canadian-built Ford Model C. I got so wet in the latter stages that I had to change every stitch of clothing on arriving at Brighton.

For many years, these two 1904 cars were the oldest Fords in Britain, and the earlier Model A (launched in 1903) was seen only as an infrequent visitor from the USA to the Brighton Run. In my Ford days, we took advantage of those rare visits to photograph the Model As in colour for the Ford photo library – on one occasion, I took the part of a pioneer automobilist, dressed in a hired 1903 motoring outfit. Gradually, however, Model A Fords began to find their way across the Atlantic. In 2001, a real gem surfaced. It was the world's oldest production Ford, sold on the company's first day of trading, and it had amazingly been on loan to Ford of Germany for several years without their realizing its great historical significance.

Henry Ford was no stranger to car manufacture when he and a small group of investors founded the Ford Motor Company in Detroit on Tuesday 16 June 1903. He had already had the Detroit Automobile Company fold under him, after producing a handful of cars, and in 1902 had walked out on the Henry Ford Company as it prepared to go into production to work on his '999' and 'Arrow' racing cars. Frustrated by the attitude of his backers, the mercurial Ford had complained, 'I can't make cents at manufacturing while I can make dollars at racing.'

The directors did not seem too bothered at his departure; they simply hired in the elderly but well-respected engineer Henry Leland – 'the Master of Precision' – and renamed the company 'Cadillac' after the French adventurer who had founded the city of Detroit; it seems they did rather well in Ford's absence....

Henry Ford had not given up his dream of car manufacture, and in the summer of 1902 he went into partnership with a successful Detroit coal merchant named Alexander Malcomson – a rough diamond, by all accounts – and began planning a third venture into production.

Alex Malcomson was a go-getting Scottish hustler, impatient to make his fortune and ready to diversify into ventures that promised financial reward. Ford's vision of mass-market motoring seemed an ideal avenue for investment, although Malcomson also realized that Ford's tendency to keep tinkering with his designs, never quite readying them for production, had to be kept under control. In October 1902 he laid down the law: 'Our salvation for next season will be getting the machine out quickly and getting it on the market early.'

The basic idea was simple enough: it involved building a prototype that would attract investment to establish a company that assembled cars from bought-in parts. Little outlay on plant or machinery would be called for, since all the skilled work would be done by the suppliers, who could be screwed down on price.

Ford's little workforce had a prototype engine running by Thanksgiving and a crude angle-iron chassis was assembled by Christmas. On 28 February a contract was signed with the rumbustious Dodge Brothers, who were among the largest suppliers of components to Detroit's infant automobile industry. They agreed to manufacture the chassis and running gear for the new Ford car for $250 per unit, with an initial order for 650 chassis to be delivered at the rate of ten a day from the beginning of July.

Contracts for wheels, tyres and bodies followed. Wilson, the body suppliers, also made the bodies for the rival Cadillac marque, and the two were apparently so similar that a Ford body would fit a Cadillac chassis, and vice versa. However, all the eloquence of Malcomson and his meticulous bookkeeper James Couzens – the industry's first and most diligent bean-counter – could not persuade many people to invest in the proposed Ford

The 1904 Ford reaches the Crawley staging point during the 2004 Brighton Run.

In November 1973 I played the role of veteran motorist for a Ford Times feature when this Model A Ford came over from America.

Henry Ford's principal associates when he established the Ford Motor Company in June 1903 were John Gray (left), Alex Malcomson (centre), and James Couzens.

Henry Ford's early workforce, in a photograph probably taken around the end of 1904, as components for the first four-cylinder Ford, the Model B, are being worked on.

One of the earliest American Ford dealerships in 1904, proudly promoting Henry's 1904 land-speed record of 91mph (146km/h), and offering to buy '2nd hand automobiles', and to grind skates...

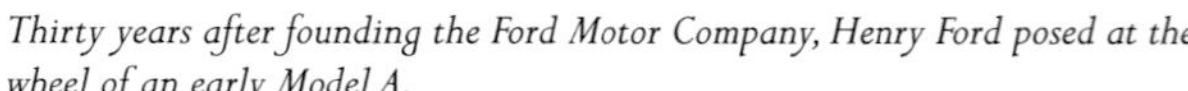

Thirty years after founding the Ford Motor Company, Henry Ford posed at the wheel of an early Model A.

Herbert McNary proudly shows off his historic Ford in 1935.

Motor Company, for Henry Ford was not exactly regarded as an asset. His previous manufacturing record made potential investors nervous – many of them had already lost money backing his earlier ventures.

Malcomson eventually found ten investors, including James Couzens, who only put up a total of $28,000 in hard cash, plus another $21,000 in promissory notes. Ford and Malcomson divided the remaining $51,000 of stock between them, but they put nothing except their partnership contract, their few machine tools and their patents into the business. Inevitably, the money quickly ran out. By 10 July there was just $223.65 left, suppliers' bills were falling due and, despite the company's advertised promise of 'IMMEDIATE DELIVERY of the NEWEST and MOST ADVANCED AUTO manufactured today', not a car had been sold.

Couzens, who had been promoted to Secretary and Business Manager of the Ford Motor Company, at a salary of $2000 a year, effectively read the riot act and told Henry Ford to complete some cars that could be sold, rather than simply tinkering with them.

At last, just as the money seemed likely to run out, the first three orders arrived, on 13 July. More importantly, the envelopes contained cheques totalling $1320. The trickle soon became a flood of sales that made Ford an industry legend, with $99,000 of profits recorded in its first year of trading. That early success persuaded Ford and Couzens to elbow Malcomson out of the company. He had become convinced that the way ahead was to build expensive luxury cars and had become disenchanted with Henry Ford's vision of building light, strong, cheap cars 'for the great multitude'.

Nobody knows which customer's envelope was opened first on that historic July day, although Ford hailed Dr Pfennig, a Chicago dentist, as 'customer number one', because he had paid the full $850 asking price of his new Ford car. His name is consequently at the top of the list of three purchasers neatly written in the margin of the Ford Motor Company's first chequebook by James Couzens. Also on that short list is one H.L. McNary, who had paid a deposit of $150 against delivery of a new Ford car.

Herbert McNary was the buttermaker at the Creamery in Britt, Iowa – a responsible position in a small rural community – and his new Ford was eventually shipped from Detroit on 4 August. It was the second car in Britt, a typical small mid-West town whose slogan is 'Founded by rail, sustained by the plough' (the local barber had bought the first, a Stanley Steamer). It was a place where the usefulness of cars was hampered by the appalling state of the unsurfaced local roads, which became impassable after heavy rain. Maybe that was what persuaded McNary to resign his job at the creamery and open a repair garage.

McNary's family kept his 1903 Ford until 1954, when it was bought for $400, 'after three years of talking', by property developer and former automobile dealer Harry Burd, of Waterloo, Iowa. Burd had been collecting antique cars since the mid-1920s and described Ford Number Three as 'one of my biggest finds'. He restored the car, which he sold in 1961 for $6000 to Swiss Ford dealer Ernst Ruegg of Zurich, who in turn loaned the car, in 1988, to Ford of Germany, to put on show in the little museum at their Cologne plant. In 2001, Ruegg decided to sell the Ford after forty years of ownership.

Jungle drums have nothing on Mike Timms, whose remarkable 'Brighton-Early' collection of veteran cars includes some of the rarest pre-1905 cars in Britain, when it comes to hearing of rare cars for sale. 'I was the first to hear about it and I bought the car on the spot,' he told me. 'You can't imagine how surprised Ford Cologne was when I turned up and told them I had come to collect my Model A!'

Like all the cars in the Brighton-Early collection, Ford No 3 is maintained in full working order by his engineer Russ Pain, who used to work with the well-known engine tuners Weslake. Its underfloor flat-twin 8hp engine starts easily with a couple of turns of the side-mounted

ABOVE: This historic 'licence plate' is still affixed to Mike Timms' 1903 Ford.

LEFT: Mike Timms with his newly acquired 1903 Ford Model A.

starting handle. That goes against the legend, says Mike Timms: 'This car has a Kingston carburettor, which was only fitted to the very earliest Model As, and according to all the history books, Ford replaced the Kingston because it was unsatisfactory. However, the car runs very well, and I wonder whether there was a purely financial reason for the replacement of the Kingston carburettor.'

The Model A is true to Henry Ford's vision of making cars as simple to drive as possible, with a two-speed and reverse epicyclic transmission controlled by a brass lever on the edge of the seat. That eliminates the clutch pedal and the difficulty of gear-changing with a conventional transmission. Indeed, the system was so easy to use that that, back in 1903, Henry Ford's ten-year-old son Edsel drove a Model A around Detroit 'with easy competence'.

Just 1700 Model As Fords were built in 1903–04, and probably no more than 100 survive worldwide. To mark the centenary of the Ford Motor Company, in 2003, Mike Timms drove the world's oldest Ford in the Brighton Run for the first time in its long life.

LEFT: In 2003 Mike Timms celebrated the centenary of Ford by driving the world's oldest Ford to Brighton in the rain.

OPPOSITE: Like the Model A Ford, this 1903 Cadillac was bodied by the C. R. Wilson Company of Detroit; the bodies can apparently be transferred from one marque to the other without alteration.

BS-8391
Cadillac

CHAPTER THIRTY-SIX

Genevieve

Back in 1970 the Veteran Car Club held an ambitious rally to celebrate the 70th anniversary of the Thousand Miles Trial of 1900. I scripted the film of the event, which was sponsored by a then-prominent insurance company named Vehicle & General, but the project was destined to end in tears. Shortly after the film was completed, V & G collapsed and was found to be insolvent. Although the film was finished, without a sponsor it never really got the prominence it needed, but there was one compensation: I had had the chance to work with John Gregson, who read the voiceover from my script, and he had been one of the stars of *Genevieve*.

It is perhaps difficult for someone who was not around at the time to appreciate the effect the film *Genevieve* had on the old-car movement when it was released in 1953. It transformed the Brighton Run from a get-together that attracted a handful of connoisseurs and eccentrics into the world's biggest motoring event. Maybe the run had always attracted crowds of spectators; after *Genevieve*, actually owning a veteran car and taking part each November became the smart thing to do.

However, the path to stardom of the eponymous Genevieve had hardly been an orthodox one, for she had been discovered at the age of 41 by a bailiff called Bill Bailey, lying naked and badly the worse for wear in a hedge beside the Lea Bridge Road in East London. Genevieve is, of course, a twin-cylinder 10/12hp Darracq, built in Paris in 1904, and she had fallen on hard times when Bailey quite literally stumbled upon her.

He was on his way to serve a court order one day late in 1945 when he barked his shin on the rusty dumb iron of a very old car lying on the edge of the pavement; it seemed to be mechanically complete, but the body was missing and the chassis had been robbed of everything removable by the local children. Bailey collected old motor cycles, so naturally his curiosity was aroused, and he discovered that the ancient car lay on the edge of what looked like a sunken builder's dump, full of rubble, old bricks, chimney pots and doors – and half-buried antique motor cars in varying states of decrepitude.

He passed on the news to two friends, Bill Peacock and Jack Wadsworth, who collected veteran and vintage cars. They hurried to the scene and found the owner of the yard living amid piles of junk in the scullery of a nearby house.

After much haggling, Peacock and Wadsworth bought every car in the yard – there were fifteen of them, dating from 1903 to the late 1920s, mostly without bodies – for £45, which even by the standards of the day was a bargain. With the

ABOVE: Dinah Sheridan and John Gregson, the two leading human stars of the film Genevieve.

help of their friends, the cars were hurriedly rescued from the yard and taken to Wadsworth's yard in Isleworth, Middlesex. Wadsworth and Peacock kept the two best cars, a 1903 Sunbeam and a 1903 Argyll, for themselves, and sold the rest on.

One friend, a young man named Peter Venning, bought the Darracq chassis that had started it all, plus another, badly rusted, Darracq chassis for £25. He took the lot to a friend's yard not far from Kew Bridge, and dismantled the pair to use their best parts to make one good car. By coincidence, while he was taking the Darracqs apart, the yard's owner unloaded another veteran, a Dutch-built Spyker, which had been discovered behind a garage in Brentford. A few years later it would be Genevieve's rival in the film.

Venning discovered front wheels of the correct size on an old Model T Ford

RIGHT: This 1903 Argyll was one of the cars rescued from the same junk yard as Genevieve.

BELOW: In her original state, Genevieve would have looked like this 1904 Darracq.

As first restored by Norman Reeves in 1951, Genevieve still wore the old gig body unaltered.

abandoned on a chicken farm near Dunstable Downs. When he got married in 1949, the rolling chassis could be towed to a new home in a shed at Cannons Farm, in the hamlet of Start Hill, near his new home, in the village of Takeley in Essex. As luck would have it, old farmer Cannon had a home-made horse-drawn gig in his barn whose body had been taken from a veteran car, and Peter Venning found that the old body fitted his Darracq chassis perfectly.

At that point, as he told me in 1992, Peter Venning decided that 'I had to acknowledge that I did not possess the facilities or the money to continue and complete a proper and worthwhile restoration', so he advertised the part-restored Darracq in *Motor Sport* for £35.

The purchaser was Uxbridge Ford dealer Norman Reeves, who already owned four veterans – two Benzes, a De Dion-Bouton and a Dürkopp. He entrusted his new acquisition to his mechanic Charlie Cadby, borrowing a 1904 Darracq 'Flying Fifteen' from his near neighbour Bob Gregory to copy its radiator. Unfortunately, the four-cylinder 15hp Darracq had an entirely different radiator from the 'Type 0' 10/12hp twin, but authenticity does not seem to have been a prime concern with Reeves, who was more concerned with getting the car ready to rally. The rebuild was completed in 1949 and Reeves, who had nicknames for most of his cars, christened the Darracq 'Annie'. The car proved so reliable that in 1950 Reeves took it on a veteran rally to Le Touquet, and that year Annie also completed her first London-Brighton Run.

However, Norman Reeves thought the old gig body on his new Darracq lacked style, so he told Charlie Cadby to replace the simple backrest of the bench-type seat and transform it into a more attractive 'tulip' shape. Bob Gregory recalled that Reeves also tried to improve the steering by altering the camber angle, with the result that, while the cornering was wonderful, the car had problems going in a straight line!

Around that time, a South African-born film producer named Henry Cornelius, already successful for films such as *Passport to Pimlico* and *Hue and Cry*, asked for the help of the Veteran Car Club in providing cars for a film he planned to make about a fictitious London-Brighton Run. The club was suspicious, worried that Cornelius simply wanted to make fun of their hobby, but after they had read the script, members were approached to see whether they would loan their veterans. Although Cornelius wanted the protagonists to drive British cars, no one was willing to lend the Wolseley or Humber that he had written for his hero Alan McKim, or the Lanchester he had planned for McKim's friend and rival Ambrose Claverhouse.

Norman Reeves saved the day by offering to lend Annie for the starring role, while his friend Frank Reece was willing to lend his Spyker – which had once shared that yard in Uxbridge with the Darracq – for Claverhouse's car. Annie had to change her name to 'Genevieve'

RIGHT: The famous scene in the film, in which Dinah Sheridan is soaked by coffee as John Gregson tries to start Genevieve.

BELOW: Yet another breakdown for Genevieve on her ill-starred run to Brighton.

LEFT: When Australian millionaire Paul Terry acquired Genevieve, he took the enlightened decision to restore her to the condition in which she starred in the film.

BELOW: Fifty years on, Genevieve returns to the One Pin pub – but this is Buckinghamshire, not the Brighton Road!

for the film. Reeves also provided his mechanic Charlie Cadby, who had to perform more than mechanic's duties, for when filming started they found that John Gregson, who played Alan McKim, could not drive. Charlie Cadby had to double for him in some of the action scenes – and, as Charlie was shorter than Gregson by a head, the joins did show!

When I contacted John Gregson's co-star, Dinah Sheridan, who had retired to California, she recalled Gregson's difficulties: 'Although he was the "owner" of the main character, the whole story being about the annual journey from London to Brighton, John couldn't drive! I had learnt to drive at the age of 17, and spent the whole film time trying not to be seen giving him instructive help out of the side of my mouth. At the end of the film he could have taken his test on Genevieve, but he still couldn't drive a modem car!'

The film was shot between September and November, with the real-life 1952 Brighton Run being filmed at the end. The 'Brighton Road' featured in the film was a figment of producer Henry Cornelius's imagination. Apart from a couple of days' location shooting on the Brighton seafront, with a handful of veterans to add authenticity (there were so few available that Genevieve herself featured in crowd scenes when she was supposed not to have made the finish at all), most of the film was shot close to Pinewood Studios in Buckinghamshire. Looking at the other locations where *Genevieve* was filmed, it appears that the final script was dictated largely by the availability of decent pubs – Ye Olde Green Manne, The One Pin, The Jolly Woodman, The Yew Tree and The De Burgh Arms all feature prominently, no doubt providing sustenance, shelter and warmth for the film crew and actors in the bleak autumn and winter of 1952.

The film opened on 27 May 1953 at the Leicester Square Theatre. Its gentle humour, centred round the Brighton Run and a subsequent (and highly illegal) race back to London by McKim and Claverhouse, with Genevieve as the prize, caught the public imagination and *Genevieve* was voted top comedy of Coronation Year. According to Veteran Car Club secretary Elizabeth Nagle, 'Maybe the fiction and the fact bear only a remote resemblance to each other; maybe the world's audiences wonder where the one begins and the other ends!' The credits summed it up neatly: 'Any resemblance between the deportment of the characters and any Club members is emphatically denied – by the Club.'

The success of the film was worldwide: in Colorado the Horseless Carriage Club organized a run from Denver to a nearby town named Brighton. Australians loved the film, too, and in Melbourne *Genevieve* played for months. One old lady who attended every matinee for thirteen weeks was eventually awarded a free pass by the management.

With her two-seat bodywork, flared front wings and twinkling brasswork, Genevieve became regarded as the typical veteran car, and her image appeared on every conceivable type of souvenir. The worldwide popularity of the film turned this little veteran into a star but Norman Reeves, who became known as 'Mr Genevieve', found the publicity more than he could handle. At the end of filming he offered Genevieve to Henry Cornelius and his wife Marjorie for £450, but, as Mrs Cornelius recalled in 1992, 'We had no suitable garage for her and anyway we had no idea that the film would make her so famous. We had also invested our last penny in making the film.'

After Norman Reeves failed to sell Genevieve in 1956 to the Mayor of Brighton, whose town she had done so much to publicize, he sent her 'down under' for the Australian Blue Mountains Rally in 1958, subsequently loaning her to New Zealand enthusiast George Gilltrap. He displayed Genevieve in his car museum at Rotorua, and eventually bought her from Norman Reeves. When the New Zealand authorities presented Gilltrap with an excessive demand for import duty for Genevieve, he simply shifted his museum – lock, stock and 1904 Darracq – to Australia, relocating to Coolangatta, in Queensland. After George Gilltrap died, in 1966, Genevieve remained in the ownership of his family until 1989, when she was bought by the late Paul Terry for a record Australian price of $A580,000 (£285,302), bidding against Lord Montagu and the financier Robert Holmes à Court. Terry made Genevieve the centrepiece of the car museum in his $A11 million Esplanade Extravaganza in Albany, Western Australia, and completely restored her. He took the enlightened decision to keep her in the condition in which she had starred in that epochal film rather than fit a replica 1904 Type 'O' radiator and body. 'We really only agonized over keeping the car as "Genevieve" for five minutes; it wasn't a big decision,' he said.

A 'whispering campaign' among elements in the Veteran Car Club had cast doubts on Genevieve's age, implying that she had actually been born in 1905, and was therefore ineligible for the Brighton Run. Certainly the Spyker had been redated as 1905, and it was equally true that Genevieve was as about as unauthentic a restoration as could be imagined. Nevertheless, the differences between 1904 and 1905 Darracqs were clear-cut, and during the restoration Genevieve was carefully examined by a committee of experts from the Veteran Car Club of Australia (who know as much about veteran Darracqs as anyone, for their

Fifty years after making the film, Dinah Sheridan, last surviving human star of Genevieve*, is reunited with the famous car.*

ABOVE: *Another episode on the fictional Brighton Road – but this time it is really Southall Broadway!*

LEFT: *Genevieve's rival, the Spyker, was later found to be a 1905 model, and so was ineligible for the Brighton Run (although it has taken part in recent years as a 'guest entry' by popular request).*

country was a prime export market for the marque), and they confirmed the date of 1904 she had been given by the Veteran Car Club of Great Britain while she was in Mr Reeves' ownership.

Sadly, Paul Terry was killed in a helicopter crash in 1993, shortly before a planned run from Albany to Perth with Dinah Sheridan as passenger, and the decision was taken to sell Genevieve. Later that year she came back to England for the first time since the 1950s to be auctioned and, as a curtain-raiser to the sale, she completed that year's Brighton Run – with far less trouble than in the film!

As a consultant to Brooks Auctions (now Bonhams), I was given the agreeable task of compiling the provenance for Genevieve, which, apart from examining the car's specification, involved contacting all the surviving players in her saga. On 2 December 1993, Genevieve, 'the mascot of the old-car movement', was sold for £143,000 to Evert Louwman to become a star exhibit in his Dutch National Motor Museum, one of Europe's premier old-car collections. The atmosphere at the auction was electric, enhanced by a guest appearance by harmonica virtuoso Larry Adler playing the well-known theme tune from the film, just as he had back in 1952.

Evert and his daughter Quirina have regularly campaigned Genevieve in the Brighton Run. In 1992 she was the focus of a splendid rally organized by the Mid-East Section of the Veteran Car Club to celebrate the 50th anniversary of the making of the film, and was reunited at Pinewood Studios with Dinah Sheridan, last surviving human star of *Genevieve*. In a neat touch, Genevieve's rally number ('27') in the commemoration event was the same as the one she had most unauthentically worn in the film fifty years earlier.

The team organizing the rally had spent three months searching out the filming locations and devising routes to join them together, although some were clearly unjoinable, recalled rally organizer Stephen Curry: 'In the scene when the small girl drops her ice cream on the zebra crossing, the cars are clearly racing along the Old Kent Road in London. When they slam on their brakes and come to a stop at the crossing, they are in Southall Broadway, ten miles away!'

As an appropriate tailpiece to the Genevieve story, in the summer of 2003 Evert Louwman, who already owned the most important collection of Spykers – Holland's best-known pioneer make – acquired the 1905 Spyker that had co-starred with Genevieve back in 1952. Louwman was delighted to report that, 'After so many years apart, the two cars will be able to renew their historic movie rivalry!'

Seen on the 2002 Genevieve 50th anniversary rally, this 1903 Model N Mors is powered by a 4.6-litre four-cylinder engine.

Originality

Most Brighton Run cars have been rebuilt and restored at least once in their long lives, but a few 'sleeping beauties' remain just as they were delivered over 100 years ago. They may be faded, their paint touched by the 'craquelure' of extreme age, but they should be cherished like the priceless jewels that they are. These are the Old Masters of the motoring world, a precious link with the craftsmanship and construction methods of the dawn of motoring. One of the finest collections of unrestored veterans is displayed in the famous 'Dark Tunnel' of the Louwman Collection (the Dutch National Motor Museum) at Raamsdonksveer, near Rotterdam.

LEFT: 1895 Peugeot Phaeton with Canopy: this is car number 139 built by Peugeot, which left the company's factory at Valentigney (Doubs) on 8 June 1895.

BELOW LEFT: Similar to the winner of the 1895 Paris-Bordeaux-Paris Race, this 1895 Panhard & Levassor Phaeton is powered by a 1206cc twin-cylinder engine. It has never been restored since it drove out of the Panhard factory in the Avenue d'Ivry, Paris, over 100 years ago.

BELOW RIGHT: 1895 Panhard & Levassor Phaeton avec Capote: a true horseless carriage with a twin-cylinder 1206cc engine with 'hot-tube' ignition.

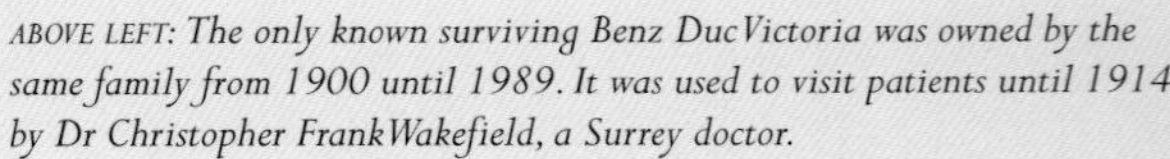

ABOVE LEFT: The only known surviving Benz Duc Victoria was owned by the same family from 1900 until 1989. It was used to visit patients until 1914 by Dr Christopher Frank Wakefield, a Surrey doctor.

ABOVE RIGHT: 1900 FN 3.5hp Victoria: famous Belgian arms manufacturer FN unveiled its first car in March 1899 and built a series of 100 3.5hp cars in 1900, including this remarkably preserved example, with its perilous 'spider seat' at the rear for the mechanic.

RIGHT: 1900 De Dion-Bouton Tricycle: 'What an embryo the car would still be if the De Dion-Bouton tricycle had not been born!' boasted the De Dion company in 1899, claiming sales of 22,000 tricycles since 1895.

BELOW: 1900 De Dion Bouton 3.5hp Vis-à-Vis: 'Light, simple, manageable but possessing a certain amount of comfort', the rear-engined De Dion 'Petite Voiture' was unveiled in 1899. Its passengers sat facing one another as though playing cards, in an arrangement known as 'vis-à-vis' (face to face).

RIGHT: 1903 White Model C Steam Demi-Limousine: They called this closed-body style 'The Ideal Car for Winter Use'; when summer came, the chauffeur – a most appropriate word for the driver of a steam car, for it literally means 'stoker' – hoisted the winter body from the chassis and replaced it with an open 'summer' body with tulip-back seats.

CHAPTER THIRTY-SEVEN

Enter the Dragon

They say that when Henry Ford and Barney Oldfield met in old age – it must have been when they shared the top table at the May 1946 banquet that celebrated the Golden Jubilee of the American motor industry – Henry said to Barney, 'Well, I guess we made each other's reputation.'

'Yes,' replied Barney, 'But I did a better job than you did.'

Back in 1902 Henry Ford had recruited Berna Eli 'Barney' Oldfield to drive the monstrous 18.9-litre racing cars '999' and 'Arrow' that he had constructed in partnership with racing cyclist Tom Cooper, to promote his ambitions as a motor manufacturer. They were crude in the extreme, with no gearbox, a basic in-and-out clutch and exposed bevel gears on the back axle, and not much in the way of brakes. Anyone with experience of motoring would have balked at driving such a high-powered deathtrap. 'Barney' Oldfield, billed as 'The Bicycle Champion of Ohio', seemed the ideal candidate. 'He had never driven a car before,' recalled Ford, 'but he liked the idea. He said he would try anything once... One life to a car was enough. The roar of those cylinders alone was enough to half kill a man... Going over Niagara Falls would have been but a pastime after a ride in 999.'

Oldfield – described modestly by his biographer as 'rogue, rule-breaker, braggart, sentimentalist, gambler, showman, bar-room brawler, dirt-track daredevil', who would almost certainly have gone over Niagara Falls in a barrel if the money was right – proved a natural. To promote the name of Ford, he barnstormed his way around the dirt horse-racing tracks of the northern states at the tiller of one or other of Henry's crude racers, which were so alike that they often swapped identities. (It was actually Henry Ford who achieved '999''s greatest success by setting a new land-speed record of 91.37mph (147.01km/h) in January 1904, when the Ford Motor Company was little more than six months old. It was, incidentally, the only time that the land-speed record had been broken on water, for Henry – unconventional as ever – set the record on a track scraped across the frozen surface of Lake St Clair, an inlet of the Detroit River.)

Barney Oldfield first made his name as a racing driver with Henry Ford's terrifying 18.9-litre '999', named after a famous express train. Henry Ford stands proudly by his creation.

The association between Henry Ford and Barney Oldfield was already over at that point, for Oldfield had been recruited by Ford's racing rival Alexander Winton, another aspiring motor manufacturer. In the same month when Henry set his record in frostbound Michigan, Oldfield was driving Winton's fearsome eight-cylinder 'Bullet' at Ormond Beach, Daytona, achieving a speed of 83.7mph (134.7km/h) in the pale Florida sunshine.

Their relationship foundered when Oldfield failed to turn up to race 'Bullet', lured by a more profitable engagement elsewhere, and Winton refused to renew his contract. He was quickly snapped up by the Peerless company of Cleveland, Ohio, whose engineer and sometime Gordon-Bennett racer Louis P. Mooers was anxious to publicize the company's luxury cars with a racing programme using a specially constructed car and a well-known driver. It is a formula that is as good today as it was back then.

The 'Green Dragon' in all its glory.

Oldfield's 'Green Dragon' was a low-slung racer loosely based on the company's production cars – or so Peerless claimed in a booklet extolling its virtues: 'Heretofore racing cars have been freaks. Of tremendous horse power and abnormal design, they have represented entirely different types of construction than the touring cars put out by the same manufacturer.' The claim, of course, overlooked the fact that the Green Dragon had little more in common with the firm's touring cars than the basic design of its 60hp power unit.

Barney Oldfield and the Green Dragon began their record-breaking career in August 1904, when, over a memorable eighteen-week period, they ran at twenty different tracks. Barney was 'clad in Lincoln Green, as were the dare-devils of Robin Hood's band', and the car broke all records from 1 to 8 miles and 11 to 20 miles; indeed, if there were no more existing records to break, Barney's publicity huckster Bill Pickens would invent one. Barney won sixteen races, crashed twice, broke his rear axle once, and only appeared without racing on one occasion – at the Nashville, Tennessee, racetrack on the Labor Day holiday in September 1904, where a heavily-bandaged Barney turned out just to please the crowds. Only a short while before, he had crashed Green Dragon through the fence in a ten-mile race at St Louis, twisting its chassis into the shape of a question mark, and breaking several ribs. But he had wasted no time during his convalescence, for he had courted and married the girl who had been his nurse at the Baptist Sanitarium in St Louis.

On one golden October day on a New York City racetrack, Barney Oldfield and his Peerless Green Dragon faced three of Europe's greatest drivers: Italian champion Satori on a 90hp FIAT, Bernin on an 80hp Renault, and Théry, winner of the international Gordon Bennett Trophy, on his 80hp Richard-Brasier. Barney 'outrode the three great speed creations of European factories and the drivers who attempted to dethrone him', covering ten miles in 9 minutes 12.2 seconds. Peerless' boast was unequivocal: 'The only way to catch Oldfield with a contestant is when standing!'

When racing, Barney Oldfield, the 'dare-devil dean of auto drivers... the man who can't spell fear', always kept an unlit cigar firmly clamped in his mouth. It became his trademark, but it also had a practical purpose, cushioning his jaw against the bone-jarring vibration of the Green Dragon on the rough surface of the dirt tracks.

Off the racetrack, the Green Dragon was still a star. It (and Barney, the 'Speed King of the World') made a dramatic appearance in a Broadway musical, starring the glamorous Elsie Janis, that was based on the Vanderbilt Cup motor race. The high point of every show was the thunderous appearance on stage of the Green Dragon, running on a treadmill in a cloud of white exhaust smoke. Barney, ever an opportunist, pocketed a fee of $500 a week for his 'guest appearance' in the play.

Because of the crashes and the mechanical wear and tear imposed by racing, there were several Green Dragons. Inevitably, there came a point when Barney's crowd-pleasing antics became too much for the Peerless directors, and the 'world's champion automobilist' was shown the door. It appears that that he took at least one of the Green Dragons – a monster with an 11.2-litre four-cylinder engine – with him to continue its barnstorming progress around the dirt tracks. When it

ABOVE: The most prominent feature of the Dragon's dashboard are the many oilers controlling the complex splash lubrication system.

LEFT: The boat-like bonnet lifts off in one piece to reveal the massive 11.2-litre engine.

BELOW: Short exhaust stubs controlled by butterfly valves pass the exhaust gases direct to the atmosphere for increased performance.

finally ended its racing days, around 1910, the old Green Dragon was given to Barney's boyhood friend Bill Long, of Lorain, Ohio. There was little sentiment about old racing cars in those days and Long fitted his Green Dragon with a new radiator and rebuilt it as a more modern-looking raceabout. He kept the car for over sixty years, but it was eventually abandoned in a wooden shed on the local airport at Lorain. Around 1970 it was discovered as a bodyless chassis, and although its stub exhaust pipes and liberally drilled lightening holes in the rear axle casing provided mute evidence of its racing origins, no evidence of its original configuration could be found. As a result, it was restored as a touring car, and that was the guise in which I saw it take part in the 1974 Brighton Run.

The old Green Dragon was subsequently fitted with stark two-seat bodywork, and was raced at Laguna Seca, Lime Rock and Fairmount Park in the USA by its American owner Don Meyer. He brought it to Britain in 1991, where he won the Edwardian class in the Vintage Sports Car Club's Pomeroy Trophy contest, and competed at the Prescott and Shelsley Walsh hillclimbs, recording excellent times of 65 and 58 seconds respectively.

The car was then acquired by British veteran expert Tim Moore, who decided to rebuild it as closely as possible to the condition in which Barney Oldfield had raced it. Because the original form of the racing Peerless was not known, Tim took for his model the most dramatic version of the Green Dragon, with a fearsome streamlined bonnet like the prow of Captain Nemo's science-fiction submarine Nautilus. The wood-spoked wheels were shrouded with wind-cheating discs, and the proud slogans of Oldfield's heyday were painted on the bonnet and tail of the re-created car.

When I visited the Dragon in its Cambridgeshire lair, Tim lifted off its massive bonnet, as big as a rowing boat, to reveal the immense engine with its fully exposed valve gear – mechanically operated overhead valves were very much state-of-the-art engineering in 1904 – and four separate cylinders, each one housing a six-inch piston the size of an ice-bucket. Also on view was that amazing exhaust manifold, with its linked row of butterfly valves, which could divert the hot gases straight to the atmosphere through the exhaust stubs rather than through the silencer.

We climbed aboard and headed out of Tim's village on to a local main road, where the monster could be unleashed. 'I'm told that when the Green Dragon was discovered thirty years ago, it had back-axle gearing good for 120 miles an hour,' said Tim. 'But, as the father of a young family, there's no way I'm going to find out whether that's true!' Then he popped open the straight-through exhaust stubs and four perfect smoke rings blew out of the ends of the pipes as we accelerated out of a roundabout.

With its mighty engine turning over at a leisurely 1400 revolutions a minute, the Green Dragon could cruise effortlessly at 85mph (137km/h), making it the biggest and fastest car ever to take part in the Brighton Run. A century after it first made the crowds roar, Barney Oldfield's old racer is still capable of astounding the public.

The Dragon in repose on Madeira Drive.

CHAPTER THIRTY-EIGHT

'Cars of the Old Brigade'

'Something of the spirit of thirty years ago will be recaptured this weekend,' claimed *The Autocar* when it announced a run from London to Brighton for cars over twenty-one years old, organized by the *Daily Sketch* and *Sunday Graphic*, to take place on Sunday 13 November 1927. Robert Beare, the paper's genial motoring correspondent, had come up with the bright idea of a run to determine the oldest car in everyday use, and had been surprised to receive an entry of fifty-one cars. Their owners were sometimes a little optimistic in estimating the age of their car: the '1893' Panhard that claimed to be the oldest entry was actually a Clement-Panhard dating from 1899–1900, while the '1895 Renault' was an impossibility, for the Renault company was not founded until 1899.

While several of the entries were obviously in good running order, and some were even in the hands of their original owners, others were more worthy of the *Sketch*'s unkind label 'Old Crocks', such as the 1904 Wolseley that had been awarded 'First Prize in the Comic Car section of the Lowestoft Carnival'. Nevertheless, forty-four of the fifty-one entries started. While some of them played up to the 'Old Crocks' image, with their crew in comic costume or with jokey banners on board, most of the 'cars of the old brigade' astonished the considerable crowds of onlookers by showing such reliability at what was then considered to be a very great age for a car.

Terming the run 'a real romance of the road', *The Autocar* remarked that the fact that, of the cars that had started, thirty-seven had reached Brighton and twenty-one had made non-stop runs, was 'truly a record of which the makers and owners may be proud'.

THE AUTOCAR, November 18th, 1927. 1063

THE "OLD CROCKS" STEP OUT.

Mr. John Bryce's 1893 Panhard, which made one of the best performances, passing through Reigate, followed by another competitor.

The reports of the 1927 Brighton Run launched the unkind description 'Old Crocks', which it took many years to shake off.

Looking back to 1927 from a twenty-firt-century viewpoint, it is quite apparent that there is still no answer to Robert Beare's question, 'How long do cars last?' Many of the entrants in that first modern Brighton Run still take part in the event eight decades on, when all of them have become true antiques of the road by passing their first century in fine running order.

There might have been an element of mockery in that 1927 'Old Crocks' Run, but the event proved immensely popular, and was repeated the following year, with *The Autocar* joining the *Daily Sketch* and *Sunday Graphic* in promoting the event. A more formal element was introduced by the Royal Automobile Club, which organized the run under its General Competition Rules, and the huge advertising placards and comic costumes that had been a feature of the 1927 run were banned.

Other important innovations of the 1928 run included the first official use of the word 'Veteran' to describe the entrants, which now had to be over twenty-five years old, for it was realized that the 1927 limit allowing cars built up to 1906 to take part had been too generous – 'far too modern to attract notice' was the verdict. Also for the first time, the cars were given the privilege of driving through the Royal Parks. The competing cars, which were scrutineered and garaged overnight in Notting Hill Gate, entered Hyde Park at Victoria Gate and ran down the North and East Carriage Roads, Constitution Hill and The Mall to Storey's Gate and Parliament Square, before crossing the official starting line at Westminster Bridge.

That year also saw the first overseas participants, Frenchmen Jean Terouanne

ABOVE: This 1903 De Dion-Bouton ran in the very first 'modern' Brighton Run in 1927, when its nurseryman owner proudly boasted that it had 'run to Crediton (Exeter) from Lewes, nearly 200 miles each way, at an average of 15–16mph'.

RIGHT: Originally built for Panhard & Levassor director and racing driver the Chevalier René de Knyff, 'Le Papillon Bleu' ('Blue Butterfly') was given its romantic name by the daughter of its second owner, Leslie Bucknell, when it came to England in the summer of 1901. It was still in regular use in the 1920s and took part in the very first commemorative Brighton Run in 1927. On August Bank Holiday 1934, the old Panhard became the first car to be damaged in the Mersey Tunnel after its opening by King George V, when it was hit by a motor coach.

BELOW: How empty was the Brighton Road in 1928, when the curious 1901 Sunbeam-Mabley, with its offset diamond wheel layout ('steered from the rear seat, designed after the mid-Victorian sofa'), was entered by the Sunbeam Motor Car Company!

ABOVE: *Britain was not the only country to experience a surge of interest in very early cars during the 1920s; on 18 November 1923 this early Peugeot and the famous 1891 Panhard of the Abbé Gavois took part in an old car rally at Croix de Noailles in the Forest of St-Germain, to celebrate the unveiling of a memorial to pioneer motorist Pierre Giffard.*

LEFT: *Mrs Mary Miles with her 1897 Benz on the 1927 run; as a teenager I regularly used to walk into South Croydon to admire this one-family-from-new veteran in the corner of the little showroom of the Miles family garage, Onward Motors.*

BELOW: *In the early days of the old-car movement, historical accuracy was scarcely important. This '1900 MMC' taking part in an early Veteran Car Club rally was 'restored' after being found holding up an old barn in East Peckham, Kent, in 1932; it has a c.1912 Singer radiator and a 1920s steering column, among many other anachronisms.*

and Robert Treille on their Léon Bollée voiturette. It arrived too late to classify as an official entry, but the Léon Bollée was driven to Brighton anyway, and its sporting crew was 'cheered like anything' at the dinner following the run.

Among the 1928 entries was a vehicle described as an 1896 Benz, which had been 'rusting in an outhouse for many years', the property of electrical engineer H.J. Dowsing ('the inventor of the electrically heated sock') who had long ago fitted it with the world's first electric starter. Dowsing died in 1930, and the new owner of the 'Benz' soon discovered that it was actually the prototype Arnold from the 1896 run.

In 1929 the Brighton Run took place for the first (and only) time in October. It was poorly organized by the *Daily Sketch* and *Sunday Graphic* and only thirty-six cars started, of which six broke down on the way to Brighton. The organizers had allowed the comic element to creep back, with some of the crews wearing 'disreputable umbrellas and concertina top hats'. Fortunately, a car 'smothered in Bass advertisements' was abandoned in a field near Reigate. In contrast to earlier runs, several of the cars had been restored to something like new condition. Richard Shuttleworth's Paris-Amsterdam Panhard 'looked beautiful in yellow and black in spite of its 'hen-coop' saloon body... in marked contrast to the scarred, paintless decrepitude of an 1895 MMC.. proudly supporting hood sticks without a hood'.

There were money prizes for the best performances, with the *Daily Sketch* awarding the considerable sum of £100 (the price of a new Morris Minor) to the 1897 Benz entered by Mrs Mary Miles of South Croydon, whose family had owned the car since new (and would ultimately only part with it in 2003). An award of £50 went to the Shuttleworth Panhard and £25 to an obscure Yorkshire-built car called a Vipen, which had apparently been buried at the foot of Hindhead for twenty-two years and had the slogan 'The Golden Marrow' scrawled across its tail.

Despite the generous prizes, the Brighton Run was obviously in danger of sinking into oblivion. A change of organization was needed, and in 1930 the Royal

Richard Shuttleworth's 1897 Panhard & Levassor was first owned by Lord Rothschild and took part in the 1898 Paris-Amsterdam race. In 1901 it was fitted by Morgan & Sons with the closed body it still wears, and King Edward VII rode to Ascot in it. It took part in the 1927 Brighton Run before Richard Shuttleworth bought it for £1.25 in 1928.

F.S. Rowden's 1898 Star Dog Cart, seen here on a 1931 VCC rally, was said to have won an award in the Thousand Miles Trial of 1900.

Brighton Run sponsor Sir Ray Tindle and his faithful 1904 Speedwell, which he has owned for over 40 years. It was discovered in the 1930s hidden behind bushes in the garden of a Reading coachbuilder, with its original single-cylinder De Dion engine removed to drive a saw. With its engine reinstalled, it took part in the 1933 Brighton Run. The Speedwell served as a liaison vehicle during both World Wars.

Automobile Club stepped into the breach, for ever fixing the definition of the word 'Veteran' by imposing a fixed cut-off point of 31 December 1904 for entries. The run was moved back into November, and the number of entries was almost double that of the previous year. Of the fifty-eight veterans, an Oldsmobile, a De Dion-engined car and a 1900 Clement had been used as hen-roosts, while a 1902 De Dion-Bouton had served as a dog kennel. The owner of a 1901 Renault that had been used to deliver petrol on a daily basis stated mournfully that it had been 'fitted with its present body to participate in a fair'. Lord Ridley's 1903 Lanchester had served as an ambulance in the Great War, while the little 1903 6hp De Dion-Bouton acquired before the Great War by the second Lord Montagu of Beaulieu, among the effects of a departing tenant, made its Brighton Run debut. It would become the first exhibit in the present Lord Montagu's Motor Museum – now the National Motor Museum – which opened in 1952.

The Brighton Run had become a highlight of the motoring calendar. *Motor* magazine reported that 'For the first forty miles out of London the roads were blocked with the cars of enthusiastic spectators, while all along the route the sides of the road were black with onlookers. It was like a royal procession.'

However, the greatest success of the 1930 event came when it was all over, and three of the participants met in the Old Ship Hotel in Brighton for a well-earned beer to swap yarns about veteran cars:

When Richard Shuttleworth discovered that pioneer racing driver S.F. Edge had once driven the family 1903 De Dietrich – which had been acquired second-hand for £50 from Sir Charles Mackenzie in 1906 and had lost its original bodywork in a 1912 fire at Maythorn's coachworks – he had this replica Paris-Madrid racing body built for the car, in the mid-1930s.

ABOVE: In 1934 Autocar *sports editor (and winner of the 1927 Le Mans 24-hour race) Sammy Davis and his co-driver L. V. Head pushed their 1897 Léon Bollée 'Beelzebub' 11 miles to the finish after the engine failed. In recognition of their stout effort, they were given a finisher's medal each!*

RIGHT: Over 50 years later I saw Beelzebub in the reserve store of the Indianapolis Speedway Museum, to which Sammy Davis had willed it.

BELOW LEFT: A very damp John Dennis on the 2003 Brighton Run with the 1902 Dennis car that his family has owned for over a century.

BELOW RIGHT: Used for many years by the estate electricians at Beaulieu when it was just an old car, this little 1903 6hp De Dion-Bouton was acquired before the Great War by the second Lord Montagu of Beaulieu, who drove it frequently. It had been left behind by a departing tenant. It made its Brighton Run debut, driven by P. McEnteee and Captain Henry Widnell, agent to the Montagu Estate, in 1930, a year after John Montagu's death. It would become the first exhibit in the Motor Museum – now the National Motor Museum – which was opened by his son in 1952.

In 1933 G. H. Eyre was driving through Gillingham in Dorset when he saw this Mulliner-bodied Napier, which he had driven daily between 1902–09, in a scrap yard, bought it and entered it in the Brighton Run.

This 1903 Clement has close links with the beginnings of motoring in Britain, for it was originally owned by Willliam Coker Iliffe, who with his brother founded The Autocar *in November 1895. The magazine is still going strong after 110 years.*

Medals

There are no prizes for the Brighton Run, just the coveted Finisher's Medal 'for punctual arrival in Brighton'.

'Sammy' Davis was Sports Editor of *The Autocar* and the owner of a temperamental 1897 Léon Bollée aptly named 'Beelzebub', which had been found in a French farmyard and bought for a few francs; Jackie Masters was Secretary of the Motor Cycling Club; and Captain John Wylie was the owner of a Wolseley that had been found with rats nesting in its undershield. The three men decided to form a club for like-minded enthusiasts, 'to keep up a little flow of competitions and rallies suitable for machines built up to 1904', and on 23 November 1930 the Veteran Car Club, the world's first club dedicated to the preservation and use of historic motor vehicles, came into being.

Unquestionably, the Brighton Run remains the world's premier old-car event, and its ever-increasing entry list bears remarkable tribute to the continuing interest in the very earliest cars. Entries passed the hundred mark for the first time in 1938, exceeded 200 in 1954 following the release of the film *Genevieve*, which encouraged many to acquire veteran cars, and the increasing popularity of the event has mirrored the growth of the old-car hobby. While the number of starters in the run was restricted by the authorities for many years, there were always more entries than potential starters. In 1984 entries exceeded 400 for the first time and the police forces along the route allowed 330 cars to start. Fortunately, there is now no restriction on the number of starters, which passed 400 in the early 1990s; in the centenary year of 1996, an all-time record of 660 cars entered.

Although the source of eligible cars is obviously finite, there seems to be no end to the number of people wanting to enter the 'Brighton'. My analysis of entries in the years that I have been watching the run suggests that worldwide there are at least 1100 pre-1905 cars in running order eligible to take part!

It is no longer enough to claim that a car is old enough to qualify without further evidence: the checks are strict and the days when guesswork ages were accepted without question are long past. In the 1930s, a 1909 Humber ran several times as '1904', a 1909 White steamer took part for many years before its true age was determined, and in the 1950s a 1920s Slaby & Beringer electric car took part. But now such documents as original order books have come to light, the Veteran Car Club has undertaken a programme – not always popular – of re-dating 'borderline' cars in the light of new evidence.

Even so, 'new' cars appear in the Brighton Run every year, a remarkable tribute to the dedication of the owners who restore these ancient cars to running condition, and to the enduring appeal of this unique event.

CHAPTER THIRTY-NINE

The Red Flag Revolution

Surely an event as well-established and popular as the Brighton Run would be a controversy-free zone? Not so. In 2002 a statement by the event's organizers threatened to change it for ever.

For some years the Brighton Run had been organized by the Motor Sports Association, the wing of the Royal Automobile Club responsible for administering competitive motoring in Great Britain. The MSA had recently set up a subsidiary named International Motor Sports, to run commercial events, thus avoiding any conflict of interest between its administrative and commercial interests. Its new Chief Executive had plenty of commercial experience but admitted that his knowledge of the Brighton Run was limited to having followed the event the previous year in his modern BMW. Nevertheless, he announced a new strategy for the run that was to provoke an explosive reaction:

> International Motor Sports (IMS), the commercial arm of the Motor Sports Association (MSA) and the Royal Automobile Club, are injecting a new lease of life into the ever-popular London to Brighton Veteran Car Run, with the announcement of new entry regulations for 2002. Previously, only cars, tricars and motor tricycles manufactured before 31 December 1904 could enter the historic event. But from 2002, Edwardian vehicles manufactured before 31 December 1906 will also be eligible. The move opens up this world-famous event for even more owners of very early cars.

To the faithful, this was sheer heresy. The ground rules that had been laid down three-quarters of a century earlier had not only become sacrosanct, they had defined the very first category of historic cars to be created, the pre-1905 Veteran class.

The reaction of Doctor David K. Gast, Professor Emeritus at San Diego State University, California, was typical:

> With this decision the MSA has opened up the proverbial can of worms. There are a number of issues beyond the fact that this decision violates the integrity of a world-famous historic re-enactment limited to automobiles built prior to 1905.
>
> In the years 1905 and 1906 mass production of automobiles accelerated. Today, there are large numbers of Cadillacs, Buicks, Maxwells, Oldsmobiles, and Reos, to mention the more prolific

The call to arms for owners of veteran cars opposed to the change of rules for the Brighton Run.

Heading the stand for the status quo was Daniel Ward, proudly flying the Red Flag on his 1896 Panhard.

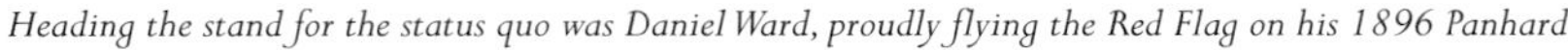

Everyone who signed up to the Red Flag Run received a souvenir flag when peace was declared.

> manufacturers. The inclusion of the above marques alone could swamp the Brighton Run. I have been a passenger on the run and I have seen the congestion that already exists with 400 entrants....
>
> In my opinion, the MSA's decision to allow later cars on the Brighton Run will be a disservice to the public, to motoring enthusiasts, to the event itself and to all of the organizations associated with the run. It will call to question the values and real motives of the decision-makers in the IMS Ltd, MSA and RAC. It will open a wound that will not easily heal. It will engender divisiveness among veteran car enthusiasts. Does the MSA wish this to be its legacy? I hope not. I hope that this misguided decision will be reversed.

Despite the many protests it received, the IMS stuck to its guns and refused to reverse its unpopular decision. Its statement that 'We are including Edwardian cars this year because they are very similar to those already eligible' revealed a lamentable ignorance of motoring history and technology. Comparing the 1906 Rolls-Royce 'The Silver Ghost' with the twin-cylinder 10hp Rolls-Royce of late 1904, for example, shows the speed of the progress in design that took place after 1904.

Dozens of concerned veteran-car owners, among them Evert Louwman, the owner of 'Genevieve', responded to the change in the rules by announcing that they would withdraw from the Brighton Run. Heading the protest was Daniel Ward, whose family's involvement with veteran cars and the Brighton Run went back over fifty years. He made his views very clear:

> The IMS has, without proper consultation or approach to the participants, decided to kill the London to Brighton Run as we all know and love it. They have decided, against the wishes of a large number of the active participants, to introduce later, larger, faster cars into the Veteran Car Run in order to improve their profits... The annual London to Brighton Veteran Car Run – the world's oldest and largest such event – has never been more popular. A total of forty-four cars started in that original 1927 commemoration run and now over 400 cars regularly take part each year – in the Centenary Year of 1996 nearly 650 cars took part. We have analysed the entry lists over the past thirty years and found that well over 1100 different pre-1904 cars have taken part in the Brighton Run in that time.
>
> Indeed, in their press release announcing this totally unnecessary rule change, the IMS state: 'In 2001, the event had a record number of spectators, and 400 cars took part making it a truly memorable year.' If that is the case, why change this historic event which is envied and admired throughout the world?
>
> A separate Red Flag Run in the true spirit of the 1896 Motor Tour is being planned as a protest against this ill-conceived change so that spectators will not be the losers. I and others intend to conduct a personal motor tour on Sunday 3 November 2002 from London to Brighton in our legally licensed, tested and insured veteran cars.
>
> Hopefully, even at this late stage, the IMS will realize the error of its ways. Tradition dies hard in this country. For the sake of a few extra pounds, why kill this wonderful event?

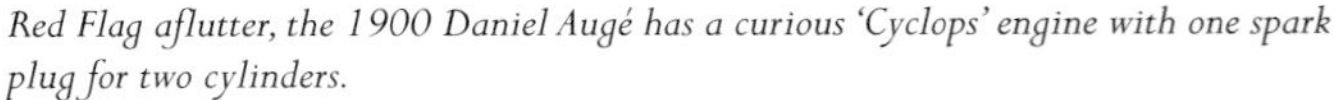
Red Flag aflutter, the 1900 Daniel Augé has a curious 'Cyclops' engine with one spark plug for two cylinders.

This 1902 Mors was one of many entrants in 2002 to fly the flag for tradition.

Among the handful of 'too modern' 1905–6 cars allowed to take part once and for all in 2002 was this 1905 20hp Rolls-Royce.

True to his word, Daniel Ward began organizing his 'Red Flag Run'. To be held on the same day as the 'official' run, it would start from Pall Mall outside the Edwardian clubhouse of the Royal Automobile Club (a building, incidentally, designed by the same architects as the Ritz Hotel) and finish on Brighton's Palace Pier. The protest had results of seismic proportions: by midsummer, the Red Flag Run had attracted over 200 entries and sponsorship from Bonhams auctioneers, while the IMS event, so well-founded rumour had it, was struggling to reach 100.

At that point, the Royal Automobile Club, of which International Motor Sports is a subsidiary, stepped in. With the closing date for the IMS Run looming, the Club realized that something needed to be done quickly if the world's oldest antique car event was to be saved. Since the IMS had acted without consulting its parent and was clearly getting further off track, complaining that those who opposed the rule change 'didn't understand the history of the run', it was up to the Royal Automobile Club to act as mender of fences.

As the Press 'voice' of the protest movement, I arranged for senior Royal Automobile Club officials to meet Daniel Ward and Brian Moore, past-President of the Veteran Car Club (and another of the prime movers in the Red Flag protest). To its credit, the Club quickly agreed that the eligibility rule should revert to the established pre-1905 standard. However, the IMS wavered and said that the '05–06' rule would remain in place for 2002 and that 'for at least the 2003 event, the eligibility regulations for the event will revert to those of 2001'. That, of course, was not good enough for Daniel Ward, and, in the ensuing 'process of consultation', the Royal Automobile Club decreed that the rule that had dictated the entry qualifications for the Brighton Run since 1929 should stand in perpetuity.

In return for this, the Red Flag Runners agreed to cancel their rival event and confirmed that the 'interested parties' in the London to Brighton debate were all now speaking with one voice for the good of the run as a whole.

At the beginning of the discussions the IMS representatives affirmed that they had received twenty-three entries from owners of Edwardian cars and expected another thirty-five, but eventually only twenty 'guest' entries materialized. This was in addition to the AA's 20/30 Renault, a car misdated many years ago as 1904 (which it could never have been), which had run by special invitation ever since the error was rectified. The Royal Automobile Club set up a steering committee of regular Brighton Run entrants and Club officials to safeguard the future of the run, and, as a goodwill gesture, the Red Flag Runners on the committee agreed that this handful of 1905–06 cars could be allowed to enter by special invitation for 2002 only.

The IMS were somewhat remiss in not explaining the presence of the 1905–06 entries in the run's programme, but the size and power of several of the vehicles was eloquent proof of the rightness of the Red Flag protest. The Brighton Run represents a real challenge for most of the entrants, for the vast majority of veterans are low-powered, and the 60-odd miles from the start in Hyde Park to the finish on Madeira Drive in Brighton offer more than their fair share of to a driver who has only 6 or 8 horsepower to play with!

To respond to criticism of the running of the event, the steering committee put its organization out to tender. The

Among the overseas entrants who stood up for the true veterans was a Murray Runabout from Germany.

Obviously, Genevieve was a keen supporter of Brighton Run tradition!

Principal overseas supporter of the Red Flag Revolution was Evert Louwman of the Dutch National Motor Museum, seen at the controls of his 1895 Peugeot, carrying the cherished starting number '1', as the oldest car taking part in this world-famous event.

The Saturday Concours in Waterloo Place introduced in 2003 was a huge success; for 2005 it was moved to Regent Street to give even greater publicity for the Brighton Run.

successful bidder, Motion Works UK, brought an enthusiasm to the task of revitalizing the 2004 Run that was greatly appreciated by the entrants. All the acrimony of 2002 was forgotten as the new organizers extended the run (formerly a weekend) into a three-day event. It began with a sale of veteran cars and accessories by Bonhams, which saw several Brighton-eligible cars, including a delightfully patinated 1900 De Dion-Bouton and a 1904 Franklin, find new owners and repeated the previous year's popular innovation of a Saturday concours in Waterloo Place, not far from the Royal Automobile Clubhouse in Pall Mall. This part of the event attracted some seventy entries, and was enlivened by several veterans giving short passenger rides around the Pall Mall block and Trafalgar Square. Among those who took advantage of this 'interactive' event was the Mayor of Westminster, who rode down Pall Mall aboard Evert Louwman's immortal 1904 Darracq 'Genevieve'.

The following morning, starting at 7.30am, with the weather set fair, the cars were flagged away from Hyde Park by sponsors Sir Ray Tindle and Vyvyan Harmsworth, radio DJ David Jensen and veteran actor Sir John Mills, who, at the age of 96, was making virtually his last public appearance. It was a milestone year, for every entry was now a full 100 years old (apart for the tiny handful of 'grandfather rights' cars that had once been incorrectly dated at 1904 and had taken part in the Brighton Run before having their natal year amended to 1905). It was a true 'antiques roadshow'.

The appointment of a new organizer had made a big difference to the Brighton Run, motoring's best-loved annual event.

Many Marques

More than 140 makes take part in the annual Brighton Run. Some of them are described below.

Arrol-Johnston (Scotland): With backing from Sir William Arrol, engineer of the Forth Bridge, locomotive engineer George Johnston built a heavy motor dog-cart whose flat-twin engine had four pistons and was started by pulling on a rope through the floorboards. The dog-cart was built until 1906; a 1905 dog-cart built as a searchlight tender for the Sirdar of Egypt survives in Khartoum, Sudan.

Audibert & Lavirotte (France): Audibert & Lavirotte began making Benz-like cars with rear engines and belt drive in Lyon – once France's second-biggest motor manufacturing city after Paris – as early as 1894, and catalogued one of the world's first production saloon cars in 1898.

Clément-Panhard (France): The Clément-Panhard was a rear-engined mechanical nightmare designed by airship pioneer Commandant Krebs, a director of Panhard & Levassor.

Clément (France): Adolphe Clément made a fortune from the new-fangled pneumatic tyre, and from 1898 began building Clément and Gladiator cars in Paris. He signed away the rights to the Clément marque in 1903, and had to change his name to Clément-Bayard in order to resume production. (The Chevalier Bayard was a medieval hero.)

This six-seater 1902 Arrol-Johnston dogcart is powered by a 12hp twin-cylinder opposed-piston engine.

This 1899 Audibert & Lavirotte double phaeton is a rare survivor from a total output of some 50 cars.

The eccentric little Clément-Panhard was described as a "fiendish contraption" by pioneer motorist St John Nixon.

This 1903 Clément tonneau seen at the start of the 2004 Brighton Run is powered by a 14hp four-cylinder engine.

Designed by Henry A. Law, the 1903 Columbia was the sole petrol-powered model produced by a company specialising in electric cars.

In 1904 a Franklin runabout drove from New York to San Francisco in 33 days, setting a new record time.

For many years this 1900 Gardner-Serpollet double phaeton has been a regular participant in the Veteran Car Run.

With a four-leaf cloved as its emblem, this Georges Richard rear-entrance tonneau is powered by a 7hp twin-cylinder engine.

Columbia (USA): In 1895 a young inventor named Hiram Percy Maxim who had built a 'gasoline tricycle' arrived at the factory of leading cycle maker Colonel Albert Pope and was asked to design a motor car. Pope's group tried to control the American motor industry through its Selden 'Master Patent', a plan ultimately thwarted by Henry Ford.

Delaugère et Clayette (France): Made in Orléans, this marque began production in 1900 with a motor tricycle. In 1902 it had produced four-cylinder cars that could run on petrol or alcohol, a fuel encouraged by the French government to use up agricultural over-production.

Franklin (USA): Every Franklin ever built was air-cooled and from the start of production in 1902 until 1922 they, all had wooden chassis. Veteran Franklins had transverse four-cylinder engines. Full-elliptic springs gave exceptional riding comfort and exceptional tyre life.

Gardner-Serpollet (France): Steam-car pioneer Léon Serpollet's first four production cars were made by Peugeot in 1889, but he concentrated on steam trams and buses until 1899, when he got backing to build cars from American financier Frank Gardner. His steam cars were fast and refined, and even took the land-speed record in 1902 at a 'phenomenal' 75mph (121km/h). Serpollet died in 1907 and his company died with him.

This 1903 10hp Gladiator, originally registered BW-255, was re-registered CE-1229 on 10 June 1910 by Ben Thorp, who sold the car to B. Greene in the early 1930s.

One of two surviving examples of the 1903 16-hp Peerless, this rear-entrance tonneau was discovered in Hawaii.

This 1899 3hp Pieper was first entered in the Brighton Run in 1932 by a Mrs E. Wood, who was still using the car regularly for shopping in Crawley.

This 1901 Schaudel is a rare survivor from a total production of about 100 cars; the company was taken over by Motobloc in 1902.

Georges Richard (France): This Parisian firm began in 1897 by copying the Benz Velo, then built the Belgian Vivinus under licence. The company's founder Georges Richard quarrelled with designer Brasier and resigned in 1904 to found the Unic company.

Gladiator (France): Originally bicycle makers, this French firm was British-owned from 1896, when it built 4hp voiturettes. Aster engines were fitted from 1899 and four-cylinder models followed in 1903, when 80 per cent of Gladiator's output of around 1000 cars was sold in Britain.

Peerless (USA): Peerless began in 1869 making clothes wringers, turned to bicycles, then built single-cylinder 'Motorettes' in 1900. Louis Mooers became chief engineer in 1901 and shaped the policy of the company with strikingly modern designs. Peerless ended production in 1931 but reopened in 1934 as Peerless Corporation, brewers of Carling's Ale.

Pieper (Belgium): 'Once seen, always admired,' the Pieper was made by one of Belgium's biggest cycle manufacturers. Britain was the firm's main export market, where marketing for their 6hp single and 12hp twin targeted lady motorists.

Schaudel (France): Former armourer Schaudel set up a bicycle works in Bordeaux in the late 19th century and built his first car in 1897. In 1901 he exhibited the world's first car with engine, clutch and gearbox built as a single unit. Schaudel also pioneered the use of interchangeable parts to create 'a car which can be dismantled like a military rifle'.

Star (England): Wolverhampton was once a major centre of the British motor industry, and Star progressed from cycles to cars to become one of the city's leading makers, starting in 1897 with a 3½hp model based on the Benz. By 1904, Mercedes-like cars were being made.

Stephens (England): Cycle and general engineer R. Stephens of Clevedon, Somerset, made a few 8hp cars with independent front suspension in 1898–1900.

Waverley Electric (USA): These electric cars were built in Indianapolis by the Pope-owned Indiana Bicycle Company. General Lew Wallace, author of *Ben Hur*, bought a Waverley Electric in 1902.

Wolseley (England): Herbert Austin, the works manager of the Wolseley Sheep-Shearing Company, built experimental cars from 1895–99. He had helped machine-gun inventor Sir Hiram Maxim with his giant steam aeroplane in the 1890s and Sir Hiram's associates Vickers, Sons & Maxim bought Wolseley's car division in 1901, when it built 323 horizontal-engined cars. A second factory at Crayford built a little 6hp model. Austin resigned in 1905 to found his own company.

This 1904 7hp Star was discovered under a pile of fish boxes in a bombed underground garage in Ramsgate and restored in 1954.

When its working life was over, this 1900 Stephens was sawn up by its maker and stored in packing cases. It was rebuilt around 1980.

Electric cars like this 1903 Waverley Stanhope were popular for town use in the USA, where roads were poor (or non-existent) outside city limits.

This is a 1904 example of the 6hp single-cylinder light car that Wolseley built in their second factory at Crayford in Kent.

CHAPTER FORTY

Postscript – 1905 Star (Why the 1904–05 Watershed Matters)

Back in the autumn of 1992 I had the opportunity of driving a leviathan from the golden age of motor racing, a mighty chain-driven 70hp Star, built for the 1905 Gordon Bennett race. Completed in the spring of 1905, it misses the Brighton Run watershed by a few weeks, yet in concept and performance it is a world away from the cars that make the annual pilgrimage to the Sussex coast. For several unforgettable laps of the Chobham Fighting Vehicles Research Development Establishment test track, I handled this 10.2-litre monster and experienced a power that seemed utterly relentless. Sean Danaher, the restorer who rebuilt the Star to full race condition for Richard Smith, had estimated that, with its current gearing, the car's top speed would be almost 100mph (160km/h); it had certainly recorded speeds in excess of 80mph (129km/h) in Vintage Sports-Car Club speed events.

The Star's driving position was perfect – almost. Sitting high up in a close-fitting bucket seat, the driver is able to see the concrete surface of the track rush by beneath the front wheels. The right-hand four-speed gear change was easy, the multi-plate Hele-Shaw clutch was not too heavy, the steering was pleasantly direct, the bi-block engine responsive; the only fault I could find was that the pedals were set too high up the footboard, so that I had to lift my feet off the floor to operate the throttle, brake and clutch.

Owned then by Richard Smith and today by Mike Timms (it is the biggest car in his famous 'Brighton-Early' collection), the Star is one of the oldest surviving British racing cars. It is one of two built by this once-famous Wolverhampton marque to compete in the eliminating trials held in the Isle of Man, where road racing was – and still is – permitted. (Why did they not hold the 1903 Gordon Bennett Race there, too?)

The Stars were driven in the Isle of Man by the Goodwin brothers, better known as racing cyclists, because Joe Lisle, son of Star's chief executive and owner, had lost his licence following a much-publicized crash on British roads while driving the development car for the Gordon Bennett racers. F.R. Goodwin, incidentally, had already established his particular niche in motoring history when his Gladiator voiturette had been commandeered by a police constable at Moor Edge, Newcastle-upon-Tyne, on 15 August 1900, for what is believed to be the first police pursuit of a criminal by motor car. The constable ordered Goodwin to chase a drunken horse-rider, who was caught and arrested after a mile!

The 70hp Stars were as fast as the Napiers that were selected for the Gordon Bennett race, but both failed to be selected for the British team. As late as 1907 one of them was advertised as being suitable for racing on the new Brooklands circuit.

At some stage the car I was driving was exported to India, where it languished for many years until it was found lying derelict in the 1970s; it had been acquired by a German enthusiast who thought it was a Mercedes (which it closely resembles), but who decided to sell it when he discovered that it had been born in the Black Country rather than the Black Forest. It then came to England, but was sold overseas in the early 1990s. Now it has returned to England.

Although it is a much appreciated part of Mike Timms' collection, the Star's owner is adamant that the idea of altering the rules to make such cars eligible for the Brighton Run was a big mistake. An enthusiastic supporter of the 2002 'Red Flag Revolution', Timms voiced his opinion firmly: 'The Star, which was completed in the spring of 1905, shows the foolishness of the proposal that post-1904 cars should be allowed to do the Brighton Run. Development was so rapid in those early days that there is a staggering difference between 1904 and 1905 models.'

And that 'staggering difference' is just what, for me, constitutes the charm and the abiding interest of veteran cars.

Built a matter of weeks after the end of 1904, the Gordon Bennett Star racer underlines the staggering difference between 1904 and 1905 designs.

Index